Yes to Beyond

SO WHAT NOW?

Norma J. Ervin

ISBN 978-1-957943-58-9 (paperback)
ISBN 978-1-957943-59-6 (hardcover)
ISBN 978-1-957943-60-2 (digital)

Rushmore Press LLC
1 800 460 9188
www.rushmorepress.com

Printed in the United States of America

A PERSONAL NOTE

Welcome to our togetherness through these pages. If you are experiencing some confusion as you see the title of this book and feel that you have seen something very similar before, you may have. This book, 'Yes to Beyond — So What Now?" is a republished version of "Yes to Beyond — Create a New Road" with a different cover picture. The content of the book is the same; the timing of initially entering and re-entering the market, is different. This book is being republished and distributed in a more appropriate timeframe for it's value as a tool, as well as, through an outlet with the potential of reaching more avenues of different life experiences for the offered tool.

Within these pages the Shift of the Ages is more clearly defined/ expressed. The Shift of the Ages involves a major change in the energy of Mother Earth herself as we move on in our cosmic patterns of cycles. Every so many thousands of years one cycle ends and another begins. At the point of that particular shift there is a 36 year of dynamics that transpires cosmically which also includes the tribe of humanity as a major participant.

The first 18 years of the 36 years is designed for humanity to come in touch/review, internally/externally with all that is no longer serving as their truth. In actual calendar time, we have already completed the first 18 years of the 36 years. This first part ended 12/21/2012. Even though we have already began the process and learned and let go of a lot, we are still cleaning up the field, so to speak as, we move forward. Yes to Beyond — So What Now? is a tool for the individual's review of what was needed and the clearing process progress. This book can be a guided map through various major journey's life as we began the major shift.

The initial Shift of the Ages may leave us feeling:

Oh, so many times I have come to the edge.
There I stand waiting, listening, wondering.
I scream, I cry, I look for someone to hold me.
I plead for life, beg for forgiveness.
I search in my old tool box for one more available tool.
Nothing comes forth except my extreme emptiness.
I gaze out into the vast expansion of nothingness!
Do I jump or just sit here and dangle my feet.......?

Poem: The Edge
By Norma Ervin

SO WHAT NOW??

JOIN ME ON THE ROAD TO FREEDOM!
DON'T FASTEN YOUR SEAT BELTS
SO YOU WILL BE FREE
TO MOVE AROUND!

CONTENTS

ACKNOWLEDGMENTS

I acknowledge the value of all religious practices. Each and every one of them have some points of valued guidance for different ways of discovering who we really are as a Created Image from the same Creator God. From a young age up into my adult living years, I have gained many pieces to my life puzzle from the beliefs, practices, and theories of three or four different religious churches. As my life journey progressed Mother Nature has become may main sanctuary where the choir sings with all of the tones of water, birds, wind through the bushes and trees, along with the voice tones of other animals and people. There is nothing to join and no belief rules to follow in order to be present. The love of All that IS is right there beside me. I feel free, blessed, loved, fully known, peaceful, and necessary with a purpose for Being when in the presences of the Creator in Mother Nature. I acknowledge Mother Nature right along with the value of all religions.

I acknowledge Mary Morrisey. She is the founder and owner of Life Ministry Institute. Mary has 40 years of experience in empowering individuals in achieving new heights of spiritual aliveness, wealth, and authentic success. Prior to taking on this path of helping people, she was a minister of a large church for a number of years.

Her life goal could be quoted as "Transforming Possibilities into Realities!" There are many paths she has taken and many ways she has helped people.

I participated in one of Mary's classes called "The Dream Builder, Creating the Life of Your Dreams" A quote from Mary that really spoke to me was, "Even though you may want to move forward in your life, you may have one foot on the brakes. In order to be free, we must learn how to let go. Release the hurt. Release the fear. Refuse to entertain your old pain. The energy it takes to hang onto the past is holding you back from a new life. What is it you would let go of today." I will be eternally grateful for all she had to offer that spoke to me in an encouraging, healing and spiritual way! You can find out a lot more about her on www.marymorrisey.com.

I acknowledge Gregg Braden. I give Gregg my deep heart felt gratitude. A deep truth from Gregg from July 29, 2019, "People who are reluctant to release the security of doing what is familiar to them is missing the opportunity to create even greater security in the New world that is emerging."

Gregg Braden is a five-time New York Times best-selling author and is internationally renowned as a pioneer in bridging science, spirituality, and the real world. As a former geologist ad computer systems designer, Gregg has explored high mountain villages, remote monasteries, and forgotten texts to merge their timeless secrets with the best science of today.

I have read some of his books, and I have met him personally at several occasions. What he has to offer has been huge to me on my Life Journey of discovering Who I AM. He is very authentic and easy to understand in all that he has to offer, be it in person or in books. Find out more about him at www.greggbraden.com.

With much gratitude, I acknowledge Dr. Bruce Lipton, PhD. He is an internationally recognized leader in bridging science and spirit. He started his career as a cell biologist. In the early 1990's he began examining the principals of quantum physics and how they might be integrated into his understanding of the cell's information process systems. He has been blessed by hundreds of audience members who have improved their spiritual, physical, and mental well-being by applying the principals he has discovered. He has a number of very practical, valuable, and easy to comprehend books out as well as beings a very good speaker who gets around to many places. I have resonated a lot with what he has shared and all that he has learned about our body and how it works. He has helped me a lot in really getting to know Who I AM.

With much gratitude, I acknowledge Patricia Cota-Robles for who she is and what she has to offer as a teacher from her training as a counselor and her sharing the information that she receives as a channeler or intuitive. Patricia is the co-founder and president of the nonprofit, educational organization New Age Study of Humanity's Purpose, also often recognized as Era of Peace. She was a family counselor for 20 years. Patricia now spends her time freely sharing information she is receiving from the Beings of Light in the Realms of Illumined Truth. The Divine intent of this Celestial Sharing is to give humanity greater clarity and understanding as we progress through these wondrous, but extremely challenging times on Earth. Patrica is an internationally known teacher and has facilitated groups in various places in the United States and the world.

Her philosophy is, "Every person is precious and divine regardless of how far his or her behavior patterns and life experiences may be reflecting the Truth. We are not the victims of our lives. We are the co-creators of our lives!" The giving of herself in the purest of authenticity, is a wonderful and valuable gift for life that Patricia has a way of sharing. For more information about Patrica Cota-Robles and what she has to offer can be found on www.eraofpeace.org.

With a huge gratitude over a number of years, I acknowledge Lee Carroll as the channeler of Kryon, a loving angelic entity of magnetic service who is coming in through Lee. Lee Carroll was a degreed technical audio engineer operating his own business for many years in California. He started channeling in 1989, and he is known as the original channel for Kryon. Since the word Kryon is not proprietary, in the last years there have been others in many cultures who have come to use the name Kryon in many forms. However, Lee is not affiliated with any other Kryon channelling by any other person, school, or organization using the name Kryon

Watkins "Mind, Body, Spirit" magazine from the UK listed Lee Carroll as one of the "100 most influential living people" more than once. During a trip to McCaysville at Delphi Metaphysical University, Lee was surprised with a honorary doctorate degree of Science, Trans

Personal Psychology, and Metaphysics. The award indicated "For his extraordinary contribution of love, wisdom, and spiritual understanding". The energy of Kryon given through Lee is filled with total Love for Humanity! A website for more information is www.kryon.com and www.kryonmasters.com.

Another acknowledgement is Geoffrey Hoppe who has brought in messages from angelic beings who lovingly assist those who are going through spiritual transformations while seeking to integrate their divinity with their humanity while discovering the God within. Geoffrey's channeled messages come as a collective known as The Crimson Circle. To see all that Geoffrey Hoppe and Linda Hoppe have to offer, go to www.crimsoncircle.com.

In giving my acknowledgments I give the information for the purpose of showing the scope of their value to all who are out-and-about searching for their own heart and soul! This Yes To Beyond journey has been me and my search as I looked for a New Road to So What Now? All of whom I have acknowledged, have been big players to me. I feel deep gratitude for All of them!

DEDICATION

I dedicate this book to all these family members who are so important and special to me: My two Sons and their families. They are, Bobby Ervin, Wife Kristin, their sons, and my grandsons, Connor, Tommy, and Tanner.

Son Gary Ervin, Wife Sheila Ervin, their two sons, DJ and Dalton, and their daughter Whitley as my grandsons and granddaughter. Also included in this family and this Dedication is the Memory of Spencer Ervin who left this Earth in 2007.

Another very special person that I bring into this Dedication is my very dear Sister who is also my very best friend, Shirley Pickering.

My life would not have been as blessed as it has been without each and every one of you playing your part! Thanks to each and every one of you!

TO ALL OF YOU,
I LOVE YOU MORE THAN WORDS
CAN EVER
EXPRESS!!

FORWARD

I am not writing this book because I just want to tell my stories and /or my experiences to as many who choose to read it. My experiences and stories are my creations for myself. I am putting out words of experiences and expressions on these pages with my intention, that with all of us walking as human beings with a heart, may we have a way to resonate with each other and consciously open our hearts to, and with, each other whether we actually ever meet each other in person. As a collective of individuals, we are as *one* in the Consciousness that plays a major part in how we orchestrate our life and the life of all humanity. We have many things to unlearn and much to remember regarding our truth. From a new perception of consciousness and with an open heart, we can restructure our reality closer to who we were really created to be. After reading any of these pages that speaks to you, I desire that we resonate with what connects our individual hearts together. Just remember and value what helped you to feel in your own life path without you having to remember my story or my expression. We are the co-creators of the New Earth. We are the New Earthlings! We do have a responsibility in this process, but our intellectual mind is not our CEO or the master of the life journey. There is an essence in the invisible that is our guide with our mind, switching jobs to being the conduit for the New to flow through for manifestation of a new living reality!

Welcome and may we resonate through open hearts somewhere along the way through these pages as our Human/Divine heart continues to find our potential to embody all that is there for us on our life journey as we find our *self* and serve as the emerged cosmic Human Beloved that we are. We are not our stories. Our true value is not a collective of what we have and what we have done. We are not designed as Human Doings. We have and do from our position as a Human Being, and all the rest is designing us to recognize and understand the difference between who we are not as we learn more by remembering who we really are. Our goals (external desires) and our intentions (more inner desires) will be invisibly and intuitively guided to bring about a stage of harmony and balance for us to have the main outcome be that of our 'becoming' rather than our doing or having. Becoming does not eliminate us from having or doing as all are important in living life on planet Earth. It just switches the position of the powerful, power-giving, living life dynamics! Let's know and become more of who we were immaculately conceived to be originally from and by the Master Creator, and from that state of being, as we have become more, may we stand back and 'Watch and be Amazed' as to how our 'Doing and Having' are enhanced and perhaps serve us in a whole new way.

Consequently, we are a Human Being. Being brings in the essence of our Divine so we can become a Divine Human Being. Our journey together through these pages is for our resonating together to implement our Becoming more and more of who we really are as a human (visible) and a being (invisible) balanced together presented in form as a Human Divine Being or a Divine Human Being. They are one and the same with both being the necessary form on Earth from which we all utilize as we play out the scripts of our own lives upon our own chosen or, guided to, stages. There are many actors and actresses on the stage with us in many of our scripts. However, regardless of the number involved, our part is for a purpose uniquely for us as we play our part of the one! Our scripted part in our own stage play is to learn to be the Star of our own show. Being this Star means: **S**urrender, **T**rust, **A**llow or (**A**lign), **R**eceive. All of the gifts for us to receive are already present for us to receive. Our journey to them is to just keep moving forward as we know, and feel, to do from the pushing and pulling of our heart's yearnings and discontentment accompanied with an active intention and intended vision of life as our heart feels it. On this journey, always keep an active awareness that the intellectual mind, the memory bank, and active reflector of all pieces of past points of reference is not our primary guide or the pure truth reflector of who we are. However, the mind does not go away. Just drop the intellectual adjective and let the pure mind of the Invisible, that which is the All-Knowing component of us, play into our Human Being, now Divine Human Being, form as a major player within us that keeps us going as a valuable member of the tribe of humanity.

> Having just planted a lot of seeds in the rose garden,
> let's allow the gestation of the rose,
> its beautiful flower as well as its thorns,
> begin our new reality of becoming!

I want to be with you, really *be* with you. Words are merely symbols—symbols representing ideas, feelings, or emotions that desire expression. Sometimes, the truest expression is just Being in each other's space in silence and feeling the connection of the presence as us. It is my heart's greatest intention to create an active sharing through these pages whereby your own experiences will speak to you. These are not just words to add to your database of knowledge, rather intended for sharing of experiences.

We have all traveled on a journey through life whether we called it that or not or whether we did it consciously or unconsciously. We were (are) writing our individual "Book of Life" as we are sojourning. Each individual book represents someone's dot and cell in the universe, which is the Oneness of All that Is. Everyone has a purpose and everyone is playing according to some script. Just as we are made up of cells connected in certain patterns which are designed to perform certain functions, the universe is designed with a similar plan with each of us individually being a cell of the design. Thus, our person is a cell of the whole, the One which is representing our function or purpose, and our position is our dot in the plan as the dot-to-dot structure is connected within the whole. Each and every one of us is necessary for purpose and position!

All of life is a journey but sometimes is more intense than others, and it is in those times that the biggest insights can come. Recognize these as somewhat unusual or different, perhaps with insights, meaning something inside of us speaks, and it is not just our brain reflecting what it knows from past points of reference or what we have intellectually learned from different sources. These intense times are usually not designed by us consciously. They are happenings that just seem to be dropping in, and in their presence, we are required to dig deeper into the very core of who we are or think we are than we ever thought was even possible. This core is beyond the capability of the brain; therefore, inside sight, in-sight, through and from some undefined source within us that knows us is called upon to participate for our understanding and well-being. These intense times which at first appeared as unfortunate can now appear as, and prove to be, fortunate. These happenings are usually not just quick overnight events but usually have some length of duration to them.

Life is an opportunity for exploring, experiencing, and expressing. This is how we grasp another aspect of who we are, play with it a while, do what we will with what we have found, and move on, always taking with us more of who we are while hanging on to nothing to hold as a definition of who we are. Well, in theory, it would perhaps be ideal if we did play that way, but it seems once we have developed an understanding from one point of view that seems to work for us, it is hard to not let it define us in some fashion. Therefore, we want to hang on to it and form it into an ego component, facilitating a personality trait that further builds an identity of who we defined ourselves to be. Consequently, according to how we play, we could be living through false images of our truth. These images are made up of thoughts, beliefs, and identities which combined formulate our personality or ego. I will use these words interchangeably in this book but representing the same thing which is our perception of ourselves as we think we really are. Our ultimate question to ask ourself is where did these come from, and how do they match up to the truth?

This book is written with its messages for you, hidden in the space between the lines, between the words, between the letters. These words are literally put together as a word expression of sharing some of my experiences from my life journey, and I share them because I know I am not the only one looking for a life with more meaning—one that makes more sense, and one that really does reflect the Love that I Am! Are you ready for a trip that seems to be orchestrated by something or someone that is you at some level, but certainly, not all aspects of it are consciously known by you yet?

I know there are many writings out there that speak of life in these changing times. I intend for there to be some unique silent messages for You to You on these pages. These pages are for an experience, not an intellectual exercise for gaining more knowledge. Feel with me, don't learn with me. In doing this, you can also have greater insights into your life. From this place of connection, we can be the co-creators that we are together. Our gifts then become a twinkle and/or a spark for others to find a gift for themselves and so goes life as we evolve into a new consciousness that has the potential to transform a fear-based infrastructure into one of Love not Hate!

LET THE JOURNEY BEGIN

WELCOME

Super Market, Cabinet, Pantry, or Refrigerator

Upon opening the cover of this book, you have stepped through a big electromagnetic circular opening located somewhere on one of the sides, top, or bottom of your 3D Human Reality Box of Life. It is an opening flexible enough for any size of a human to pass through. However, it is designed to mostly accommodate the individual owner of the box as no two individuals' 3D Human Reality Box of Life is the same. There is no door swinging for opening and closing this freedom portal. As you step into, venture into the words of the pages of this book; allow yourself to be going on new exploration in your life for your life. There is a 'You to You' journey potentially present here. These pages are not about you adopting my story as your story or all of these words being experienced as your words too, but rather for you to see the words, feel into what resonates with you as you allow the power of the space between the lines and/or between the words to become speakers for You to You as potentials or insights facilitating your Yes to Beyond unique journey. Utilizing this realm of invisible presence, aspects of your own life may begin surfacing as clarity or guidance. Through your journey within these pages, these words, these less than coherent or even smooth flowing of snapshots of concepts that make up something in some reality, may not be your life's journey as you know it. Or is it? A question for all to ask oneself who is inclined to have a different view of reality and live a different life is, "What is Yes to Beyond, what is different there, and where is there"?

This book isn't designed to be read as a story with a beginning and an ending or to even necessarily be read in page order. Perhaps, see it as a Super Market, a kitchen pantry, cabinet, or a refrigerator with all having the potential to nourish, nurture, and sustain you in some way that you feel the need for in various ways in multiple moments as you traverse your daily 24-hour cycle in time. That cycle is a given truth for all of us. Our journey has variables; however, all of our days are a cycle of 24 hours measured by our need for the structure of time measurement. The Super Market is for the larger picture with the pantry, cabinet, or refrigerator facilitating a more condensed space for exploring what has already been purchased and is being used or prepared for use. Super Market, pantry, cabinet, or refrigerator, any one of which is your choice as you pick according to what you feel, is needed for nurturing yourself in any given moment. It could be one bite or a whole meal. It could be already purchased from the store, or from something you must shop for to prepare for consumption.

What do you desire as you have the opportunity to say "Yes to Beyond" as you walk through your freedom portal opening into the unknown to find your expanded God-given birthright within and as Infinite Love expressing Self? If God isn't the word you use, then state it as you know it—Universe, Creator, Source, Infinite Love, or whatever fits. It is all the human names for the same place we all came from regardless of race, color, creed, or belief. We are all of the similar functioning bodies as the systems inside of us all function biologically, the same that enables us to be what we term "alive."

Read these pages as you feel to read them. It may be one bite as one word that resonated with you; it may be an appetizer, a main course, a dessert, a salad, a bowl of soup, or even a candy bar snack (probably chocolate preferred!). Whatever is up for you, and wherever you have gone to find it, be it at the Super Market—searching the whole book as an overview whenever needed or desired — or in-between meals snacks just wanting something because your inner system is calling you forth for something so you look in the pantry, cabinet, or refrigerator which may be on a particular page. If you are ready for a meal, it may be multiple pages. Read it, be with it; however, you choose to allow it to be a part of your 'Yes to Beyond' journey.

Here are some points to ponder as you may be contemplating if you really are on or even want to be on the 'Yes to Beyond' journey:

1. Is there a **feeling in your heart** fueling a **yearning,** a knowing, that there has to be more than what our current mass consciousness is displaying? Nothing will ever change if nothing is felt out-of-balance.

2. Are you wanting to **bring clarity** to understanding what is presenting as a false appearance as our truth?

3. Consequently, declaring and embracing your personalized 'Yes to Beyond' journey is knowing you are not alone as **we play as ONE** in the collective tribe of humanity.

4. Are you ready to consciously and voluntarily step through the huge, (remember it is big enough for you to walk through **standing tall** and **fully empowered**) freedom portal of your own human 3D linear reality box.

5. Let the (your) journey begin, or recognize it has already begun, as you step into the **"unknown to you"** to find that which has **always been known as you!** It wasn't visible in the box of perceived reality that we as humanity players have (had) mis-created over time through using our free choice to be something much less than we are and much different than we were created to be. Within and from this limited reality box, orchestrated by a false energetic way of living life, we have been experiencing and continually exploring a perceived reality of false truths about ourselves. All of this has been holding us to a survival mode which has kept us doing all kinds of unloving ways of playing just so we could stay alive, aka survive!

6. While you (we) are 'out' there now and are feeling as a trapeze artist swinging, flailing, or randomly floating between 'holding points' which feel foreign but necessary, know that the significance of one of the power points of the New Reality is, **"Take in as absolute truth and fact, 'we don't know what we**

don't know until we do know more, and some we will never **know. It just IS** and IS is Infinite Source and we are all a part of this 'Creator's Creation.' There is much of the how's of our journey that the human intellectual brain can't comprehend let alone deal with in any intellectually-logical fashion.

7. Happy traveling and be aware of another "powerpoint" to grab ahold of as we are experiencing a different reality. It is that of freely offering **compassion for and to ourselves** as an individual on this our journey, our piece as a part of the ONE. This directive will become more and more not just clear but necessary as our journey gets further and further away from our (the) reality box and all that is, or was, familiar.

8. Last (maybe) but not least—always know and feel without any doubt (to the best of your ability) that **you are safe** and **you are never alone!** You may be saying, "How can that be when I live alone? Or how can that be or what does that even mean when I have a partner and family and friends all around me and yet I feel as though I am all alone in this journey and not even connected to those around me?" The answer I get to my quiet inner questions comes to me with clear recognition as "Watch and be Amazed." I pause here as I clearly took in these words as they fully registered with me and in me without anyone's voice speaking them to me. I knew them from somewhere, somehow, something or someone beyond my sight. In the realms of the invisible, I AM known, seen, and must be understood. Consequently, this is proof that I am never alone! I see that I have completed, finished, am done with my old energy 3D box of reality, and must get going (or keep going) on through my circular freedom portal to my new version of life as I am on with my 'Yes to Beyond'!

9. Welcome to 'Yes to Beyond'. **Be present in the Now** as you Watch and be Amazed! What else can you (we) do as all landscapes are changing and every mirror is tilting?

10. **Be at Peace!** You (we) will be seen, heard, and felt whenever, wherever, and however the opportunity is present in Divine Right Order which includes Divine Right Timing. I have a hard time with this right timing part because I want it when I want it as I speculate my stated directives are all that is necessary for the change to occur. I am learning to give my intention and then just water my intention, but not demand that it grow and be ready to harvest overnight or in a week.

All is RTG, Ready to Go!

Watch and be Amazed as you traverse streams that become rivers that flow into the ocean. Quiet calming pools, ponds, or lakes on our journey are helpful and restful space to be quiet and regroup, breathe, and feel peaceful. However, know that if we, or as we, attempt to stay in the space of the quiet calming bodies to avoid the flowing water, we are holding back a large piece of ourselves. We will never experience or even express as a vital piece of creation itself—flowing water—if we resist moving forward as a flow of a living life journey! It is told that the human body is 70%-80% water in its healthy state. Most of this has to be flowing in some way inside us!

As we step into 'Yes to Beyond,' we will be guided to explore, experience, and express it all in many ways, all of which will be for our highest good and the highest good of all living things, mankind, animals, and plants on our planet Earth home. As we consciously see and know ourselves as a unique piece of the peace of the Oneness of All That IS, collectively, we are co-creating a New Mass Consciousness. This New Consciousness will show us more of the truth that we are as we actively participate in Living Love Consciously, knowing that Love is far more than we have previously understood it to be! Beyond our old paradigm, eventually, all of the false concepts of our human nature will be renewed to what we were originally designed to be with a much, much bigger understanding of what the Love that we are is really intended to be! God, or whatever you choose to call the Master Creator, is not punishing us.

We as humans and through using our free choice life-gift that we were given at the inception of our creation as life in form are the ones that have messed this up. That doesn't mean our choices were all bad ones even though they were not always reflecting love. The reason we were given free choice is that we could have the opportunity to create enough non-love creations like lack, war, greed, separations within the whole of global humanity through all kinds of belief systems and more. The gift in all of this is for us to see more clearly who we aren't and what is not love so we can now be more prepared for what love is. From here, we can see and declare what we want the reality of our life experience to reflect as more of who we really are—a creation of Love which is what is meant and intended by being created in the image of God. It is not to look in the mirror and see our physical body face having a resemblance to our creation ancestor, so to speak. God was not, is not, human form, but IS pure essence that is the Live Source of All That IS and that Essence is Love!

PLAYING HEARTS IN NEW CONSCIOUSNESS

Presenting Myself

My Truth:

1. I was Born
2. I Am Alive
3. I Am Continuing to Choose Life
4. I Am Allowing and Accepting many deaths and rebirths within me as my Life Journey
5. I Am Designed for Freedom
6. I Am Love
7. I Am Aware of the Love in You that I See in Me
8. I Know We are a Part of God Also
9. I Know We are still in Process
10. I Know as The ONE We Are Consciousness Evolution

I am one of those people who has a deep heartfelt connection to water, so much so that it is as though it is actually almost as necessary to me as my own heartbeat. I greatly value and appreciate nature's waters as a part of Mother Earth, and I also am highly attuned to the calm and rushing waters inside of me as I flow or stagnate on my life's journey paths.

Now as I am experiencing the water as the river inside of me, the flow is so deep and swift that I almost feel unable to navigate with it or even to negotiate with it. However, I am becoming aware of all that is present as the emotional components of depth and swiftness. This is where I have been in writing this book. When the dynamics of all that I want to share seem to come in as a presence all at the same time, it just becomes too deep and swift emotionally for me to handle it in a logical way. Therefore, previously, I have just closed the door and gone away because I can't swim and the fury of the water's power feels not safe. When identifying this as a scenario I have experienced many times in endeavoring to get this book written, I recognized my reaction in my writing journey. I would shut off my mind and go into a blank mode when my inner emotional-driven life got so deep and swift that it felt completely unmanageable and impossible to accomplish. Having said that, and having recognized that space yet again, I am making a new choice here and now which is "keep going because I know I CAN manage this and it is possible!"

Well, enough reasoning for excuses, One more time I am RTG — Ready to Go!

I came into the world on December 19, 1944. That was during the energy of the World War II era closer to the ending of the war than the beginning of the war. Therefore, I arrived when peace was more of the focus than perpetuating the fighting and destruction. My birthplace was a small farming community in southwestern Colorado. I must have had a strong determination to get here and be here in this now as I gained the knowledge later in life that my mother had attempted to abort me, and obviously, I didn't allow her to be successful. She was not a bad person, but she was a scared person facing all of the dynamics of war and the potential of raising two babies alone as I already had a less than two-year-old sister at the time. My father was choosing to enlist even though that did not become his path. This is a little bit about my beginning as to when I arrived on planet Earth this time and where I arrived, and now the journey begins.

In and on this journey of life, it seems from the very beginning of the time that I had the capacity to have my own imagined vision of life. I really was living within parallel lives. One is my outside life doing what I was taught to do and what I was told to do. By utilizing the free choice that we were given as a birthright from our Creator in the original conception as a human being, I went on to form my identities and roles based upon my country's culture, my acquired beliefs, and my programming, much of which was the dynamics of our mass consciousness as our guiding book for living. This all played into the making of my outside parallel previously mentioned. It represented the visible part of my existence. The other one was going on in my inner, invisible to the world, life. My thoughts and feelings hardly ever matched what my outer life was playing out or expressing. I began to wonder if these parallel lives were just my experience or were they the norm for humanity, and if so, what does all of this really mean?

I left my small hometown after high school and basically never went back other than to just visit, plus the fact that my parents also moved out of the town at the time that I was in college. While growing up, I always felt inside of me that there was more to discover about the world than I was experiencing. This inner parallel seemed to always be speaking to me from a very young age! After high school graduation, the journey began as that inside-outside conversation about reality was never quiet and questioned me every step of the way as I played out my external life. Most of the time, the only thing that my parallel lives had in common was that they shared existence and/or life from and within the same biological/ physical body. Mine! However, for the majority of the time overall of the years, they, the parallels, may have been in the same book but they definitely were not on the same page!

Over the years, I had many changes including major family changes, many location changes, job changes, relationship changes, and self-employment experiences and changes. Also included were religious/ worshipping changes where I never left God out. I just gained more insight as to what/who made in the image of God really means. I found it is so huge and way beyond the capability of our biological minds to even comprehend all of it. All of this is to name a few of the outer visible changes that are not without impact on my inner parallel invisible life! I tried to keep up with my taught and programmed external world of 'to do' and 'to be' what 'I should do and could do and be.' All along the way through all of these life explorations, experiences, and expressions, my inner parallel was always expressing to me that there was much more to discover than all of this that I was playing out.

As a result of my two parallels seemingly not in alignment with each other, I always had been uncomfortable deep inside in some way, with a deep sense of the urging to truly find myself in the space of more than this or beyond this, that I kept hearing was real. I just couldn't seem to get there for some reason. I was aware that I didn't even know where "there" was, but I knew many scenarios where "there" wasn't. I knew (know) that when I arrive "there," I will absolutely know I have arrived as I will experience being in it. It is the heaven above and/or the heaven on this Earth! It may not even be a specific place, rather it may be that I will experience myself as BEING the Human Being that I was originally designed to be regardless of where I am or was. In the mass consciousness that we have designed over thousands of years, we have displayed our importance as that of a Human Doing rather than a Human Being with our designated value measurement of value being Money as we play it and define it.

In these pages of sharing time and thoughts with you, I am going to be speaking mostly of my life as I began walking and playing more with the urges of my inner parallel as I moved to give it more and more attention. I estimate the timing of this period of my life beginning sometime in the year 1980. The catalyst that kicked me into motion after the major regrouping inside and outside of me was a divorce and the deep love for two small children that were affected by this happening. At this time, and leading up to this time, that still but loud voice inside of me was calling out, and sometimes screaming out, "You have to find yourself! You have to live from a sense of self and you have to love, honor, and respect yourself too!" I got the message and began stumbling around to find my answers.

My was-band, as I now refer to my ex-husband, was (is) a good man. Our decisive factor was that he was very clear on who he was and what he wanted to be and play out in his life, and I was clueless for the most part about who I was and what I truly wanted out of life. Therefore, in our journey together, I did my very best to make and live his life as my life and make his interests mine because if I didn't, we had very little in common other than two small precious sons! I tried to change to make it all work but just couldn't get the job done. I walked on to find who I was as my internal parallel had directed, and I got the reality of the message. I walked on with my biggest prayer being that the heart, mind, and soul of these two small boys would not be damaged beyond repair with a wound that would negatively or painfully affect them the rest of their lives. Along with their lives being healed and blessed, I prayed that I would find, know, and love myself in that perceived bigger and more world where my internal world would be reflected in my external world and there would be a balance that would support a life of peace inside and outside of me.

1992—A Deep Calling for Change!

As a child growing up and moving into my adult years, I had never had the desire, dream, or even vision of being self-employed. As a part of a baton that I felt was passed to me by my dad, I became self-employed within a short time after my father's death. He had been his own boss through multiple businesses spanning many years. At this point of time in my life, I had owned and operated a bookkeeping service, Harmane Bookkeeping Service, for multiple years. I had started this in the city of Denver, Colorado. After having been born and raised in a small Colorado farming community, it seemed that my soul was calling me back to the quiet of my Being. Therefore, even though the bookkeeping service had served me well over the years, I was burned out and ready for change. My body was tired, my spirit was once again crying, and my soul seemed to be putting up a new 'next' signal for me! After having been my own boss for a number of years and knowing that I could satisfy my own longings and experience something new and different to me in this world that I was still exploring, I orchestrated a plan!

1993—Unusual Experience

This was the year of the occurrence of an 'unusual experience' that was the **gateway to a new road.** I had spent a concentrated period of time getting all of my clients to a place where I could take a much-needed vacation. I had my plane ticket and was going to go to Sedona, AZ for a week. I had heard of the dynamics of the energies there, and I felt just being there and resting in that space would facilitate my understanding or awareness of what was next for me. I felt the call for something new and different at such a deep place, but I was still unable to grasp it in 3D reality. I was so excited on many levels—going on a vacation, embarking on a strongly felt mission, exploring a place I had never been before, just stepping out of my routine life of being ever-present for the demands of others, to just being with myself in a different environment where no one I knew, but for me, could get to me. This felt like the ultimate gift to me!

Several nights before leaving, with almost all of my preparation for going done, including most of my personal packing, I went to bed feeling tired but good and excited. What happened next shook my world! Just before going to sleep, I heard these words and had this conversation. I heard very clearly from inside of me, **"How is your fear?"**

I responded, "What fear? What do you mean? I am not afraid!"

The very clear inner voice replied, **"Good, hold onto that feeling of not being afraid and know all is well and there is truly nothing to be afraid of!"**

I thought how strange all of that was, but oh well, whatever! Maybe I was more concerned about my venture in front of me than I thought I was. Perhaps, this was just an unusual confirmation letting me know that all was going to be okay on my trip. However, before actually going to sleep, I had the most excruciating pains in my heart and chest! I don't know how long this lasted, but it was certainly more than just a few seconds. It was like I felt the pain while at the same time I was somehow the observer as well. I clearly remember stating to myself, "If I didn't know better, I would say I am having a heart attack." But I never felt afraid. Sometime later, after this had all passed through, I had great clarity on the earlier dialogue, as well as tremendous amazement of the entire happening.

The next morning, I was up and at it, still amazed but feeling okay. I had no concern, but the thought did cross my mind that I must really need a vacation more than I thought if these weird occurrences were going to start appearing! During the course of the day, I did call the lady who was the practitioner of the yoga class that I was taking at that time. She had told us previously that as the life energy in us shifts, it could cause physical happenings so don't be alarmed, but do be cautious. I relayed my experience to her and ask if that could have been what happened. She indicated it could have been, but she highly suggested that I see a doctor before going on vacation.

Herein was the dilemma. I didn't have a doctor and had not even been to one in about ten years. Plus, I didn't have time to schedule an appointment before leaving. I wasn't so keen on doctors anyway. I gave her the main points of my 'truth according to me;' hence, my version of my dilemma. I thought I had thoroughly covered and pretty much settled the issue. Well, not entirely I guess as she urged me to promise her that I would see some medical professional just to be sure. She gave me the name of a doctor who practiced Tibetan Medicine and alternative ways. I did call but couldn't get in for three weeks. I said I would make an appointment when I got back. I then called my instructor back with the updated information, and she accepted my decision. I do not know if she agreed or not, but she accepted it, which I appreciated.

In moving on . . . the night before flying out around midday the next day, I gave myself the gift of a relaxing massage. The masseuse stopped at one point and stated, "We are not supposed to offer anything up as a diagnosis, but I am being strongly guided to tell you that something is going on with your heart and you should see your doctor soon."

I couldn't believe what I was hearing because I had told him nothing other than the massage was a gift to myself as the first piece of my vacation. For me, it was work done, time to relax, vacation, and all of its facets up for exploration and experiencing! He then thoroughly questioned me about my plans: Where was I going? When was I going?

How was I going, driving, flying, and on and on? After I gave him some answers, he was very adamant in his directives, and inside of me, I was just as adamant with my responses! The dialogue went something like this with his part being out loud verbal and mine loud but kept inside of me!

1. Postpone your vacation—OH NO!
2. Go to a doctor now—BY CHOICE, I DON'T HAVE ONE!
3. If you do insist on going on vacation now, it would be better to drive than to fly—THERE'S NO WAY I WOULD DO THAT!
4. If you do fly, upon arriving, find a doctor just in case of an emergency later and you will know where to go—WHAT THE HELL IS REALLY GOING ON HERE!
5. He leaves saying to think about all of this, and we will connect in the morning—DON'T CALL ME AND I WON'T CALL YOU!

I went to bed an absolute basket case, and this time, I was not the observer of the situation but felt like a battling participant. I was not experiencing physical pain, but I was steeped in confusion and was very distraught! I called a friend of mine as I tried to find answers within me. Should I cancel my trip? Should I go find a doctor? Did I really need a doctor as I was told "all is well and don't be afraid" as the experience was happening, and that is how I went through it? Therefore, was I caught in the fears of others, and was I trying to override my truth, or was this for me to find and strengthen myself in my truth?

My friend tried to find some intuitive responses to my situation when she thought of something in some book that may be of help. When she went to the bookshelf to find the particular book, another book just fell off the shelf in front of her opening up to a particular page. I don't remember the name of the book now but on the page that fell open, the message pertained to our higher purpose and the importance of listening. This piece spoke to me as a vote for I did not need to go to the doctor. Somewhat resolved but still not totally clear on what my answers were about canceling my vacation or not, or the doctor pieces (should I go, and who would I go to), I went to sleep seemingly totally exhausted which was completely opposite of the original intentions for the evening!

During the night, I had a dream where I experienced myself as a member of a Cosmic Star Group. Now I must tell you that I did not live my life espousing far out things at that time. I was not a science fiction advocate, or a system buster, or a rebellious individual. After all, for goodness' sake, I was an accountant where everything must balance to the penny, as well as in the extremes of that life. There is black or white and even gray doesn't easily fit. So, my being a Star Being through conscious imagination, I don't think so! To me, my only far out ways were: I had some differing philosophies around the western model of medicine, and I was exploring and had been for about 10 years some changing views around my religious beliefs.

Upon awakening on travel day, I was so tired at such a deep level that it felt as though my very soul was asleep. I knew there was no way I could even make it to the airport so I called and canceled my flight. At this point, one question was seemingly answered by default. Consequently, disappointment then flooded over my tiredness and I felt paralyzed. There were the still-unanswered questions of the doctor pieces hanging over me like a black cloud. While I was still in bed, feeling I couldn't get up, my phone rang. Figuring it was the masseuse calling me, I chose not to answer it. I immediately got an 'inner punch' to answer the phone. It was not him but instead a lady whom I had not spoken to for over a year. She told me who she was as I did not recognize her voice. I immediately recalled the situation of our original meeting.

I had gone to watch the movie The House of Cards. By the time the movie started, it had become close to a sellout crowd with only a few empty single seats dispersed throughout the theater. One of these empty seats was beside me. Sometime shortly after the main feature had already started, a lady arrived and occupied that seat. At some point in the movie, she started sobbing, quietly at first, and then downright uncontrollably crying which she was still doing when the movie ended. I didn't know what to do or say, but I knew I had to be with her in some way. I stayed seated as all the other people in the row left climbing past us. I then, saying nothing, just turned and put my arms around her and held her. The theater cleared in preparation for the next showing as she remained out of control and I continued to hold her. The graciousness of the theater staff even held the people at the doors so we were the only two in the theater for a period of time. She finally took a breath, regained some composure, and expressed deep gratitude to me.

Knowing they were waiting to start the next movie, I ask her if she would go into the lobby with me, where we could talk there. We did that. Her story was that her fiancee had died some time back, and she had been unable to grieve for whatever reason. There had been something in the movie that had opened her up to that grief, and there was nothing she could do to close the flood gates. I learned no more details at that time. I gave her another big hug, we exchanged business cards, and moved on our separate ways. I had not seen or heard from her since that day.

Inside of me, I shouted, "So today of all days, why is she calling!" Trying to be present and somewhat pleasant, I reluctantly entered into the conversation. She indicated that she was moving and was in the process of packing when she ran across my business card. She realized we had never talked again after that day in the theater over a year ago, and she wanted to thank me again. I accepted her thanks and expressed that I hoped she was doing well.

She then continued. "Did I ever tell you how Dennis died?"

"No," I replied.

Her immediate reply was, "a heart attack."

You can only imagine that at that instant, my psyche went into another tornado spin! I immediately thought "so why am I being awakened with this out-of-the-blue call on this already precarious day? Why was I urged to take the call?"

Before I could regain any semblance of composure to speak or hang up, she continued, "I am doing very well now and my healing came along lovingly and quite rapidly after I was able to open my heart to the grief around all facets of the loss of him, so once again, thank you for your part. In my packing, I have found something that I want to give to you.

I had a book that I had bought for Dennis that he wouldn't read because he was afraid. I want to give you that book because I want to gift it to someone, and you were there when I was afraid. The book is on healing the spiritual heart. Will you accept my gift?"

You can see who was crying then! Doing the best I could to talk and cry at the same time, I accepted her offer of the gift and told her my current situation and the divine timing of her call. We tried to coordinate our schedules for a meeting to give and receive the book before she left town. We were unable to arrange our schedules so we could meet in person for the gift exchange so she left it at my office. We never spoke or saw each other again.

After being, yet one more time, absolutely stunned by the turn of events, I saw that we had been angels for each other at appropriately designed moments. I recognized we were not the ones who consciously designed and orchestrated our connections in precisely the critical moments of need for each one of us! I now had the answer to my still lingering question. After putting all of my situational pieces together, I chose to not seek out a doctor. I did not see a western medical doctor as having the tools to facilitate, or even recognize, the components of spiritual heart healing. This healing was about a personal opening and healing, not about medicating or cutting 'according to them.'

The masseuse did call later in the morning and was pleased to hear that I had canceled or at least postponed my vacation. He did ask about my seeing a doctor as I told him I didn't have one. I was feeling resolved with my decision to not go to one at this time. He respectively listened to me and seemed to honor my decision while at the same time feeling it was still important that I do something. After revealing to him that I did not have a personal physician, he offered me an alternative which happened to be a well-known (in the field) Bioenergetic Practitioner who was doing some pretty amazing things for people in the healing field working with the body, mind, and spirit. Knowing that I had not set a for-sure appointment with the Tibetan Doctor, I agreed to at least call this person.

So, what now? I am up and functioning on my first planned day of vacation with all plans canceled and my insides somewhat lighter in resolve but still heavy with disappointment. I could give myself the day off and then go back to work. However, all of my clients' work was caught up, and no one was expecting to see me for ten days! A new dilemma now—what could I do that would still be fun and give me the break that I so needed? At the same time, I was feeling like another big piece of the disappointment that was now raising its voice to be heard was that a big powerpoint on my 'vacation agenda' was to find the answer to what was next for me in my life's manifesting path. I still desperately desired new experiences to explore. Deep inside, I knew that I was so through with my Harmane Bookkeeping Service. I felt I had now been shown that it was not time to see my next change because I wasn't going to the rich and powerful energy of Sedona, AZ to get insights for my answer. I had felt guided to go there. I felt like a huge boulder had been dropped onto my path in front of me!

I had some fun-loving friends who lived in a beautiful, loving home in a remote place up on the side of a mountain. He was a professor in the doctorate department of the local University, and she had various roles in the community. As I scrambled around to see what potentials there are for my next ten days, I decided to call them and see if anyone was home. If there was, I would invite myself up for a cup of tea. If I stayed in my house, I felt I would go down too far to keep moving, and I certainly didn't want that! My phone call had a good outcome as she was home and welcomed me with open arms. I didn't share all of the aspects of my present situation other than I said my plans had changed and I needed to get out and talk to someone so I could regroup.

She indicated that this was an excellent time to come as she had a house guest from Brazil. She indicated they would be having brunch soon, so please come join them. With great gratitude for a lighter aspect of my day, I took off up the mountain. When I arrived, my friend was still preparing the delicacies for our meal as I engaged in a delightful conversation with her Brazilian friend. In the course of our conversation, it was revealed that the lady was a healer and was clairvoyant and did readings as a part of her healing practice. While we continued to visit, she turned to me and stated that she would really like to do a reading for me while we were waiting for the food to finish cooking. Strictly looking through my own consciousness filter in that present time, I told her that was very kind, but knowing and feeling that she was on vacation, I didn't want her to be working. Therefore, I declined her offer, but she insisted. Keep in mind I had not shared any of the details of my present happenings with either lady. All they knew was that I had a plan that did not work out and I was regrouping as I was happy to be able to be there with them for lunch and visit.

Her intuitively guided message to and for me went something like this: I had been preparing to go someplace that I definitely should not go to now. She saw that I had recently had a phase of a spiritual heart opening and that my heart was not stabilized yet. If I had gone to this place at this time, the strong energy could have caused my death. I was to rest for 5 or 6 days and to just be quiet and if possible, be by myself as much as possible in that time. Needless to say, I ended up sharing with her the details of my then-current situation. She then indicated that it would be beneficial still to take some type of an out-of-town vacation but to go somewhere I had been before—no place that was new at that time. It would be good to have this place be someplace that my heart loved to be, and it wasn't stressful getting there. Once again guided to another answer, I made my choice that night and left the next morning to a beautiful mountain town that I loved which was about 200 miles away. I also graciously accepted the additional piece around the dynamics playing out pertaining to my heart.

The final episode to this chronological piece of my inner and outer parallel balancing journey was my appointment with the Bioenergetic Practitioner that I did go to two weeks later after returning from my reconstructed vacation. The initial body scan was done with modern technology which read the body's energy pathways. This, coupled with the intuitive knowingness of the practitioner, gave me very valuable insights about my body, mind, and emotional self with information for my health that did not involve labeling anything as a particular diagnosis.

I was so deeply impressed by this concept, the information available, and the modality. A few days after my appointment, I called to inquire as to what the training and process were to become a practitioner. I was asking myself if in the biggest stretch of my imagination, was it anything that I could conceivably become? I was informed that in two or three months, the well-known man was going to open a school for the purpose of training and certifying Bioenergetic Practitioners. A medical background was not only not necessary, but not preferred, as this was a new way of maintaining and understanding health and healing, and sometimes, those with previous medical training had a hard time releasing their healing beliefs in order to embrace something new. After some discussion, I was enrolled for the first official series of classes of the International Academy of Bioenergetic Practitioners, later referred to as IABP.

Now you see, I got the answer to my last question—What is next? It came through my original vacation plan but after seemingly all avenues had been altered. I ultimately got all that I had set out to get and much more. It was truly as though a different plan encompassing all of my main known-to-me points and many of my main points yet-unknown-to-me were executed as an overlay onto my original plan. It was as if the main part of the original plan was to design some downtime, i.e. available space, for my higher Self, my God Self, or whatever I wanted to call it, to come in with the new information already available for my next Divine Human Creation. The Divine plan was laid over mine but not canceling out mine. It was amazing to me how I was guided to keep playing until all of the pieces, known and unknown to me, were put together, recognized, cognized for, and as the answers to all of my questions. I felt my internal intentions all in a newly balanced internal-external package ready for living in the next chapter of my life journey as I learned even more of who I am and what I have to give and receive.

I did take the courses given for certification, and I was one of the students in the first series of classes to graduate. I received my Bioenergetic Certification, moved forward to downsizing, eventually closed my bookkeeping service, and became a full-time Bioenergetic Practitioner with my own office. I later followed this adventure by having a mobile traveling clinic where I served Amish communities in three different states. It was an interesting and very valuable chapter of my life's journey that was at the core of my giving and receiving Divine Human reality for a little over ten years.

Following is a poem and some shared thoughts that were written by the founder of the International Academy of Bioenergetic Practitioner, Spencer Woolley. He made his transition from this Earth lifetime in 2001.

A Word from Spencer

Life's goal is not to outwit death and disease, or 'get out alive,' but to become conscious and self-actualized: aware and able to handle any and all changes without fear and with an understanding of the message contained in the change. To be a self-actualized person means to break free from the limits of the self by surrendering self-will to the divine will. It means to be aware of the body as an expression of the spirit, a physical carrier of consciousness. It means to live life with love, honor, and forgiveness, to accept change as it comes, and to understand that what is needed and appropriate will always manifest in its own time and way. There are many lessons to be learned on the way to achieving the goal. Let the physical world and your body be your teachers. Align them with the spirit—and don't skip school.

> Someday, in our attempts to master
> the earth, the wind, the waves, the tides,
> the rivers, the seas, gravity of the atom,
> we will find God.
> And with Him, harness the energies of His Love.
> Then, for the second time in the history of the world,
> God will have said, "Let there be light!"
> and we will have discovered fire!

A poem by Spencer G. Woolley

Thank you for letting me share my journey with you as you showed up to see if there were any bread crumbs here in-between the lines or words that resonate in any way with a journey that you may have had, or are having in your book of life that was allowing you the opportunity to see more of who you really are and who all of us are as ONE Creation coming from the same Source!

A NEW ROAD

I'm off to see the Wizard, the Wonderful Wizard of Oz,
So, how do I find my way - the yellow brick road you say,
No, I am not going to that Wizard, I am going a different way!

I am taking the road where every brick is a different color,
Some reflect faces, some reflect places and some are mirrored
spaces,
This path does not lead to 'over the rainbow' rather it is the
rainbow!

So is there a Wizard at the end of this road too?
Is it the same Wizard or one New?
Oh yes, there is most definitely a Wizard I hear say,
But there is no end to this different way!

While skipping and dancing on the journey, I feel the I AM
That I AM
As the mirrored spaces reflect the Wizard all along the way
- ME!

Poem by Norma Ervin

Do you want to come let your heart play?
Become Like a Child today and Don't
Over Complicate the Truth!
Remember....
Your Life is Your Choice
So....
Your Choice is Your Life!

Expanded consciousness creates new potentials for Divine Humans and Mother Earth!

It's about the Heart - Not just the Will
It's about Allowing - Not constantly Efforting
It's about Acceptance - Not always Processing
It's about Awareness - Not always Analyzing

As the ebb and flow of all that is now, has ever been, and even perhaps of all that is to be in and as the future, who are WE? The answer starts out with yet another question, Who AM I? Life is like a puzzle with each piece having a crucial place to fit in order for the picture to be complete. This is a fact regardless of what the picture of the puzzle is. Each piece has a special, exact place to fit with its perfect offering for the whole. Right now on planet Earth, new paths of thinking, living, communicating, and perceiving all the way to the very core of existing are requiring of us, demanding of us to find a workable answer to 'Who We Are!' This challenging journey seems to be taking us away from the yellow brick road where we have been told from some fairy tale land that we could travel down the magic road and find our Wizard of Oz. The change wasn't so extreme in those times in the past nor did it happen constantly.

So why a New Road? Where does this idea come from? Is it just the perception of a few, or does it have a more universal beginning? Who voted what systems failed or brought about the need for us as humans to view the dynamics of our collective life differently? Following is a piece of information that some of you may be aware of, and it may be new to others, but it does propose answers to the questions just asked.

There was a time in history that is known as the Harmonic Convergence which was on August 16-17, 1987. This is a documented timing for the gateway leading into the changing of times on Mother Earth that would be involving us as the tribe of humanity. Science can explain how the elements of the Cosmic Universe itself were changing in a cyclic manner at this time and the years to follow. 1987 led up to the ending of a cycle on Earth as it moved into a new cycle and a new beginning. This cycle was a 26,000-year period of time. Each 26,000-year cycle has a 36-year cycle of time when the first 18 years of that 36 years are the ending of the current cycle. The second 18 years of the 36 years is when the energy is being set for the energetics of the cosmos and the Earth for the next 26,000 years. That first 18-year period began in 1994 and ended on the well-known (to many) date of December 21, 2012.

In the awareness of all of this, it has been shared that many human beings would consciously, or unconsciously, experience these 36 years as a major shift in their lives. The first 18 years would be when we would find ourselves completing, finishing, being done with a lot of what had been major, or even minor, ways of being in our living life reality. What we were completing was referred to as an old energy cycle of mass consciousness that we had created as multiple cultures at a global level with each culture having pieces of their own uniqueness in the whole. The 12/21/12 ended the completion period. Following that date, the transition would be us as human beings and mother earth, moving into living and defining ourselves from New earth energy. From this perspective, we would be a part of discovering and developing a new mass consciousness. We are in that period now, and it will go on until 2030.

In this second 18-year period where we as a human race are co-creating the patterns for a New Earth as we play our part in the creative dynamics of the shift of change, it is not only happening to man, but is also a part of the cosmos, our galaxy, and Mother Earth as Gaia. Science can prove the moving of planets, suns, and other forms in our galaxy and outside of our galaxy. We can watch the weather changes of Gaia in our own communication systems or various other ways with some even personally experiencing some of the major happenings. Recorded history over ages of time can also prove the timing of cycles of life on planet Earth. Much of this history has come from the indigenous Indian tribes and other indigenous tribes with science confirming a lot of what has been documented.

Therefore, in this time when so much is happening that seems to be presenting hell on earth, could it be that it is all appropriate as the dark and evil, which is just that which is not love, is being pushed to the surface for recognition by the masses? Could we be being directed to move back toward the light for us to play out as our Master Creator intended? In that change, hate can become love, war can become peace, the lack can become abundance, greed can become cooperation and/or compassion, and even more good can be our truth!

Now consider what you perceive is happening and exercise your free choice as to how you want to play your part as an individual piece of the collective, the ONE. One indicates a whole together, not separated. My choice is to allow myself to say 'Yes to Beyond' and to travel many unknown-to-me roads to learn and experience what this all really means. For me, these new ways are facilitating me to bring a balance to my inner and outer life and to know both in a way that has my 5 senses as life tools stretching their capacity. I want my external world to reflect my internal world. I want to know and understand who I am from my heart and feeling self as a human being, and transfer that to my external reality as a human doing as I play out my many scripts on my own chosen stages. Much of our mass consciousness pattern has implied that we are basically human doings and that our external values are our life and to Be doesn't even make sense.

WELCOME TRAVELERS
LET US GET ON WITH THE JOURNEY OF CHANGE
AS WE TRAVEL OFF THE FAMILIAR
YELLOW BRICK ROAD
TO A NEW ROAD!

WELCOME ABOARD!
DON'T FASTEN YOUR SEAT BELTS SO YOU WILL
BE FREE TO MOVE ABOUT!

I am not here with my intention being to guide (facilitate) you to have any of the experiences I have had. I am not your God, your preacher, your master, your guru, or even your teacher. What I am is one of your co-creators as we are Divine Human Being Co-creators. We are here to be co-creating together. That is our purpose, our mission, and whether it is felt by us or not, our passion. I am not coming to you out of theory. It is the process of my journey through my 'Book of Life' that has me here now to share, express, explore, experience, and evolve with other co-creators who choose to play together to discover the depths of our Being, our potentials, and what it is that we are truly playing out and creating. At this current time of all landscapes changing and all mirrors tilting, is there a world between the worlds where some heavy-duty refining is taking place? I feel there is and together, we can see with new eyes to see the messes that are appearing as beauty evolving. We all have written, as well as are currently writing, our 'Individual Book of Life.' If we are alive, that is a fact. Therefore, we are all authors and publishers. Our Book is our Life Journey. We publish it without book form for others, as well as ourselves, to see us by how we walk, talk, or otherwise reflect who we think we are and how we feel about life.

In this now on planet Earth, we are in the midst of evolutionary changes as they have never happened before. These changes are huge including the cosmos, our galaxy, our planet the home of mother Earth and all of her gifts of nature, and our divine human's physical self, to mention some of them. We are changing and are somewhat challenged by all of this whether we want to or not, whether we are consciously participating or just trying to stay asleep. I want to join with many of you as co-creators in these exciting times which could be termed the best of times and the worst of times.

These pages are my passionately designed mission for a co-created journey for those who are 'up' for the ride. Following are some highlighted points to keep in tune with for the journey to, and with, the New Road.

1. That we **become fully enchanted or mesmerized** by this new world coming up on our horizon even though at times it may seem more alien than real.

2. That we **consciously become acquainted** with it by allowing our five senses to expand their functions. This is how I suggest that could be accomplished:

   A. **Touch-reach into the seemingly nothing space**
   B. **Hear-listen in the silence**
   C. **See the Invisible**
   D. **Smell the breath**
   E. **Taste...this expanded sense collective allows a new taste of creation**

Stating it another way but expressing the same thing, is it possible that we can utilize our five senses to go and experience spaces within us and outside of us that reveal Us to Us in a realm beyond our five senses?

Could it work expanded like this?

See—Insight
Hear—Awareness
Taste—Nourish (Nurture) Life
Smell—ignites recognition
Touch—hones it to matter, form, physical, human

We can experience the 5 senses as singular aspects that stand alone but can also be easily connected with each other. We utilize them as the grand gifts of creation that they are. They take us through a door from the invisible to the visible. They are the keys to the door of the threshold into the space where they aren't but where they were created from. Perhaps, at that very intersection, they literally exist and yet they don't. Senses are human dynamics designed for us from our divinity realm but not needed there. The threshold is not a swinging door but rather a revolving door that opens up to a whole undefined, undivided space. There is no box appearance.

3. We expand our senses when we receive and accept a new way to read our own Book of life, as well as a new way to observe our fellow co-creators' books of life where we could read between the lines and the spaces between the words. In this mode, we are understanding beyond the thoughts and words of the definitions from the brain. When we sing together, we hear the tones of the note between the notes even when we are not together. Is this intuition? Is this clairvoyance?

4. As authors continuing the writing of our own Individual Book of Life that we sense and use our words as mere symbols of the nothing visible but everything present space and has this all make sense as a new paradigm for living life...

This would all be the journey. What are the benefits for the sojourner to utilize for exploring, experiencing, and expressing? Some potentials are:

1. Experience all kinds—not just words for analyzing. Feel it as an alive book where we are together.
2. Awareness of a new reality beyond duality where we can take up residency.
3. Create New Life tools.
4. Arrive at a place of knowingness of how the now times are the whole and perfect times of the ultimate Creation playing out and recreating All in Divine Right Timing.
5. Know Your SELF as a whole and perfect.
6. Know and BE your SELF as, with, in, and from LOVE.
7. BE FREE.
8. Know who you (we) are and what that really means—I AM That I AM.

Now I am going to share with you my journey in that 36-year core period of ending and beginning times starting with the first 18 years on our journey!

DISCOVERING MY PERSONAL TRUTH

The Journey in a Nutshell starting in 1996

I owned a condo in the city and I lived and operated my bookkeeping business in a nearby town. All seemed okay in my life with no serious challenges, and I was comfortable just doing my thing. I was searching for more meaning in life as I explored more and more avenues for more experiences. Nature became one of my greatest teachers as well as my most friendly and sincere companions. I love the water as rivers, lakes, or ponds; I loved the trees along the hillsides out in nature, and I was always brought to peace by the singing of the birds. I just loved the outdoors! The spirituality of the Native American Indian also gave me deepfelt insights into looking at life in a more expanded way. I was not in a relationship at this time and was quite content with becoming my own best friend even though I was open to being in a relationship.

One October night I had gotten up, and I heard so very clearly the words, "It is time to sell your condo!" I actually turned around to see who was there even though I knew no one was present. Where is this coming from and how can this be were a few of the questions that were racing through my mind. I had always said that when the time was right to sell it, I would know, but I never expected to be told this way! Therefore, I just chose to ignore it and chalk it all up to my imagination, even though I had not even been contemplating any sale. I had a good renter in it, and after all, that ownership gave me 'financial value!" All was well, and I intended to keep it so! After dismissing it, so I thought, other peculiar things continued happening until I had given my full attention, but not without complaining and arguing!

This was all happening in the middle of the night around 3 or 4 o'clock. Upon going back to bed, I received another message from the same voice that had given me the original message just a few minutes before. This time, I was told that in a moment, my phone was going to ring but I was not to answer it. It was just ringing as proof that my earlier message and this message really were happening and that it was not just my imagination. Well, sure enough, within seconds after I got back in bed, my phone rang. I did not get up to answer it (this was before cell phones) but just laid there, and it rang one more time and quit. Over the next few months, I continued being deeply stirred inside with the battle inside of me presenting the very strong feeling that I really did not want to sell my condo, and yet, I did have this deep, not so well known or strong, feeling that I was getting the answer to what I had asked all along. I was asking for something higher than my intellectual mind to let me know when it was the right timing to sell. I had no concept that this is the way the answer would come to me, and I had no real point of reference that it would be anything that would require me to interfere with my comfort zone because that condo was my symbol of self-worth and it was generating extra money for me. Somehow, my inner self was seemingly saying, "All of you mysterious players, just move on!"

At this point in my life's journey, I was downsizing my bookkeeping service and slowly starting my Bioenergetic Practitioner Clinic. Therefore, my plate was already pretty full and a little unsettled in the transition of finishing one self-owned business and starting another one, the alternative health one. Being late in the year when it was time, I started getting my bookkeeping client's books ready for income tax time and W-2 forms out for all of them. I saw no way that I could deal with anything else. However, my internal nudge did not stop. Finally, I thought I could negotiate with the universe, so I started my own time frame. I internally declared that I would consider the sale, but it had to be after the first of the year and closer to April because by then, I would have all tax preparations done.

This worked for a short period of time, but I never did regain peace within me. Still contemplating the possibility of a sale, I decided to go to my rental tenant and tell him the possibility of my putting it on the market, thinking that perhaps he would be interested in buying. I did go, and he was not interested in buying. He also shared with me that he was getting married soon, and they were going to look for a different place to live anyway. Wow, one more sign to me. It was going to be empty anyway! We had a friendly chat and thanked each other for being there for each other, and I went my way with another whirlwind inside me, or maybe it was just the same one whipping up again. Before leaving the condo, I ask for permission to walk through it and see any repairs it would need before putting it on the market for either a buyer or another tenant. What this walk-through really turned out to be for me was a huge 'past life review!' I had quite a lot of dynamic, dramatic, traumatic circumstances that had led me to buy that in the beginning and the few years that I had lived there allowed me to find new parts of me and who I was and to do a lot of healing. I had loved my solitude and the privilege of finding and supporting a 'Me to Me' life. After leaving there and reflecting on the day, I immediately recognized that there was a lot more of me there than just a bottom-line money measurement of my value. I had found a new path to living life from that space. After this visit, was I ready to move on to yet another new path to life? I had recognized the gift that I had given to myself and all that I had received there. I now owned all of that inside me; therefore, of what value was it really to keep it as a memorial? Going into negotiations again with the universe, I stated that I was now more willing to sell, but I needed another clue if that truly was the right direction to go at this time. I ask that the clue be in the ease of finding a realtor that I felt comfortable with and could easily work with.

On to next—'Yes, I will consider selling.' It is time to move on to next even though I have no idea what this change will be or what it means. The next step is to find a realtor. Another big step is I don't even know all of the questions to ask in that process. I don't remember if I had a visit with a friend or a client for ideas and suggestions pertaining to a real estate agency and/or a realtor. Someone did recommend a realtor to me, and he came with good recommendations not only business-wise but also as a very kind and personable person. That all sounded good to me, so I called him. The initial meeting was good, and he was immediately ready to meet me and move forward. At this point, I was still nervous around the whole situation, but I was resolved to the fact that I had received my answer pertaining to being informed when it was time to sell, and now I was ready to just jump in and do what it took. Therefore, I had jumped in at some level but still asking for verification. We met at the condo, walked through, had a discussion, got some questions answered on both of our parts, and went on our way to meet again soon after he has put together more details for the process.

I received a phone call from him the next morning stating that he does have some information for me and would like to meet with me personally again as soon as we could arrange it. We did meet later that day, and the information that he gave me after a friendly discussion on all of the good that he saw in the condo literally shocked me as well as brought me to tears! He and his wife had been considering buying an investment property. He had taken her over to see it the night before and she also really liked it, and they would like to buy it. One more time, the universe gave me what I had asked for and more pertaining to a realtor and a definite answer to selling! The end of that story was that after they were open to taking the leap and purchasing an investment property, they decided they would prefer a two-bedroom one, and mine was a one-bedroom. Therefore, they did not buy it, but he immediately brought me a buyer who did. My condo sold in early 1997.

Now that the directive to sell the condo had been completed and I had recognized a lot about me, my life path, and more of who I wasn't as well as who I AM, my 18-year journey of change continued. I finally was completely through with my bookkeeping service business and was getting more and more engaged in my Bioenergetic Practitioner practice and was feeling good about the potentials of that business. Early on in my new business in the alternative health field and after I had my first computerized scanning device, I took part in an alternative health fare. Another one of the graduates from the first IABP (International

Academy Bioenergetic Practitioners) and I had a booth at the fair where we were demonstrating our devices and sharing what their value was in the health field. The fare ended with an open banquet for all participants and attendees who wanted to attend. Sitting at the same table where I was sitting was a gentleman who was a truck driver that was interested in these kinds of things and had come to the two- or three-day event as it had fit in his schedule. We got into a good conversation about all that we had experienced in those few days, me from my booth and meeting the people, and him from being able to go around and gather information from so many of the vendors and presenters. This was the beginning of a friendship for us that continued over the next four years.

As time went on, we discussed buying some property together. This was another new step for me as I recalled my journey through selling my condo. At the beginning of this path in my life journey, I was also alerted by my invisible guides as I began facing the fact of leaving everything, everyone, and everywhere that I claimed as my life and chosen surroundings. The response that I got was, "You will be going someplace you have never been before." My anxiety started as I had no past point of reference to help me through this, and I wasn't even absolutely sure that I even wanted to go. However, the subtle directive remained powerfully present letting me know I would be leaving my known and going into my unknown and believing it to be good or not. I was going!

We explored different options in Colorado as that is where I was comfortable. In fact, that is where I had lived all my life except for a short period of time that I lived in New Mexico not too far from the Colorado state line. Not finding anyplace that we both really liked or that we felt we could afford, we begin to search out options around where he was from which was Missouri, and guess what, I had never been there before! We eventually did find a place that seemed to satisfy factors that each of us individually desired, and between the two of us, it was affordable. For my part, I could manage because I had sold my condo. Preparing for the move was very emotional for me as I was truly leaving everything and everyone I had ever known as family, friends, clients, home, and land surroundings! Consequently, I was back to internal storms of all kinds.

However, by the time we actually were ready to go, I did feel sadness in leaving my two sons, their families, and all of my friends, but I was also a little excited to be experiencing something new even though all in front of me was unknown. Talk about 'Yes to Beyond' with everything unknown; I felt truly in the world between the worlds leaving everything that was and not knowing anything or anyone in front of me. Even my truck driver friend would be going over the road after a few weeks off.

The first moving adventure was actually on the road the first day of moving day itself. I was driving my car following my friend who was driving a U-Haul truck that had inside it everything that I owned as of that now. I was feeling some strange feelings particularly as I had just left my boys and I had never been out of reach at any distance from them before except when my younger son was in the military and was stationed in Spain or another state in the US. I was already missing them. I also had a strange feeling inside me when I looked at the back of the truck in front of me knowing that every material thing I owned was in that truck, and I didn't really know anything about the area I was moving to as I had only been there once. That was when we went to look at the house that we chose to buy. I saw that I needed gas in the car so I pulled into the first gas station that I saw thinking that I could fill up quickly and still catch up with the truck. Well, I was wrong! When getting back on the road, I drove as fast as I could and never reconnected with the truck. It was before the days of cell phones so I could not call.

I became distraught as I really did not know how to get to our destination for that day. I knew how to get to Kansas City, but beyond that, I was clueless as we were meeting at his folk's house outside of St. Joseph, MO. I became very emotional and had to pull into a rest stop and regroup. Crying by this time, I went into a conversation with my unseen partner adamantly asking what was going on! I had just left everything I had ever known to move on, and I had left with a subtle feeling that it was all in divine right order. Why now was I disconnected from my friend and the only stuff that I still had as well as I was now a foreigner in a foreign life, having nothing, and nobody. My heart was crying and asking why had I been guided to take this step? My answer was, **"All is in**

Divine Right Order. This move is not about relationships. It is about you leaving all that you knew and thought you had in order to move into a new reality and see much more of who you really are and to expand your world and be willing to walk beyond your own limits." Somehow, this did give me peace. By now, I was exhausted so I just took a short nap before getting back on the road. When I got to Kansas City much later that day, I just kept stopping and asking questions as to how to get through the city and keep on my way. I did have a phone number of my friends' folks home so after I thought my friend would be there by then, I did stop, find a phone, and call and was guided the rest of the way.

This journey led me to a 6 ½-year period that was definitely one of the most intense periods of time that I had experienced up to this point. I did not plan it, at least as far as I knew then, and I did not go willingly in the beginning. I was like the cat being pulled out of the tree by her tail with every claw embedded as deeply into the tree as was possible and feeling that I had lost the fight. Hurt, angry, confused, and somewhat feeling defeated, I settled in for the ride. The interesting part of this is that no one was making me do anything! I even heard myself making some of the decisions out loud that were moving me on my way, when at the same time, on the inside, I was screaming, "What is happening!" There seemed to be a 100 lb. foot in the middle of my back that would not let me turn around or stop!

Remember, the year of the beginning of the crucial change within the 18-year period began in 1994. This move was happening in 1998.

We settled into our new location and did some house repainting and a few other things to make it our home and then my truck driver friend had to go back to work and his journey took him over the road and he was gone weeks or a month at a time. That was hard for me, but I really kept hearing what this journey was really about for me, and it was not relationships. Consequently, I kept endeavoring to look through the unknown until I felt I fit somewhere, and that at some point, I would see what I was supposed to see and learn what was up for my learning.

In the next four to five years, I had many opportunities to review and reflect on my life up until then as I was alone in our home in the country the majority of that time. I did make a conscious effort to get my Bioenergetic business going but was unsuccessful to create a practice in the local communities. In fact, several times in taking part in various health fares, because I was representing a faction of alternative health that had a different approach than western medicine, I was actually told that I was of the devil. I became discouraged, but I did find a group of people that were interested in pure essential oils, and we made a connection that did give me a feeling of communicating with the outside world.

Back in Colorado, the Bioenergetic Academy had designed a website listing all of the people who had become certified and were open for business. From that website information and my location, I received a call from a person that introduced me to an Amish man who was interested in talking to me. He lived not too far away in an Amish community in a town less than 100 miles away from me. This started my journey working with Amish communities in 3 different states. Through another set of circumstances, I had purchased a new-to-me motor home that was like new with only 17,000 miles on it. I made that into a traveling clinic and went to the Amish and was able to service them from my clinic motorhome as I had electricity from a generator and a series of connected batteries and I could utilize my equipment for them this way as they did not have electricity.

Sometime in 2001, my connection with my truck driver friend ended and I moved on to another adventure, taking my motor home with me now not only as a clinic but as my home as well. I moved on to doing scans for a doctor in a local clinic in Springfield, MO and giving the doctor the information that I had found from my electronic computer scan. At this time, I was endeavoring to live nearby in an intentional community where I had my motorhome as my residence. This was my scene for a short period and in Oct. of 2001, I went to Germany with three other people, one of whom was a German from Germany. This Germany journey had a duration of six weeks. On this adventure, I learned a lot about biodynamic farming and that way of life. I became much more educated regarding intentional communities and their value particularly the ones that were developed in Germany with some of their ways being practiced in the US. I was there in Germany soon after the 9/11 World Tower Bombing in the US. It was really interesting to feel and see how this had an impact on other countries as some were in the process of deciding to support the USA or not in our fight against terrorism.

From this adventure, I left Missouri altogether and moved on to Arkansas. Within this time, I was still going to some Amish communities periodically in Missouri and one in Arkansas. After moving to Arkansas, I was beginning to wear down. I really began to say to myself that I was really paying a price for something, but I didn't know what the hell I was buying! I knew I had some really good experiences, that I had been playing new, that I had certainly stepped out of my comfort zone, that I had found more of my power, that I had discovered a lot more of myself, and yet within me, I was tired and I was not content. I felt empty somehow as I didn't feel like I really belonged anywhere!

I recognized that I had gained a much bigger understanding of knowing that God is within me and not just outside, somewhere away from me. I was recognizing more and more that my true value was as a Divine Being connecting on Earth in form as a Human Being. I recognized that I had previously seen my value as a Human Doing, that my external life was the definer of who I was. Therefore, with this new insight, what was I to do, where was I to be, who was I really within this strong pushing and pulling discontent? At that time, my biggest questions to myself were when I was focused on my mental and emotional bodies. I also had the recognition that I was running out of money and my intake was minimum. I kept asking myself what have I done wrong, where do I land as home, and how do I keep going? I missed Colorado, but I felt I could not go back to all that had been known to me as my reality. I had moved on, but to what? After much more inner work, inner vision, and trusting Universal (God Inside of me conversations) I came to the realization that I could return without going back to all that it was. It would never be the same for me because I was not the same, and I could never be just who I was then or who I knew myself as then.

On Labor Day weekend in 2004, I re-entered Colorado on my returning trip ready for my next new, not old, chapter in my Life Journey.

My younger son was participating in a conference in Kansas City. I drove my motorhome from Fayetteville, Arkansas and met him there. He then drove us on the trip returning him home and my return from a long journey. A friend of mine in Arkansas who had a truck loaded up all of my belongings in the truck and towed my car back to Colorado for me.

Consequently, the 6 ½-year journey ended. I had left all, found much, and experienced a lot. I had a much bigger version and vision of life than when I left, and I now felt myself like a different person. However, I did arrive 'returned,' not back, not knowing where to land, what to do, and no clarity on how to resume being me so I could fit in somewhere! My family greeted me and were happy to see me, but it was all different somehow. I had not kept in touch with any of my friends as I did this journey. In that current now, who even really knew me as I didn't even really know myself? What could possibly be next, and yet there must be something?

Following are the highlights of the next 8 years of my life journey as I completed the first 18 letting go years of the 36-year period of resetting a crucial dynamic for the next cosmic cycle on the planet. Remember that the first 18-year cycle began in 1994, and I have just reported through 2004.

1. 2005—found a beautiful place out-of-town to live; I put my motor home in an RV storage lot; I rented a room from a doctor in town who was a medical western medicine doctor who also believed in and practiced alternative healing methods and concepts. In my rented space, I did body scans of patients and gave the results to this doctor for her diagnosis or suggestion for treatment. I was still unsettled inside and was searching for where I actually belonged as I was still learning who I was and the different me was returning.

2. 2006-2007—I moved again and took a job at a resort in Estes Park, CO. I had always wanted to live here, and I wanted Rocky Mountain National Park as my backyard. I loved living there, but I did not like my job at all. It was very hard for me to work

for someone else after having been self-employed for over 20 years.

3. 2007—Was a very traumatic year as I had an 11-year old grandson die of leukemia. The resort where I worked went into foreclosure and was purchased by a new owner. At the time of ownership change, I left and moved back to the valley. My grandson died four days after I moved back.

4. 2008-2009—I got another job through a temporary employment agency. It did not work out with that job leaving me with dwindling funds and no job. I had worked long enough to get unemployment pay for a period. I was still very distraught and lost and still could not discern where I belonged.

5. 2009—That fall after having spent a multiple month period of time going through my storage and everything I owned, I discarded everything that was no longer of any value to me physically or emotionally as I cried a river! I let go of so much that was all about who I used to be that no longer held any value to my 'unknown me' of that present time. Upon completion of that time of experiencing, I packed what was necessary into my car, gave up my apartment, and moved to my sister's in New Mexico for the winter. My goal there was to write more on the book that had been residing inside me in bits and pieces since 2003.

6. 2010—It was a big year that was the final step in bringing me to zero in every facet of my life. I was already at the bottom emotionally and mentally and was barely floating financially, but I still had the desire and intent to keep going the best I could because I did have a vision, a dream, of a different life which at moments I thought somehow it could become my reality. Getting this book written and published were a part of my desired dream. Well, my final big step of this 18-year period of leaving, re-evaluating everything was triple by-pass open heart surgery. That situation now brought me to zero physically with my health.

7. 2010-2012—These were recovering years in all ways. In 2010 and 2011, I went back to NM for the winters. My biggest challenge for these years was that I had no physical energy as all was healing. I still had my vision—my dream, but I would keep canceling it out as I would state that my mind saw it, but my physical and biological body was not able to participate in a way of helping me manifest it. At this point, I felt there was no way for me to have any kind of fulfilling life ever again. Toward the end of 2012, I was regaining a little positive attitude and my body was doing much better physically. The surgery had left me with a new health issue which at first was very hard for me to deal with and not go into fear of all kinds including death. That new health issue was Atrial Fibrillation (AFIB).

December 21, 2012 was the historically recorded time for the ending of the first 18 years of the 36 years. What had me so amazed as I reviewed all of my experiences in the earlier years of this period was the exact timing of all of my major changing events and how they had affected me. All of this started for me in 1994 which was the exact timing of this 36-year period, and those 18 years had most definitely taken me away from everything that I had ever known as me and as my life. All these had left me not knowing who I even was and how or where I even belonged on Earth, but I was very clear that I was not ready to leave (die) and was very grateful that I was still alive. Up to that point, many people on both sides of my biological parents' families had died in their 60s or before and many of them had died of some kind of heart problem. Both of my parents died in their 60s and both deaths were related to heart issues. My mother's cause of death was directly related to a heart issue and my father's was a ruptured pulmonary artery as a result of the complications of lung cancer. When I knew I was going to have open-heart surgery at age 65, I momentarily went into the space of extreme fear just knowing that I was not going to wake up because of my family history and all that had died and the circumstances.

LIFE'S FOUR CORNER STONES, VERSE ONE

Now that I was in the first 18-year period of the 36-year core of the time of change that was explained earlier, I was being guided by a mind of some kind that was way beyond my intellectual brain-mind. It was as if I had a 'Yes to Beyond' mind that was now in charge of my journey, and I just had to concentrate on moving and hanging on the best I knew how when it seemed all of my old tools for life were seemingly becoming obsolete and no new ones were yet in my toolbox for use. My main job seemed to be to stay tuned into what was coming up as my major 'Life Review'! Consequently, still living as though I lived in a box of some kind, it was time for me to look at Life's Four Corner Stones.

Here are some beneficial questions to be used as clues for the treasure hunt through one's Book of life as we reread some of the main chapters. Remember to read into the invisible spaces as well. It is not just the illusionary play itself that was (is) of importance, but rather the feeling and Divine-Human expression of the experiences that really moves consciousness on to be the same or become more.

Following are some questions for contemplation in our individual self-review:

1. How have you lived much of your life, and what motivated you?
2. Outside of your jobs and other identities, who are you?
3. Is abundance just a measurement of how money gives you your worth-value?
4. How do you relate to people, or not, and how is that serving you?

5. How are you treating your physical body, and how is it serving you?

6. Are you at peace inside and outside of yourself?

WORK IT … WORK IT …
LIFE'S FOUR CORNER STONES

RELATIONSHIPS

How can this Be?
I have given everything and every way I know how to give,
Still, it seems Love isn't enough or lasting.
My Love, Your Love, Our Love….

We came together with the drumbeat
Beating our Soul's rhythms - seeking harmony,
Beating the music for our dance together.
We cried, laughed, danced, shared, played, dreamed,
Loved, agreed, disagreed, and more.
Wasn't this a Love that mattered?
Wasn't this a Love that was real?

Now you are gone!
Gone as quickly as the wind passing through a tree,
Leaving only a ghostly tone!
Gone from my space, but still in my heart!
I hurt, I cry, I scream, I wonder, I would pray if I could, I listen,
        I go numb!
How, where, when will life be different?
I feel I am on the edge of existence with NO answers!
I want to die, maybe I will, perhaps I have somehow!
What is Love?
Who am I?

—A verse from a poem by Norma Ervin

Could these be some answers or guidelines for relationships?

A Dreamed-Up Relationship

1. Minimize the expectations.
2. Let go of the old definitions of relationship that one might carry.
3. Claim no ownership of each other.
4. Live in a way that neither person has to compromise who they are.
5. Curb judgment of each other.
6. Communication is a priority but long discussions about everything is not necessary. Much communication can just be sensed.
7. Be aware of and have a sensitivity to each other's true and deep feelings. Don't dishonor or discount this space.
8. Allow different beliefs.
9. Don't try to change each other to suit one's own needs
10. Recognize each other as whole and complete (in this now) within and as themselves.
11. Trust each other and trust the flow.
12. Respect each other.
13. Keep it fun.
14. Value and enjoy intimacy.
15. Be together because you want to be. When that time is over, kiss, close the chapter, express gratitude for all the gifts the relationship gave, and move on.
16. Individual freedom of life and expression is the ultimate.
17. Love is all there is. It is not just an emotion. It is a life's journey to discover Love and Truth and experience it as our reality, integrating all of its aspects.

How have you played relationships? How have you felt and described a perfect day that was not up for attachment but just for the value of the moment? Does anything in the following expressed day resonate with you? Can we just have a perfect moment and move on? Can we really come to loving ourselves enough when we are not in a marriage or a defined commitment that we can just go with the flow? How big can our imagination be? Remember to read (see) and feel (touch-sense) between the lines and the words. Could you be the King or the Queen regardless of the location or the circumstance? Who are we really looking for to fully Love and know? Is it Ourself?

ONE BEAUTIFUL DAY

The flow of the day was wide open to (for) any impression,
So why not go from castle to parking lot; experience to expression.
From the moment of the castle meeting, gentle magic was in the air.
Go ahead, let the imagination soar, as King and Queen we could be a pair!

Where do we go, what do we do, how do we spend the time?
Do we walk and talk or drive and talk as it is way too early to dine?
King says to Queen, "Step into my Coach, and somewhere we will go,
As the bright sun is shining, happy birds are singing, a perfect place will show."

Completely at ease, and with constant sharing flowing, we found our next stay.
After walking, talking, and eating, the parking lot was the next spot of the day.
As coaches turn into pickup trucks and castles into parking lots, what does this mean?
How will this transformation be perceived by the King and the Queen?

From the noise of a busy nearby street of constant traffic passing,
The landscape beholding many signs of McDonald customer's trashing,
As the littered french fries the seagulls are eagerly gnashing,

To the peace we were enjoying, it felt with this other world we
could be clashing.

Wrapped gently in each other's arms, we were semi-reclining,
While all of the outside world seemed to be resigning.
We couldn't be making our really because the windows weren't
steaming,
Was this all really happening or was I just dreaming?

How do Kings and Queens keep their royalty, how do Angels
keep their wings?
Are we who we are, and live how we live because we know all
of these things?
Does it matter if we travel in a stunning coach or a big pickup
truck as we move on?
Whether experiencing life from a castle or a parking lot, listen
for your Heart's song!

Live Life as though there was no right or wrong but with free
choice for what is.
Dance Life as though no one were watching as we are the stars
in our own showbiz.
Love Life as though we can never be hurt, and our Heart will
always know its song!
Allow Life to flow all its creations even when we don't see how
or where they belong!

Is this what we really experienced as we flowed our creation
of today?
No matter where we were or how we got there, we just wanted
to be together to play!

We fully lived one beautiful day
That was truly magic in every way!
Author Norma Ervin

Relationship Letter Expressing Release

Have you ever been in an intimate relationship that did not turn into a marriage or even a long-term commitment? If you have, then there has to be a healing that takes place inside of oneself. At a point after the breakup, what can one do to show themselves that they have come to a place beyond the anger even though some pain may still remain? One way to accomplish this is to write that person a letter from your heart as to how you really feel. Put it on paper from your heart even if you do not intend to give it to them, either because you don't want to, don't have the courage to, or just feel it was healing enough for you just to do it and felt there was no value in sharing it. I wrote one such letter in 2008 and I did read it to the person involved and then gave him a copy. I felt very released and complete after first, writing it, and secondly, having the courage to share it with him in person. His reactions were quite emotional but mostly nonverbal. I felt we both benefited and moved on without pent-up emotions. At least, that was my truth.

Following is some of the letter that I wrote and shared. Again, read this by checking into your own book of life and discerning if there is anything lingering inside of you from any period that feels unresolved in any way. It may be way past the time of resolving it in person with the one who was involved. However, know that you still can resolve it inside you in a way that will free your mind, spirit, heart, and soul to move forward and bring you a healed life ready for the freedom that you were originally designed to live. Another option in reading this letter is to just read it for the gathering of some 'real life bread crumbs' worth digesting as we travel our journey of finding ourself. From this perspective, the focus is not just on a broken-up relationship or unresolved or resolved pain and healing; rather, it is about living.

In my sharing of this letter, I have changed the name so as not to disrespect the person as this was written several years ago. However, the Life Bread Crumbs are relevant for wherever and however we choose to utilize them. These words may have been written pertaining to a particular situation that happened a number of years ago, but the truth that was learned within me contained lasting and active tools for my use as needed on my life journey even now, and as we are co-creators of the New Consciousness, the 'Yes to Beyond,' let's share all that we see as a way to accomplish our new oneness.

Dearest Chuck,

Thank you for listening to my birthday gift to myself. In this now, it is very important to me for you to know a big part of why my soul created you in my life as a player even though it was only for a short time. I just got all tangled up thinking there was more to discover together. I really enjoyed you as a playmate when you were still playing with me because you wanted to. I did have a glimpse of my "wild woman" who so wants out to be more known by me. I recognized the fun person you are from your heart and am thankful we had some good times.

I have given much thought to what I would like to share with you as parting words even as there is still some active pain for me that this is the parting time in our journey. I recognize that you were through a long time ago, but I am a little slower in some things, and I am just completing my letting go. In looking back, I feel you were probably through as our big trip finished. It seemed that was when changes began to happen, and you had told me more than once that you didn't want that trip to be a "commitment clause" so to speak for you. I did not think we had played it that way, but I do see our journey changed right after that and there were more and more signs of you pushing me away. Recently, when you told me you would return my phone calls but you would not call on your own "because you didn't want to give me the wrong impression," that was the dart that finally hit the bullseye right in the middle of my heart, and I got it! So having said that, let me share a few more feelings with you as I will let our journey go now.

We agreed at one point that we believed connections happened for a purpose. I truly believe that our souls brought us together for reasons that our journey would serve us as individuals to be all or at least more of what we were created to be. We weren't privy to the reasons, but we did make a conscious choice individually to check out the connection. I knew immediately for me what many of those reasons were and many more showed up as we played. My soul created my experiences that I needed to play out, and you at some level agreed to play. So, I say thanks to me for the willingness and courage to play for growth and to you for being the player that you were. Also, please know that in all of these words, I am never saying that "you hurt me" as I am totally responsible for my own feelings. If I get hurt by what I need to experience for my learning, so be it. I own that and do not project it to someone else, but I could not learn some of this without players. There is value in the pain even though it hurts, and there is so much joy in the fun of togetherness. Both are wonderful parts of growth and fulfillment.

So, how many times do I say thank you for playing as long as you did —from the time that you wanted to, up through the time that you still played out of a feel of "kind human responsibility" whenever that period began for you.

1. Thank you for being a fun, kind, good-looking, and humorous man who brought me through a huge block in my life by just being available to play with me to show me that some of my taught perceptions around some other people were wrong. I could value them as people outside of myself, but they were not ones to play with as friends, see as the same as me, and feel love toward, a love that is not just said as a generic word.

2. Thank you for a brief experience of playing relationships differently. I liked seeing that I could do it without the need for ownerships and that I truly did not want to be married, and I did live my individual freedom to be my own person. I liked allowing differences of belief systems, and we could still play and have fun without the need to make each other into a clone of ourselves. My main draw to you was that I wanted to play with you, and every other part of my life did not have to include you, and I was feeling okay around that. My playing self was emerging and I was enjoying feeling her as a part of me, and I loved the journey and its main player. I never wanted to marry you, take your money, cramp your lifestyle, take you away from your friends or any of your "other good times." I just wanted to

play when we both wanted to. I do see that I ask to play more often than you wanted to play. For that, I am sorry and regret that I might have felt pushy and relationship-consuming. But if you did not tell me and kept accepting me when I ask to play, there was no way I could have known to play differently.

3. I thank you for playing a part so I could look at jealousy which is one aspect I did not want to carry on with me.

4. I thank you for playing in such a way that I had the opportunity to go to the core of "the Ugly Duckling Syndrome." You frequently gave words with feeling comments around gorgeous women that you had been with or not or just your observations of their gorgeousness. I felt I stood in front of you as an ugly duckling, and when walking beside you, I didn't grace your presentation to the world. Even when I was in my fanciest dress in a place of elegance on the trip we took, it still was not a setting that I was seen as pretty enough and worthy of a compliment. The Angels helped me out that evening as the waiter designed me as the 'first lady' for the evening, and I enjoyed pretending the part. The Ugly Duckling felt special. I thank you for playing your part in this because I need to see much more clearly where my beauty really is, and that it is in my heart, not in my physical looks even though I do desire to look as nice as I can. I am heart first and physical appearance after that so if the Ugly Duckling is repelled because of outside looks, the heart still glows and responds as to who I really am. Ugly Ducklings are transformed to being beautiful swans when their hearts are seen and known. I can now look in the mirror and see the beauty that is as pure as the potential of the most gorgeous woman. Now it is not so important to me that someone else confirms or even recognizes my physical beauty or not, but I would like to share my heart. If anyone is interested in getting to know me and not just seeing me, we can play hearts. I hear it is a really fun game. Maybe, hopefully, someday, I will know more about fun in life because

I was just learning how to have fun and experience what playing feels like.

5. I thank you for giving me another piece for my box of special jewels, otherwise known as gifts. One is when my heart is awakened through a connection. It doesn't go away just because the circumstances changed. That awakened love spark may have to learn a new song or learn to express in a different way, but my Christmas Tree of Life which has an ornament for all of my sacred gifts will always have an ornament on it glowing with the inscription 'Chuck—Loving Playful Spirit.' I will always feel its unique sweetness every time I review my box of gifts.

6. I thank you for playing with me longer than you wanted to because some of the extra twists and turns we have done on this path have brought me additional value. I have harvested much that has and will continue to enhance my life's journey. I feel my soul is pleased with my progress. I guess part of what's up for me was not only to learn how to be together differently but also to learn how to let go gracefully and lovingly. I want to end gracefully and lovingly and not in battle or with the painting on my windshield of life that I look through every day to be reflecting the pain of the wound or the blood of the battle. I want the windshield of my journey with you to be a picture of joy and playing that I now can see as a little more real. I am going to design me a seat cover and perhaps a pillow for the house that has a button to push that will bring out arms that will wrap around me and hold me lovingly and tenderly. These will be on a timer so I can be held for as little time or as long time as I want. I am not sure yet how I will recreate the kisses. Maybe those will have to be just from memory, but that is somewhat scary because my memory doesn't seem capable of retaining long-term.

7. Another reason I thank you for playing longer than you wanted to is that it gave me the opportunity to see how I could, or if I could, play even more differently than I originally thought.

I told you after your request of asking me to step out of all intimacy and fun times and just be friends, that I would see if I could even play that way. In the interim between that time and now and through more twists and turns, we have had several good times. I was encouraged and thought I could play along. Well as it is now, I know I cannot play. I clearly recognize that I cannot just play as boring, uncaring friends that occasionally go out for a burger to talk about the weather and the unexciting mundane events of our lives. I do not want that role with anyone, and especially you! Also, if we do not share anything that is important enough for you to call me on your own from time to time without just responding to a call from me, then I too move on because I see no real value in a one-sided friendship.

I wanted to play more. I had dreams of more things that we would do and experience together. I thought there was still a chance. I didn't expect all of these dreamed adventures to be out of your wallet. I was going to do my share. But I am a big girl and I know a lot, if not most, dreams do not come true. However, I just seem to refuse to believe that I should stop dreaming. I will let these dreams go to the 'won't happen pile' and dream some more for another time and space as my heart feels excited again.

I recognize that after and since Spencer (my grandson) died that I have not been a perpetual ball of excitement and have not always been a joyful person. His death did derail my life as well as that of my family. I am still endeavoring to regroup at a deep soul level. I was plunged into that space through experiencing the physical death of someone I loved dearly. I have lost a grandson to real death, a son to a living death, and the death of friendships with dear friends due to the death of circumstances of how humans play life. I feel like I am sitting in the middle of the floor in an empty room with urns of ashes all around me. It feels like at least one of these urns is carrying my own ashes as all of my losses have taken away so much of me. I feel like I have been in a multiple-act play entitled 'Welcome to Norma's Hell on Earth'! All players have done their parts beautifully—all family and friends. I don't perceive the fires of hell as eternal punishment but rather as the fires that brought much of what was to ashes. I must believe that within the pain of all of this, there is another production that will come. I think it is going to be called 'Norma's Gifts from the Depths of Darkness.' It seems this has not been scripted yet, but many angels keep me informed that the production will happen in the divine right timing, and it will be grand! I am trusting and hoping that it will be soon.

Right now, there is a clearing that is going on in the spiritual hearts of many of us human beings. It can feel yucky, very uncomfortable, and very frightening. Many are experiencing it and many are endeavoring to deny its presence. It is bringing up anger pain, body discomfort, even disease, and all kinds of other emotions as it pushes forward to clear all that is in the way of us being all that we came to be. I see me in this clearing. Sometimes, the pain in this is so overwhelming that I just want to scream out "This so sucks and it just so hurts me!" This is another reason I am leaving you with all of these words because I have to be true to myself and express what I feel and felt as we journeyed from my perspective, even if we were not on the same page. If I have gone overboard a little, please forgive me.

If there is a gift I could leave with you from who I am from my heart, I would ask you to read the book "The Bridge Across Forever" by Richard Bach. It is a love story that may have parts that are too far-fetched for your beliefs, but there are so many other parts that can, and do, speak to the heart of absolutely any of God's created humans, male and female. I feel you possibly never really cared for me as a special female in your life, but I do know we had some times together that you too enjoyed. If I have any other regrets, it is that I kept feeling there was something of value happening here long after you were through. But all in all, I guess I kept playing long enough for me to see all that my soul had set up for me to see.

My dear, I don't know what your soul was asking for you. Maybe I'm the only one that gets tangled in complexity and turns what could be simple into the complex, but it really doesn't matter as I played our time together as I felt to play it, and you played it how you felt to play it. We rode the waves of the ups and downs in the actual external physical world as well as from our own inner waves of emotions, feelings, and actions, and now we go out to sea (see) with what is.

In wishing upon a star, I wish we could have joyfully played some more. Closing no doors, putting up no heart walls, never saying never, but saying goodbye to the journey that appears finished—I do let go!

Sweetheart, be peaceful, and may you find all of the joy and love you want in the life you create for yourself.

Goodbye. Until we meet again or not.

Relationships give us opportunities to experience all of our emotions. Following is just a short version of how they can start up one way, and then a glimpse of what they can become. This was a real-life experience for me that I internally and externally recorded in my current Book of Life. The amazing point for us here is that when the relationship has finally truly ended, one has the opportunity to look back and view the whole puzzle and see all of the value that it was to them and be filled with gratitude instead of continued anger, pain, hate, and resentment. This gratitude outcome is the one we are looking for as we learn who we are as divine human beings on earth serving the purpose of raising the mass consciousness of our planet.

A Shorter Version of Clarity

Now onto a short version of another real-life happening on my path for you feeling to reflect if in your book of life you have had any such internal storms, and so how did you resolve them and/or learn from them, or not yet, or not at all.

So it begins!

We became acquainted through more of the essence of who we are which is seemingly somewhat beyond our 'much more minutely defined' ego personality. The personality is self living out life with more emotional and physical concepts with a bigger involvement of the intellectual mind keeping all in control. We were afforded the wonderful opportunity to do a different 'courtship' so to speak because of the distance in actual land space between us. We did not (do not) know what we were courting, but in agreement, kept playing. Our sharing was not just pie in the sky fairytale and/or Pollyanna idols as we were given the opportunity to 'express freely in a safe space.' We ran with this, and I for one know I took full advantage of the opportunity. I felt my love open from my heart in a way of expression of what I was feeling as me, for me, and for you in a way I had never experienced. This was new and very exciting for me as all of this was also tempered with the smatterings of our everyday life!

Then came all heaven and hell through the flood gates! All aspects of love, from unconditional to conditional, hate, war, peace, judgment, denial, defensiveness, hurt, disappointment, sexuality, abundance, broken trust, lack of trust, doubts, fears—every aspect from 'to God be the Glory' to all of creation be damned—came rushing in loudly for the recognition of their appearances. This created erupting volcanoes and tornadoes touching down and going up, followed by earthquakes in every cell of my internal being as well as my physical body. I was trying to hang on at the same moment I was exploding. It seemed it was impossible to hold anything back from expression or inner feelings, but at the same time, some form or 'otherness' was holding my hand. I was desperately attempting to feel that presence too and hang on! It felt like all of this had rushed in to destroy the very love that had called it forth and set the stage for its arrival.

Had I not known you and experienced you first from such a place of 'new love,' one that I expressed mostly from my heart, I would not have expanded my own feelings of love for myself. I definitely flowed that love to and around you as it all opened up a path where I felt and received your feelings coming back to me. As I work through, feel through, and reflect on all that this was for me, this chapter will be closed and moved to the 'Archives of all that was' with gratitude that it happened just as it did because I gained so much and I am now a stronger, more authentic woman more prepared to be of service to the One of All that I came to be! I don't remember if I actually gave or read this to the person involved here or not, but I truly do still remember how ripped apart I was before I was able to regroup and reap the value and the understanding of the whole experience.

We learn so much about ourselves as we walk through our relationships and allow ourselves to be consciously aware of all aspects of our truth that is showing up for us to see. We must also recognize that what we pull out like us and who we are signals to us what to change, or not, within ourselves. It is not our responsibility to change anyone else regardless of the type of relationship. One of our main guidelines here is to have the intention to always be in awareness mode of how we are participating in walking and creating our own life, not only in our various relationship playouts, but when we are just being with ourselves as well. We can never truly remember and/or reconnect with who we truly are and was originally meant to be as a divine-human being if we are not consciously paying attention to all facets of living life being presented to us by and through our 5 senses and all they are instrumental in creating for us to experience in various ways.

Relationships, be they through marriage or any type of commitment or otherwise, as they are not all intimate relationships, are one of our greatest learning tools as we walk this journey called life. We author-live our book of life, but each of our relationships, be they friends, fellow workers, community co-creators for all kinds of reasons, all roles of being a family, and more, are definitely one of our main cornerstones in life! Perhaps, the biggest relationship for us to review and change is how do we see our relationship with ourselves. What do we need to see and do differently within and for ourselves changing us from self (small and limited) to SELF as we were originally created to BE and then do!

Various types of relationships have been mentioned with some being shared as they were experienced, and all of which have been with actual people involved. Have you ever experienced a really strong sense of a connection happening but there was no person physically present or even known in reality? I have had that experience, and I chose to express how it was for me in a poem. What and where is our invisible reality?

A PLACE

There is a place that is so real, but not seen,
I met you there today in a vibrant sunbeam.
We touched as a knowingness that all is well.
Feeling your presence, I feel there is more to tell.

There is a place that Love laughs out loud, you know,
I knew your heart there and knew it wasn't just a show.
Who are you, and where do you live?
Please, please tell me so I can come receive what you have to
    give!

There is a place where we felt and shared our Love, but could
    not touch it,
We were so alive and at home, but in no house did sit!
I Am with you there, but want you here,
To see your face laughing, feel your heart beating, my dear!

In this place, was it me loving me, or me loving you?
Was it all one, or were there two?
As the touch was as a knowingness that all was well,
Does it really matter if there is no more to tell?

Yes, I have a preference, as on Earth I live
Sharing all that I embrace is how I give.
I give to me, but I want a 'Special You' too
To explore, experience, and express with to name a few!

Love is all there is and cannot be divided,
How it is shared helps expansion be decided.
So as we expand the knowingness that all is well,
Love Being One and All, forms being multiples, there is more
    to tell!

Author Norma Ervin

LIFE'S FOUR CORNER STONES, VERSE TWO

Work It . . . Work It

ABUNDANCE

How can this be?
They told me to go to school and get straight A's
For them, I did.
They told me to get a college degree from their vision for me,
    not mine,
For them, I did.
A good-paying job was the name of the game…
Climb the ladder, follow the rules, gain fame,
I win—you lose, you win—I lose,
So goes the lyrics of the merry-go-round!

STOP! I want off!
What is passion vs demand, Being vs doing,
Value measured by true self-worth vs measured by dollars and
    possessions?
I ponder—I change professional paths.
The cycle starts over,
This time for me, not them.
Seems many guidelines are the same!
Duality Law: Doing + Money + Stuff = Self-worth.
STOP! I want off!

Duality Law: Quitting + Low Abundance = Worthless Being.
Are there any Natural Laws?

I hurt, I cry, I scream, I wonder, I pray, I listen.
How, where, when, will life be different?
I feel I am on the edge of existence with NO answers!
I want to die, maybe I will, perhaps I have somehow!
What are Abundance and Money really?
Who Am I?

—Author Norma Ervin

According to the dictionary, abundance is defined as 1. a great supply; more than enough 2. great, plenty; wealth. Instead of just a human definition, could this also be the truth of the birthrights that we were given from the very first vision of the immaculate conception of mankind itself? As the poem asks, where are the Natural Laws? We were not conceived to struggle and fight for our lives in order to exist as an important, (necessary) player on Earth. One of our birthrights was that through grace and ease, we would have what was needed to maintain our living existence and that would be the truth for everyone. God, the Master Creation Creator, did not change the immaculate concept of mankind, through which the free choice directive for mankind was given from the very beginning. It was mankind's decisions through free choice that created the 'less than originally designed' reality world and mass consciousness that we are experiencing and have been for eons of time.

Now recalling that this is still reflecting the 18-year period of reviewing and discovering more of what is up for closure and change through our own human understanding as well as through our hearing with new ears and seeing with new eyes, we look and listen into the silent and invisible Power Source of ourselves that delivers to us through intuition and feeling. In still reviewing some of the aspects of our own Authored Book of Life, the following sharing was written in my book in July 2005, pertaining to my fighting-arguing-searching time with abundance.

Recall here that I had previously owned two self-employed businesses and therefore, thought I understood independence as a viable and workable way of life, not just a form of existence. In review, I did realize that most of those previous years were patrolled and controlled by my intellectual mind and all of its points of reference. These included my belief systems which had a big part in forming my identities which then lend themselves to my ego as well as my awareness of all of the rules present as truth in our mass consciousness.

July 8-July 10, 2005

Personal Writing: I must have done something terribly wrong, and I must be doing it still over and over. There is a whole world around me joyfully playing, and I can't even freely buy a bottle of hand lotion. Why could I not detect such a limiting and wrong path before I was brought to this point? This is, or is it, my creation? Why did I do this to myself? Asking my higher self's invisible guides, how could I watch me do this and trick myself into believing I was hearing guidance? I still feel some of what I was feeling and discovering was a new truth, but reality remains that I have had no, or very little, revenue flow for a year now! To live on planet earth, money is not only required but is absolutely necessary! What have I done wrong? I would like to know, but at this moment, I trust nothing!

I look around me, and other than what speaks to my quiet world and heart space, all else seems so meaningless. Unless I get a money flow, I am done! What have I done wrong? I would enjoy life differently If I had some money flow. I feel and felt that I don't require hours, rules, requirements, and lots of other bullshit so that I can make a few dollars per hour and continue to live from month to month displaying a lack not being able to do what I want to do and saying "Thank you, Spirit, I am so grateful and all is well!" This isn't living! This is just existing in a system that will squeeze all life out, and I am almost there! What have I done wrong? Have I rebelled too much to recover? Right now, I don't feel like role-playing a game to make this look or feel any different! And yet, I am expecting it to make a difference! Somewhere within me, I still have some beliefs that my life can be different without me caving into duality mass consciousness.

Maybe I am supposed to learn to believe that what feels so totally screwed up and awful is okay. Maybe that is what I signed up for, and there truly is no other way. Maybe I do have to die and leave before I can experience it differently. Maybe the place of grace doesn't exist here, or maybe it is just for those who haven't done something as wrong as I apparently have. Also, there is no one on this side of the veil or the other side who really cares! On this side, all they want to do is fix me or judge me; thus, confirming I have done something wrong. I know of no one who can really help me get where I want to be. So, who am I?

I can't get new glasses; I can't get my teeth fixed; I can't play with the grandkids in the way I want to! I hear "We are never alone" from the other side, but I certainly don't know what that means! I feel the other side stood right beside me and gave energy to me as I blinded myself or they tricked me, and I bought it all, hook line and sinker, really believing life was finally going to be better. At that moment in time, we were (are) told over and over that the 'better time' was finally almost here. Oh, what a fool I am and was! I just wonder how many of you are laughing your heads off at such a grand joke and such a stupid foolish person who would fall for it all! Have I gained the highest of medals for being the dumbest player!

I don't believe we are honored. I believe we are helped to screw up by being told all of this stuff that most cannot attain. It still seems that money is what makes the world seem real. I thought I could believe it differently but see I can't, and it may have been a grand exploration and experience, but it has left me bottomed out! Speaking to my guidance, I proclaim that, "I would like to thank you for your help in all of this, but right now, it seems fruitless to thank you for anything, to ever trust you or me again, and to hope for or expect anything that will work for myself or you! And So It Is!

I really have had some really good 'New Times.' I just feel such deep, deep disappointment that I have been unable to manifest a different Earth experience. I guess I contracted with you to help me fail so miserably and completely! So, what now? Do I have to live chapters being and doing all that I said I was through with just to be here? Did my intention to live life 'New' have no real meaning? Can I truly not get there from here? It is like there is nothing to even cry about. What is just is! What has happened has happened, and the results are what they are! There is no reason to cry as my soul is so engaged in the outcome that a tear can't even be squeezed out!

There is no energy for anything extra as this now-felt reality seems to settle in solidly.

I sit here breathing, but not even knowing why. Probably all that has ever helped before is that it just has prolonged the timeframe for me to reach this place, and I have had a few moments of pleasure and several glimpses and experiences of a different reality along the way. Perhaps, someday and somewhere, someone will truly be able to live a different life. However, I am not sure it will ever be me. There is no real emotion in this so I don't feel this is just a pity-me party, but rather a resolution to a fact. May I stand graciously in the presence of those whom I know and who know me as I go through this culmination! I would rather leave than agree to live imprisoned by my own creations that I can't seem to resolve. The only thing that scares me is that I will have to come back and do this again. In this, it feels there truly is no way to win! If there really is any insight to flow to me, may I hear it! I truly have nothing to lose as I feel I have lost it all—much by conscious choice and the rest, I guess, as a result of what I was doing wrong or that I was not aware of. Consequently, feeling I have nothing to lose, I also feel I can't gain enough to really make a difference at this point in time. Therefore, all that I ask is that I don't inflect my reported outcome onto others as they may know how to create something different for themselves. For a long time, I sure thought I knew how too!

July 9, 2010

Today, I feel like Dr. Jekyll and Mr. Hyde. One moment I am scared and angry, and the next moment, I am really feeling I can stand as my God Self and get through this. I am feeling scared, really, really scared.

I am feeling humiliated because I am here in this situation and at the same time, I am really confused as to how I really landed here. I knew I was (am) walking a path that made no logical sense, but I thought it was making sense in the creation of the New, and I really thought and felt it, therefore, believed I was on the right track and all would play out so differently. I truly, truly believed this. What scares me as much as being out of money is that I can be so blind and obviously keep making choices, or holding beliefs, that truly do not serve me. I so much want to hear 'some message from higher knowing' to jump in here and assure me that all is well really and that all of this is not as it appears, and I have not been the idiot of the century! However, I do not see that happening at all. I just have to accept that I screwed up big time.

Yet even as I assess my situation, there is a part of me that is still loudly saying that grace is real, that my needs and desires can be freely given to me, and it has nothing to do with earning, deserving, good girl, dues paid, righteous, etc. We were (are) told over and over that it was designed to come to us through grace as a birthright, not an entitlement because of a free choice to not participate or be responsible. Also, our real purpose for being created on Earth is to Be the Love that we are in all of our giving and receiving experiences and expressions of living our lives while here. In my Reiki initiation, I was told through an intuitive reader that was there as a part of the process, that what I had come to Earth to pass on was done followed by the comment of 'job well done.' When that statement was stated, the lights even actually went out in the room. To me, this indicated that message was the truth.

I really feel we don't create a New World by having money be the God and the measuring stick of all worth. I have spent much soul and spirit investment on seeing and experiencing money as energy. Therefore, why, why am I out and have no flow? What have I done wrong? What am I not seeing? I am not yelling or questioning in anger at this time. I truly, truly am asking my Higher Self, God, and/or any energy walking with me in any way to please, please give me some help here. Please, please I hear myself pleading. Is my resistance that strong? Am I that asleep? I really didn't think so. I know I still have much to move forward within my evolvement, but I really did think I was doing pretty good. Why wasn't I (aren't I) able to see beyond what must be my personal prison walls? Is my life really so blocked and so much more so than absolutely anyone on the path that I know? Are all of the insights and knowings that I think I have had really just gibberish and foolish notions that truly mean absolutely nothing in my wanting to create a different life for myself and the Earth?

Have I really taken so many wrong turns that I will never, in this lifetime, in this transition between the world's time, be able to manifest any of the freedom that I so want for me and all? As I wrote that last statement, I realized that I really have lived a life of choice with much freedom over the past years. However, I have to be able to totally claim it or be in the gratitude of it completely because there was always a money-abundant overtone of lack, fear of lack, present. At this moment, right here and right now, I am grateful for the perceived freedom that I have experienced even as I am being totally and completely at the end of my money resources in this now with no flow in! Somehow, this isn't the type of freedom I thought I was manifesting. Where is the life I have dreamed of and envisioned? Why did I miss all of the doors that led there? It feels I saw the door but never found (had) the key.

In all the questioning, I still feel I truly do desire, from the depth of my heart, not just the wishing of my intellectual mind, to and will, and now am, deciding to Be the God Self that I Am, and to stand in this as the God Piece that I Am and not as a victim. However, now standing where I am experiencing what I am expressing knowing that I am co-creating with others a new consciousness for mankind, I still don't know which corner to go around to make my situation different. Because of the fact that my current supply of money is gone, and I have no answers to this from any new perspective, then I feel my only resolution is to step back into a duality piece and tolerate it! I feel I can't re-learn to like it. I am truly open to see if this is truly the very thinking that is sinking me. Should I be willing and joyful about taking a job that has some enjoyable moments and like it? Why can't I move to be the teacher, or the Being given as me via grace, and just Be the God Piece that I Am and love living life, and let my essence be my gift as the giver and the receiver? Please,

please help me understand! I ask this mainly of my Higher Self, but also of all that is co-creating with me. I think I am teachable. However, I thought I had given up suffering, and it seems I am now continually looking at controls.

This current paragraph is being inserted now in 2019 timeframe to add a bit of information as a piece of clarity to what is being shared on these pages that were recorded (written) earlier in 2005. Two points of clarity here:

1. There was a time when I was probably three years old that I had an experience that was very frightening to me, and my life was literally being threatened. I took on a deep instinctive reaction inside my little girl self in the midst of my deep fear that I obviously had done something very wrong even though I had no idea what it was. As children that young, we have not developed any signs of logic that we understand, but we do have an instinctive part of us that gets us to a point of negotiating with life through our little internal protection systems. What my little mind told me in the intensity of that fear was that it was not safe to be me. In my own way as that little girl feeling a need for protection without any understanding why but just as a reaction to the threat to my life that had been so visibly demonstrated to me, I did mentally choose to hide from the world. How this led me to live my life instinctively was just to observe how others played and follow that as my safe way— listen and watch to see how, then follow that, and let that be me!

2. Much later in my adult life after having learned a lot more about the reality of life and who I really was, I gained some awareness of all of us having a Christ seed inside us and some of what that meant. I become acquainted with this information during this time of the first 18 years of the 36 years of change that has been explained earlier. Because we are in this monumental time of change in moving out of old energy into a new one, it was revealed that in this lifetime, we all came in with a Christ seed

inside of us that was prepared (designed) to be major guidance in our individual parts as players in the change. It seemed as though there was a Divine Right Timing for us to actively play out our part. Depending on when we came in this lifetime, it may have been a little time before our Divine Right Time so we had to tuck that seed away for a little while until the time was right!

Do you see the crossroads here that my small child self could have been playing in from what seemed like a horrifically horrible situation with the energy of the old playing out big time as protection was needed? However, at the same time, how much of that protection was also needed for the Christ seed as it wasn't yet time to play the role that it was specifically designed for, which was the time of the New Consciousness creation? Which was the true story? In all of our 'crossroad' intersections, we have free choice. My young three-year-old self wasn't equipped yet with a logical mind, but her intuitive/instinctive God-Given tools were present and alive, and something was up for protection. So, what was it really, and was what seemed horrible really necessary and a gift?

Now going back to 2005 and continuing the completion of situational times. In going back to the core of my hidden Christ seed time of this lifetime, I feel it is the insight to the total depth of 'what have I done wrong' when I was faced with death and/or great punishment or great pain all through the eyes and perceptions of a child. I truly didn't know then as I don't know now. But I can look from this now onto that time and know that 'I didn't do anything wrong!' Could that also be my truth now? Could this all truly now be a progressive part of my evolution? Can I still go through it to a place of manifesting my dreams and/or living a NEW life outside of duality and the current old mass consciousness? Can I do this easily by just having some understanding here and really not having to suffer and step back into 'old' and like it?

To the very best that I consciously can at this moment, I stand as the God piece that I AM and So it Is, and So I AM! I feel I am standing here naked with nothing left to hide, and nothing to cover my butt and no crutches. If we truly have no more lessons to do and our karma days are completed and/or forgiven, then what is this and why am I here? I have and do believe I am now karma-free, and I have felt I was out-of-lesson. To that last part, I question, how can that be?

July 10, 2005

Standing as and Being as my piece of God, I have done nothing wrong! I am a very active and viable co-creator of the New Earth. This is just what is presented at this time. I do not know, and will never know, the 'how of the ultimate Creator of all Creation.' Therefore, I accept what is and allow all to flow on. I have to trust as the mind of my intellect has been loved in, that all, or many, of my ways and appearances in situations of life will seem very foreign to me. To the best of my ability, I will not put a dualistic old definition on any feeling and/or situation. As I don't judge myself, others are less likely to judge me, and more NEW things appear. As my Higher Self knows the way forward in this now, and since there really is no separation, I too know. Therefore, all is well. Accept, allow, and trust continues to be my mantra, and I truly give thanks for all opportunities that present themselves that enable me to remember and Be more of the God piece that I AM!

LIFE'S FOUR CORNER STONES, VERSE THREE

Work It ... Work It
Life's Four Corner Stones

HEALTH

How can this be?
Do this, and for God's sake, don't do that,
And healthy you will be,
Be thin, be beautiful,
Be handsome, be macho,
Look Sexy, for appearance is the ticket!

You don't fit?
Then an extreme make-over you must get!
Fill it up, suck it out, tuck it in,
Move it over, cover it up, color, and replace
All in a zip-zap,
With a chisel, scissors, drill, and sew—done!
You're happy, have fun!
Eat, drink, and be merry,
For tomorrow we will bury!

Really? Yes, there's more,
Duality Law: One is born to die!

Seems Born and Die are Oreo's with some stuff of life
    in-between.
If your "stuff" is good, so they say,
Then good health and heaven are your pay.
If your "stuff" is bad so they say,
Then bad health and hell could be your punishment every
    day!
Optional "stuffing" recipe for good health and perhaps heaven:
Drink plenty of water, exercise frequently, take your vitamins,
Eat a balanced diet in the proper food groups,
Get plenty of rest, maintain a low-stress level,
Live, be happy, follow all the rules, etc.

Optional "stuffing" recipe for bad health and perhaps hell:
There is a balance factor here,
So you better watch out!
Don't let the bad outweigh the good!
Bad Ingredients, so they say,
Drinking, smoking, eating too many carbs,
Too much sugar, fats, no exercise,
Lie, cheat, hate, break many rules most of the time,
Exist stressed out is naming a few!

STOP! I'm in trouble, I think!
Where's my help?
The directory is as follows: Preachers, Doctors, Lawyers!
They tell me much,
But I think there is more!
What is the "story behind the story"?
What is the essence of the mystery of existence?
What is my part in all of this?
I know from somewhere that I am a player with a purpose!

Oh, my gut wrenches, my heart aches, my head throbs,
All at levels that feel much deeper than my space can behold,
Or any words define!
From their definition, I know I experienced a heart attack!

Yet I heard from somewhere "don't be afraid."
From their definition, I know I experienced a stroke!
Yet I knew from somewhere to lie down and breathe into the
    very core of my Being-ness,
Connecting to the space of my perfection!

I lose all sense of having a body,
I ask for guidance and understanding.
Flute, piano, and drum music,
Plus color from nature all around me as seen through the
    windows,
Plus the energy of the trees and the wood from the walls of
    my log cabin
All reformulate me a body I can feel!
What did they say?
I don't know, I didn't ask!
My heart really hurts again!
I ask, they don't know!

I'm afraid, I cry, I wonder, I can't pray!
How, where, when, will life be different?
I don't want to die, but maybe I am, perhaps I already have
    somehow!
I feel I am on the edge of existence with NO answers!
How can I be healed?
Who am I really?

                    —Author, Norma Ervin

A Perspective Outside the Box

Regarding health, the following is an article that I presented as a potential for publishing in an alternative health magazine. It did not get accepted, but it did express what I felt. As you will be able to tell it was in the time that President Obama was in office that I wrote this. However, health concerns seem to be constant, as well as an ever-changing concept according to who is in office as President. In this now, it is Trump, and anything and everything is up for change with much of it not making a lot of sense and is accompanied by a lot of confusion. His decisions have not changed my feelings around what health care is and how we could better serve our culture as a whole by being open to expanding our perspective and understanding more about what the capabilities of our body really are and how we could factor that into our health care systems as a whole.

Health Care Reform
A Perspective Outside the Box

In our country, as well as globally, we are experiencing life in a somewhat volatile way while seemingly traveling down roads that have many twists and turns and that have never before been paved for us. Regardless of what anyone's individual opinion of President Obama is, the fact that he has been very instrumental as a leader for change cannot be denied. One big item on the agenda for change and the one that seems to be not one way up front, but on center stage, right now (during his term), is health care reform. It is wonderful that we live in a country where freedom of speech is allowed, and many are expressing their views on this issue.

While endeavoring to formulate the main arguments of the health care reform issue into an understandable whole picture concept, it might be helpful to see a box with four labeled corners that would incorporate the main factors of what this issue covers for us as United States citizens as well as world citizens. According to our cultural model, the potential components of health care could be:

1. A healthy physical body
2. A healthy cognitive and intellectual mind
3. A chosen spiritual and/or religious belief system or something that in some way gives one an understanding of their existence
4. Controls

A shortened version of this box would be Body-Mind-Belief-Control.

Here are some words taken directly from the printed media that seem to be the highlights for several of the main arguments in this issue.

"How can there be a question that govt.-run, goal-controlled health care will do anything but create inefficiencies exponentially and transform another sector of the economy into dead weight at taxpayer's expense? Our health care industry thrives now because of the freedom it has to succeed. Dedicated professionals strive to achieve. Let's turn them all into secondary figures, following the marching orders of the political hacks, special self-interest groups, and govt. bureaucrats. I want my doctors completely independent of government interference."

And yet another point of view taken directly from the printed media:

> "Change in healthcare coverage will never come to America until healthcare is divested of its "for-profit" model. In actuality, political power and greed are rooted in our uniquely FOR PROFIT health care here in the US. Pharmaceutical companies, hospital corporations, as well as health insurance carriers all answer to Boards of Directors and investors. The paradigm requires that they strive for bigger profits to keep both happy."

Not directly quoted from any media but nevertheless, an important component of the control piece would be insurance companies. We have designed a health care system that requires a great deal of money to even use and maintain. Because this system has gotten so far out of balance as well as somewhat beyond our conscious understanding, we have allowed (created) arbitrators of a type to step in, take out some of the confusion, and pick up some of **our** responsibility. We call this creation insurance. Two things could happen pertaining to insurance companies:

1. When someone else pays, one doesn't question the cost as much; therefore, individuals take less personal responsibility.
2. The costs of health care are so high that it becomes overwhelming, and the insurance company gives the perception of making healthcare manageable.

A last piece of control is how our human self actually endeavors to control our innate intelligence by dictating what the body should and shouldn't do, how it should eat, how it should dress, what it should think, as well as how medications are utilized. The result of all of these factors combined can tell the body it doesn't know how to take care of itself, and it is not a self-healing vehicle. The body is an incredibly sophisticated Spiritual Entity and knows how to rejuvenate itself, but it also allows us to have free choice.

As a group of people making up mass consciousness, we have given up our power to many different entities. Therefore, we have to argue over the methods of control until we are ready to regain our power, operate from who we really are, and return to ourselves. If our immediate world is the mirror of our beliefs, then we must presently carry the belief that the true value of our health and body is dictated to us by some power outside us, and we can go to that class or source to be healthy, but we can go only if we have enough money for the class, the treatment, or if we have the insurance that will pay.

> There are two ways to be fooled
> one is to believe what isn't true,
> the other is to refuse to believe what is true.
> Philosopher Soren Kierkegrand (1813-1855)

None of the entities within the control factor are bad or are playing a part in our life that we need to resist or go into internal or external conflict with and strike out in anger or defense. They are a part of our creation as a part of them reflect back to us what we believe about ourselves.

Two more perspectives of health care or just life outside of the box are: one from the pioneering anthropologist, Louis Leake, who once stated, "without an understanding of who we are, we cannot truly advance," and Einstein indicated that regardless of who we are or what our role in the universe may be, we're all subject to a greater power when he said, "Human beings, vegetables, or cosmic dust—we all dance to a mysterious tune, intone in the distance by an invisible piper."

Should we step out of the noise of the debate in our external world and listen for a different song—a different way of living that does already exist and we just have to hear and remember it? Do we need to quit seeing who we are as defined by the world around us to see who we are as defined by the world within us? Are we up for making new choices based upon regaining our sense of Self which would indicate we would choose awareness over ignorance? Is true change about fixing everything that appears broken, or is it about creating something new from whole different energy? Do we already know how to do this as indicated by the Gnostic Gospels dating to the 4th century as they describe a force and how "from the power of silence appeared a great power, the mind of the universe which manages all things . . ." I think this is the part of us that knows how to reclaim our own power and operate from there. This power does not include greed; it does not claim authority over anyone; it does not usurp anyone's responsibility for themselves; it has no tools of any kind to create separation among any peoples, as ultimately, it is who we are as creations from the Image of God. We can no longer be sleepers, nor just observers. We must wake up, observe for understanding, and then participate from knowing who we truly are as Divine Human Beings living life in the form on Planet Earth! In making this huge leap in seeing and experiencing the world differently, it is important to honor both our intuition as well as our logic, but the logic will not be the defensive, strictly ego side, of the intellectual mind which has previously been programmed to be our master keeper/protector. END of ARTICLE.

Personally Addressing My Life and
My Health and Body Changes
July 18, 2011

Personal Conversation with Spirit

As I am aware right now that I am an integrating 'body of consciousness,' I ask this body of mine, "How do I move forward now? How do I physically function now being more whole?" This is a big one for me as it has been years, probably eight or nine or more since I have been able to comfortably energetically function as a human with a physical body! I give thanks for some actual awareness in words of what is happening on this Earth energetically as I have known at some level that my physical body was responding to, or with, an energy change, and it was not about there being something wrong with my body. However, my heart surgery led me to doubt, and the unusual physical existence in, or as form continued (s) to be my reality. As a unified body of consciousness, what can I share with myself right now? What does my intuition bring to my mind to give me an in-sight as to what is really going on within me that is affecting me not only internally, but externally as my physical body as well? Please, please let there be something.

I receive, **"Go to your (our) heart space and be present which is more than just being silent and listening. Being present is from a heart being open to, listening, hearing, seeing, smelling, and even more. Become fully present and receive what transpires!"**

Expressing something else beyond the health issue, I am moving on now. I pray to the God essence in me for answers. I hear that it is not answers per se that I am up for, but rather for sustenance in my process, something to sustain me. Therefore, I ask my divine-human God-Self in prayer for insights that will sustain me in this New Energy and in this New World as I am also a New Earthling! As I write (state) 'New Earthling,' I have a deeply felt thought as it brings a knowingness that "I am walking, experiencing New already, right here and right now."

I hear, **"Dear One that We are; I Am, You Are, All as the ONE I AM, stay in truth here. It is the perception of the truth that is doing the big dance. You are not living without money because you already have __All__ that you need! Access through grace everything for manifestation!"**

I am seeing yet hearing like it is truly being from Me to Me—not as someone else telling me. It doesn't even feel as slightly removed as my Higher Self—it is experienced as 'All of me being present expressing to me.' Expressing serves me in a different way than speaking, hearing, feeling, smelling, or touching by themselves one at a time. Expressing incorporates all of them, all at the same time!

This flashed through me as a valuable piece of understanding: **Higher Self does not mean above us or outside us. It could be stated as the (our) Much More Informed (Knowing) Self within us! It is not removed from us, as it is inside us!**

Assurance or Insurance

What I received through an expression of truth was (is), **"In the old energy, we heard, or saw the directive intuitively from Spirit (God), and then we followed; in the new world, new energy, there will be more and more times that our (my) newly integrated BOC (Body of Consciousness) will communicate as us (me), not outside us (me). This is also experienced as though it is a combination of Being and Doing." This feels as the new precursor to manifestation.** The flash through me was really different somehow, and I am not sure that I have adequately captured it in words!

So how does all of this apply to me right now, right here today where I am in conscious space and physical reality layout space, as well as staged play performance space? I was just asked a huge question as I was reflecting and contemplating the dynamics of my perceived current situation/condition.

The question was, **"Do you want ASSURANCE or INSURANCE?"** Wow, this felt huge and all-consuming to me!

Assurance is the big package, the big deal, the whole of all. Assurance is the ultimate package as it covers everything known and seen (visible) and every perceived nothing, unknown (invisible) that is necessary for who we are and what we desire to manifest. From this place, realize that desire is not just wanting from the intellectual mind; it is the expression of the partnership of our Soul and our human heart to play our role(s) that are being called forth from the combined energies and essence of us as a Divine Human.

Insurance fills in the gap in many places where we have the perception that we aren't enough, there isn't enough, something is broken and needs fixing, and on and on. Insurance is a game—a huge human game with a multitude of dynamics within the creation itself. It has an energy of its own that it has generated due to its magnitude of rules and diversity of players for multiple reasons with the bottom line being—to take care of us when we can't—when we aren't enough and when someone or something else has usurped our power because we have allowed it to. Ultimately, we have been conditioned to shut off our memory of knowing who we really are.

At one point in my years of owning and operating a bookkeeping service, I shared an office with an insurance salesperson. One of the things that I precisely remember about that period was how many hours he spent regularly on the phone or in person, verbally convincing potential clients that something horrible was going to happen either to them, their family, their business, their vehicles, and/or something else that they owned and that the weather was always something to be aware of in fear. It seemed the goal here was the need to convince people of lack and tragedy. His whole script was to have people address fear in the highest way, with his desired potential outcome being; they would buy insurance.

In choosing Assurance, how does that play into my sustaining energy of today regarding the whole picture of encompassing my human, divine, physical, emotional, and mental aspects of living life? Included here as well could be my momentary perceptions of health and wealth and/or lack thereof. In breathing into 'Assurance' and cloaking it around my 'now' in all dynamics, aspects, and ways known and unknown, consciously and unconsciously, experienced and/or not, I feel peaceful, and have no need to worry! All is well, and I am happy and joyful. I express gratitude to be playing as a partner on Earth, and the Universe is happy I am playing too! I am enough and all is moving forward!

Right here, I am adding a thought in the time of actually writing this book which is 2019. The actual words around Insurance and Assurance were written in 2011. If one was to make an acronym out of the common part of the words insurance and assurance, here is what that could look like. The common part would be 'surance'. **S**ource **U**niversally **R**ealigning **A** **N**ew **C**onsciousness **E**nergy. Do you want to be IN it as Insurance and all of what makes it up with those dynamics being its source? Or do you choose AS it, as Assurance with its description representing the whole of all as its source? This leaves us with our own understanding and perception of the value of the source in 'surance' of each.

LIFE'S FOUR CORNER STONES, VERSE FOUR

Walk it ... Walk it
Life's Four Corner Stones

Self-Esteem

How can this Be?
I was conceived out of Love, or Not,
I took this in.
I was born and immediately Loved, or Not,
I took this in.
Early on, I expressed my Beingness,
This was accepted, or Not.
I took this in.
I loved exploring with my imagination,
This was allowed or Not,
I took this in.
The rules of family, culture, and society were presented to me,
I followed them, or Not,
They took this in.
I was rewarded or Not, acknowledged or Not,
I took this in.

Now the designing of my life is for my creativity!
I believe I can do it, or Not.
I did it, or Not.
They approved, or Not,

I took this in.
All in all, I think I am really close to who I really AM or Not.
I wonder, How do I know Who I AM?
How, when, and where will I know?
Go to the Edge!

Poem Verse, Norma Ervin

I feel the first call I would have to my Self-Esteem and the knowing of Who I AM would come from having a degree of 'Assurance' that my physical body as my personal Earth Form Vehicle will be with me in a vital and healthy way as long as my incarnated Living Love Consciously life journey lasts in this current journey. In my saved writings from years past, I found these appropriate practical words to express to my body. I did not write this. It came from a channeling of Kryon by Lee Caroll entitled Kryon Directive.

CAL
Cells Are Listening

We know each other, and I love you. I'm sorry it took so long for me to figure it out. I want you to go into the processes that you know about and I don't. I want you to come together in benevolence that would create health and a long-lasting human being. I want you to talk to me in whatever ways you can that I can recognize. I want to hold your hand and you hold mine for the rest of my life. If there is any inappropriateness of imbalance chemically in my body, I want it to go away through time and appropriate action. I realize that I have habits that are killing me and I want them to change. I realize that I have a very bad height to weight ratio . . . Dear cell structure; I want my metabolism to echo my magnificence. Help me to be the right size of the greatest health. Change what is needed, pull on the akash if you need to, in remembrance of who I used to be. Change my diet preferences if I need to. Let my body crave what it needs and not what I want it to need. Bring it to a place of balanced divinity, and I promise I will talk to you every day because I love you.

And then don't hang up the phone.
Please, don't hang up the phone!

Moving on with my own perspectives . . . with my physical form potentially perpetually realigning all along the way, what now would be another appropriate 'forever' tool to utilize for a healthy Self-Esteem? Deep in the depth of our Soul's part of our Divine Human existence is the center of our Creator's Creation Essence designed and called forth within us as 'desire' for our use on the stages of our in-form life plays. When we are internally tuned into this center, our internal communication speaks to us as desire(s) for dreams! Dreams keep us moving forward to become more of who we really are as we then play them out not only for us but for all of mankind as we are all ONE. If the dream is not of the quality that would be of the highest good for all that is, it would seem that it is not coming from a desire in the depth of one's pure soul but rather from a deep and dark place inside. Another perspective component could be from an intellectual mind space within us that is analyzing a fix for something that is supposedly not working or needs change. From and as the Master Creator, Love is All there is for all of Creation. In our existence, experience, and expression as Divine Human Beings, all of our creations that are from a true desire are from Love or from searching for Love! A true desire manifesting into a dream comes from the core of us! Within that core, we are the artist, the musician, the poet, the author, the teacher, the visionary, etc., igniting our desire and sending it forth into a dream.

Here are some thoughts now pertaining to what a dream really is from a perspective of it being a forever active component for Self-Esteem consideration. Dreams won't save you. They are not salvation. They are not who you are. A dream is a desire playing out as an expression—expressing one's version, understanding, felt knowingness of their God-Self. Dreams are a way of discovering and serving Who I AM; they are not Who I AM. They are a pathway, a Divine Human Being way for us to express 'Who I AM.' They are neither substitution nor salvation. Salvation—if I can have that instead of this, then I am saved, freed! Saved—saved from what? My perception of Who I think I Am because of my interpretation of my experiences, or what I am experiencing. Dreams are a part of the wardrobe of the paper dolls' clothing!

How do I get past the concept/feeling of the dream being me, instead of the recognition of Who I AM? From that recognition, I can have the dream from my truth, not as my truth. The feeling of the expression isn't my God Self proof. It isn't the necessary ingredient for me to be my God Piece. As God, all is possible. As God, nothing is missing. As God, no pieces have been lost or misplaced. As God, no separation has ever happened or is even possible. The Image of God could never be manifested in any way or form lesser than itself. Image means likeness, not likeness altered; therefore, Image of God is a fact. This is Who I AM!

Dreams are neither the pathway from truth down to perception, interpretation, and finally translation; My God Self Piece hopes, dreams, I will be such and such. Perception—This is Who I think I Am; Interpretation—because of how my life played out (experiences) and is playing out (expressions); Translation—conclusion; therefore, it is truth. Nor are dreams the pathway up from translation to pure Image. Dreams are not Jacob's ladder—They don't take us to heaven!

In allowing Self-Esteem to be a cornerstone as we walk life, (life live), what does that really mean? The dictionary defines self-esteem as being satisfied with oneself. In striving to be a balanced Divine Human Being, it is necessary to have a physical, mental, and emotional collective presenting as a workable form (visible) in some manner as well as the components of a spiritual life around some invisible components. The invisible would be beliefs, perceptions of our beginnings, how we got here, etc. all playing into Who are We collectively connecting the Divine to the Human part of our form equation. Perhaps, having a little different way of viewing self-esteem from a smaller version of just believing that it is just in, 'How much do I like myself or not,' we can see how much bigger it really is than that. In an expanded version of our vision, perhaps, self-esteem could become bigger and more powerful and be written as SELF-ESTEEM. Therefore, the accelerated flow of life itself could move from the core of the individual Soul as living life from all that we already are. We express this by playing out many Earth stage plays with us as the Star as we script from a set pattern of 'Soul to Desire to Dreams' as the ever-moving life force meaning to our Living Love Consciously life journeys while knowing that all of our journeys are a sharing of the giving and receiving of Love according to our free choice.

NOW AS A CORNERSTONE OF LIFE
HOW SATISFIED ARE YOU WITH YOURSELF!

Work It … Work It
Life's Four Corner Stones
A REVIEW

Relationships
Abundance
Health
Self-Esteem

I want to die, maybe I will, perhaps I have somehow!
What is Love?
Who AM I?

I'm afraid, I cry, I wonder, I can't pray!
What are Abundance and Money Really?
Who AM I?

I feel I am on the edge of existence with NO answers.
How can I be healed?
Who AM I really?

All in all, I think I am really closer to who I really AM,
I wonder, do I Really know Who I Am!
How, When, and Where will I Know!
GO TO THE EDGE

See if you find yourself in any of the experiences at "The Edge" and remember to read between the lines.

THE EDGE

Oh, so many times I have come to the edge,
There I stand, waiting, listening, wondering,
I scream, I cry, I look for someone to hold me,
I plead for life, beg for forgiveness.
I search in my old toolbox for one more available tool,
Nothing comes forth except my extreme emptiness
I gaze out into the vast expansion of nothingness
Do I jump or just sit here and dangle my feet?
I will decide some other time ...
I turn to go back!

In what seemed like an eternity,
But was only a flicker in time,
I see millions of well-traveled paths
All fading before my eyes.
I gaze out into another vast expansion of nothingness,
Is it really another space of emptiness...
Did I really turn away from the edge?

I turn ever so quickly to experience all,
To find and answer—hear a voice,
To see a foothold—a stepping stone!
Spinning, whirling, I think I stop—dizzy
Aware of no direction, where I started or
Where I stopped—I breathe.
I feel lost at a depth I have never experienced before!
Tears pour out flooding every cell
Every energy particle of my entire Being,
The flooding stops—I breathe!

Swirling, spinning once again
Into the vast expansion of nothingness,
Nothing to connect to—to identify with,
I take a deep breath as it seems air is all there is!
From somewhere, somehow, I now know,
This is Divine Space,
The space of perfection of all that is and isn't,
All beginnings, all endings,
All paths, all dreams,
All seen and not seen,
All heard and not heard.
In the stillness, I smell the sweetness of life!
Many more times, I breathe it in!
I feel such Love!

The Edge—where is it?
Am I still dangling my feet?
Have I jumped?
Did I turn back?
Where am I?
Ah, does it really matter,
For Now, I AM!

—Author Norma Ervin

So What Now

On our journey to the Edge, we have and are exploring, experiencing, and expressing many Divine Human Being in-form Planet Earth Stage Plays where we are either an actor or actress or a props person. Every one of these plays has given us the opportunity to understand more about who we really are beyond just being a Human Being functioning as though we were our highest self, functioning as a Human Doing. Once we get to our own individual edge, realize we are not alone, know we have learned more about our truth, and feel ourselves in a much different way, we then can jump over the edge and see where our wings take us.

The following poems and thoughts to share give a glimpse of the questions we may be asking as we are getting to, even maybe very close to, experiencing the (our) edge in some way either by ourselves or with others in person or in compassion. These are just some major situations of horrific magnitude that the Tribe of Humanity has experienced; there are many. If we look deeply, they could all have a gift for our growth in discovering who we are even when it is extremely hard to find as we just look through our intellectual mind's interpretation and our emotional response or reaction.

Tsunami 2004
Could It Be?

Tsunami, a natural event in the changing of the world,
Truth Surfacing Uniting Naturally All Mind Intelligence ….
Could it be that thousands came to play poor
So when the time was right, they could show so much more!
Could it be that on these very shores, they must live
In order to maximize the gift they would give?
Could it be that among the thousands, some chose to go, some
    chose to stay
As tragedy cries out proclaiming either was the ultimate price
    to pay?
Could it be that there is a Divine Plan taking a stand
With Mother Earth and Human Angels playing hand in
    hand?
God is God and Man is Man, as the image of one the other
    was made,
While within the sustainer of all life, Mother Earth, Divine
    Plans were laid!

Could it be the gifts are many, thus naming a few?
Tsunami 2004 took the world's mind off war!
Hearts immediately cried out compassionately, you see,
With many instantly rallying to serve, feeling how can this
    Be?

No doctrine, ruler, leader, system status, or perceived value
determined the demise.

With no command given stating either or what happened
came as a surprise!

There was no conscious choice to devastate and/or kill in the
name of right or wrong,

So each and every heart was free to open wide and listen to its
own song!

Love is all there is that isn't up for debate.

As Tsunami 2004 gave all an opportunity to freely and fully
let their hearts dictate!

Could it be there are no victims here, dead or alive, with
which to relate,

But rather all bold and courageous Divine Teachers to thank
and honorably celebrate?

Governments, organizations, and corporations gave as part of
their design

But what about the millions of gifts given as personal hearts
align?

I was proud when one prominent government said,

Out of the box of structure, we must be led!

So, person to person, heart to heart, much personal abundance
was put out to share,

As many received with grateful hearts expressing love and
thanks that many to help were there!

Perhaps, the Divine Plan is healing the perception of separation
of, to have and have not,

As these dedicated players played out this agenda for a lot!

All is Love, even war, as some stories must finished be,

As Tsunami 2004 has given us a chance to more clearly see!

Now that we have gone to the Edge, and feel pretty certain that we
have jumped because everything seems so different, but a good different,
are we just floating in the unknown feeling a bit lost looking for something
to hang on to? It appears in my own 'pages of history,' I could have
been in that floating-place asking for answers as some memories were

obviously still present even while much was finished and what was ahead was unknown. Seems that it is a challenge for us as 'human doings' to regularly or consistently stay in a form of reality in the Now! These found pages were titled New Year's Eve 2004. Some of these small chapters in my journey that I experienced then just maybe an answer or a guide to an answer now 15 years later as well. Our Divine Self does not have time as a measurement tool. As a human, we use it as a tool daily in some way or another. If something that was presented to me 15 years ago and still gives me more insight today, does that mean I am a slow learner or there is just more for me to learn in the energy of this time as changes are getting bigger and bigger and happening quicker and demanding more? Maybe what spoke to a human doing 15 years ago speaks differently to a forming 'Divine Human Being now.'

New Year's Eve
2004

Focus—to engage back into humanity—play and experience fun in freedom without working a perceived purpose. This is a personal writing of mine.

A Creator Spirit Guide came to me early today laughing and saying the following: **Beginning of intuitive message**

"Come on, Honey, we are going to lighten up and have a grand, not just good, but grand time. This isn't a holy heavy time (New Year's Eve). Look past what isn't happening and decrease the effect of separation.

There is much celebration on the other side of the veil with all of the thousands who crossed over recently from the Tsunami. We did it! Rejoice too as a participant!"

More of the Intuitive Message, **"Lighten up, please lighten up. This is a big command to ourselves. Many gifts of the Spirit are consciously reappearing to us now in an expanded form. In the now, they are ours to receive and embody. They are not crosses (burdens)** to bear. We are not to immediately put them into 'purpose!' All is well. It really is. So many very powerful things have happened for the Love of all. Powerful really isn't a necessary word here as what is happening without giving it definition. Divinity is flowing and active in and on the Earth herself, the universe, and in the physicality of bodies. Live is easier now as we are not holding so much! The riddle is vanishing. Clarity is more present without uncertainty.

Feel your body; your awareness is what you are told through your body. Feel it, listen, hear the God mind communicate through the heart-brain speaking inside you, not the ego-mind searching beyond you (outside you). All is well. The space around you is much clearer, as we can get close, and oftentimes embody within it. This new energy is available for anyone's use, in new or old energy. Soon, you will drop singing words that keep the two divided or separated because there really is only one energy, and the illusion will fade from your perception. The new energy is expansion, and that just is! Remember you have left behind nothing, and you have gone nowhere!

Don't effort so much to bring us in so-to-speak because we are embodied, and we don't come from someplace else. Our energy is your energy and your energy is embodied as our energy. All is expanded as a result. We don't sit outside each other but within One. Because of this, no energy can be moved in a way that has never been possible before. Not only is there NEW energy that has never been before but also the expanded capacity and capability for movement (flow) is New. In this New embodied combination, you don't so much need guidance or instruction on how to 'meet us' so to speak because we are embodied. With more awareness of our being of One energy, this One energy is of a higher frequency. There is much sweetness and light-heartedness here. It truly is time to plan and experience Love in a more complete way than has ever been possible. You saw it and felt it today. (I had had an amazing connected conversation with an out-of-town friend of mine.)

In the New Year with New implying more than it ever has been before, two things are absolutely yours to Be—BE very attentive to yourself, and BE open to consistently seeing and receiving the fruits (the beauty and the thorns) of the Rose (of your Rose). These are the gifts of the Spirit and are given to you through grace—nothing, yes nothing is required of you except for you to recognize and know your wholeness. Let your truth appear before you without judgment. Realize that the whole of you has never been separated from grace and that all gifts are of, as, and from Spirit! You have now released all hold on your Spirit so all potentials of and for expansion are yours now. You have already been told that your divinity as your darkness (not meaning evil) has already created much for you that is ready now to be manifested so you can experience more of your own wholeness. Receive all that your divinity has to give you. IS-ness is not believing or knowing, it just IS!

There is a divinity that is being expressed in the IS-ness now that has never been before. Trust that and allow all of it to be your experience for expression as it can be no other way. Don't analyze and define it to the point of diminishing it for yourself. In changing your story, you have no point of reference to tell you that all is not yours. Nothing is withheld from you and grace cannot pick and choose what to freely give you. All gives all according to the wisdom of your own core. There is no other way! Therefore, receive all. Don't ask why or how, just 'be it' and flow the 'do it'! There are no 'yabuts or what ifs'! We don't play that way anymore. If you still want to play the victim game, it is your choice, and we have no judgment around it as all is Love—either Love expressing or Love wanting expression. In energy, one moves and one holds. There is no one thing that completes everything. The flow never stops and says 'done'!" (End of intuitive message.)

My questions to my guides that are communicating with me which are some parts of the God essence that I am a part of:

The first question is, "How can I lighten up? I feel I am still too intense. The intensity seems like such a real part of me most of the time.

I really don't know my life without this. I think I have only had brief moments without intenseness."

I hear, **"Change your story—know your life without tenseness! You are still looking for something to hang on to so your body holds the tenseness and only jumps to the next thing you bring it in for it to hang on to. Right now, there are two things for you to let go of that you are grasping desperately for and energetically clinging to— Purpose and Dreams! These can be used for self-definition. Move energy here and receive what comes to you. Much will!"**

My second question is, "How do I re-engage myself and move back into humanity?"

Answer, **"How do you want to be back in humanity? We see your heart's song for play and fun, and then we see your stronghold on purpose and dreams. It seems you are holding onto that which you want to be moving."**

My response, "I feel what you are saying is that it is like I am holding the door shut and at the same time, asking for the key. So how do I see through this? Being more specific, what is the book that doesn't seem to be taking form (Purpose) and the mountain property (Dream)?"

Answer, **"You have just answered what they are."**

My response, "So what do I do here? My ship is going down."

Answer, **"Change your story. Let go of the need to swim with one arm holding the lifeboat. You don't need a purpose in the New and your dreams aren't your salvation. If you hold onto a purpose, it is presenting the belief that there is something to fix, and it is urgent. The felt urgency of needing to do something, to fix something, pushes you out of the Now into a future projection."**

I feel, perhaps see, I am "efforting" the book (writing) as I do not have a 'job' in the old, and I am telling myself that "I have a job" which is gathering myself to write the book and getting it done, and I thought I intuitively heard that from Spirit, my Higher Self, or from somewhere. Therefore, I am confused, and I am yelling, "Help!" And in the meantime, I am beginning to really feel concerned over financial abundance.

My intuitively received response, **"These are two entirely different pieces—abundance just IS. It is not tied to anything. This is a piece you are energetically clearing for humanity and bless you for this. The waiting is a giving and receiving of energy, not to be designed, motivated by abundance issues."**

"I didn't think I was doing that, am I?"

"Yes, you are in that your worry energy wraps around it and factors into the flow. You have a good imagination piece working for you. Relax around it and let it happen. Your judgment of your friend as 'tying it down to shoot herself in the foot,' is your story too! Allow it to happen!"

My response and/or reaction, "I can hear this, but I am afraid! What if it doesn't happen and I run out of money and have manifested no job?"

Answer to me, **"Again, abundance is a free gift, so quit attaching it to everything else, and you are safe. You know your safety in most, if not all, of everything except in abundance. You are living your freedom outside of the structure and others' dreams, but you are worrying about your abundance!"**

My question, "Do I need to seek an old energy job? Am I being too crazy here? Am I playing the trickster in feeling 'I just can't go there?'"

That question just seemed to close all channels of communication inside of me! I went to a space of nothing, nothingness.

"What do I do here? Help!"

Received response, **"Breathe—not to force an answer but to allow an answer. You are safe, trust, allow, move energy."**

"So how do I go out to rejoin humanity?"

Answer, **"Go out as the fruit of the rose. Go out now—just as you are right now! Go out to allow, to give and receive being the I Am that you are, and see what comes to you! You want specific answers from us and as God also. You as a God piece, us as God, now energetically more embodied than we have ever been, meaning separation is gone, which in fact separation really never was present! We are not withholding the answers so you have to search more to prove yourself and we will tell. We don't experience your** manifestations as you do, but we are your truth as God also. We work with you energetically as you manifest the form, and all is divinity at work. It is now not possible or appropriate that we give you all of your answers. Remember, there are two parts of the Rose—the fruit (beauty and fragrance) of the Rose and the thorn of the Rose. You know the difference, and you know how each feels. You know you can make no wrong decision, and there is no wrong answer; there is no right or wrong—just walk. Choose and step on, keep moving, and quit stopping to ask us if you made the right choice. We love you and are working with you in ways you don't fully understand, but it is all within the Divine plan for all that all of us have put into motion. Just trust that and allow it to unfold in all of its magnificence!

It is all so much larger than your linear world and you know. Therefore, stop endeavoring to thumbtack it to that bulletin board as though that is the only reality that exists! You are safe. Let your God-consciousness illuminate your awareness for you as to whether you are experiencing the fruit or the thorn. Use your intuitive God mind, voice, or resonance with free choice, and keep moving. The New energy that is ready for New Potentials is neutral but not stagnant, as it is ever moving. It is no longer a work of Spirit to ask a question. Hold onto its stopped energy and wait for an answer. The New Potential energy won't stop (go on hold) with us but will move on. Therefore, what we are left holding really does no longer serve us. The energy frequency it served is no longer us, and we can never return to that frequency that was what served."

Wow, I am just watching, reflecting, and being totally amazed in this 'now' day in 2019 as I have just finished sharing with you something that I recorded word for word on New Year's Eve, 12/31/2004. I had a really rough night last night and seemed to roll around all night with questions, reflections, memories, yes, some worries too, as I endeavored to quiet my tornado inner happenings and bring some peace in. I certainly was experiencing the thorns of my rose! As I went to my computer to enter this piece for the book that really is getting written now for real, I was truly amazed at all of the responses and/or answers, that I was entering from 2004 that was giving clarity to, or answers to, all of what I was experiencing last night in 2019.

Now again, I ask, "What is time really?" It obviously exists with some kind of value for measurement in the human world of reality. However, time, as we know and use it, is not present in the Divine world of our co-creating partners for the creation of a New Divine Human Being. Whatever I was dealing with as my understanding of life and my life journey in 2004 brought me those answers, and then 15 years later, they were still the essence for my answers. Believe me, much has changed in my life over those 15 years so it is not that I stayed completely on hold without movement during that period of time. My life journey has expanded my life a lot in those years. However, many of my scenarios are still in the changing process as we are a collective, which includes me as an individual, are literally still purging much from our mass consciousness which no longer serves us individuals, and the collective is ONE.

This experience has proven to me that what **IS (Infinite Source)** is, it just IS. It is the same yesterday, today, and forever, and yes, 15 years ago! Therefore, can this also show that when it comes to the Divine components as our Divine Human Being, that we can 'look back to the future' for some clarification in traveling the 'Now'? Isn't it true that from the realms of the Essence of the Immaculate Concept of our existence, all that we need to walk the journey was, and is always and already within us ready for our recognition, understanding, and use? We will not all receive the information in the same way or in the same words as each of us are on our individual path with our own way of interpreting life and who we are in it as we have had our own experiences according to our individual core and the gift of free choice. This has developed our own individual package of wisdom which is always up for expanding and showing us more of our truth that we can play in and with. No two are exactly alike, but through heart connections, they can play together.

I truly have a heart full of gratitude this day for my experience of the divine right timing of my sharing the past words in the exact moment. They were also the answer for this very day! I declare, How cool is that! I am so grateful that is the way life works from time to time on this current journey! Maybe we don't recognize the gift of our rose as much when we are experiencing the thorns! I feel I have had to learn that the deeply felt punctures of the thorn are a gift as a necessary part of the process, and not an indication that I have, or am, doing something wrong and am completely off course!

The Edge—Where is it?
Am I still dangling my feet?
Have I jumped or did I turn back?
Where AM I?
Ah, does it really matter?
For Now, I AM that I AM
SO WHAT NOW?

SO WHAT NOW?

There is no home to return to,
There is no structure to claim that name,
There is no place to view the pictures,
Look at the stuff and play my roles,
For me to find and/or remember who I am!
There is no book of definitions—no wall of reflections!

I stand in the core of a space of nothingness—nothing,
With my entire insides feeling as the burnt ashes of all that
     was!
All that remains is a smoldering, lingering smoke.
I float—somewhere, somehow—**Out of This**—I AM

The ashes are cold,
The smoke carrying the last bit of aliveness of what was is
     gone!
All seems gone!
I feel like the energy template of some form
Flying over the place of all that was.
I see nothing—no kindred forms!
Who AM I, Where AM I, Why AM I?
I float—somewhere, somehow—**Even Now**—I AM

Can I soar forever without form?
Have I died—passed out of the world of form?
Did I travel any as the last essence of the smoke?
Am I the last bit of aliveness of all that was my physical
     existence?

Have I crossed over?
Did I come by myself—was it only my home that burned?
There is a memory of emotions presenting themselves to me,
I feel a resonance, but glean no definitions, no answers.
So what does this mean?
Am I alone here?
I don't feel separated, yet I see nothing to connect with.
Maybe I don't know what separation is!
I float—somewhere, somehow—**I Know**—I AM

So What Now,
Rebuild—how, where, what
A very lovingly felt essence floods over my energy template
Whispering "come with me"
As my very core flickers with twinkling lights.
My entire being vibrates to a WOW, there are others!
I float—somewhere, somehow, **I Feel**—I AM

We go to the cosmic movies and see a most unbelievable movie
Called "Life on Planet Earth-The Possibilities in a Universal
     Experience."
What an incredible story!
Why do I feel me in every part?
I am the baby to the elder,
The warrior, soldier, terrorist, priest, dictator to lover,
I Love, I hate.
I float—somewhere, somehow—**Even in and as All of
     this**—I AM

Movie over, lights on, looking around the theatre,
Planet Earth and all its inhabitants and dynamics form the
     stage.
I observe my physical form sitting
In a comfortably padded seat in the audience section.
I feel the presence of the others
As I look around and see many of the seats filled.
We know who we are

As we watch the very well-done fairytale play out!
Grounded, here. Now **expanded,** I AM

So What Now,
There is no home to return to,
There is no structure to claim that name,
There is no place to view the pictures,
Look at the stuff and play my roles.
For me to find and/or remember who I AM.
There is no book of definitions, no wall of reflections,
The ashes are cold as mother Earth welcomed them into her
bosom
There is no reflection of the last particle of smoke,
As the air breathed it in and let its essence free!

So What Now
Love.
Love will find a way.
Love is the way!
What does that mean? How can that be?
BE—BE still and know!
Love can make itself known in and as the Silence.
Love is All there IS!
Now, as a Human Angel transitioning on Earth—I AM

So What Now
IS ness
I AM
Love!

The Bold Letters Message . . .

Out of this
Even now
I know.

**I feel
Even in and as all of this
expanded.**

**Now, as a Human Angel transitioning on Earth
I AM
LOVE!
By Norma Ervin 11/11/04**

Now that we have reread our Book of Life regarding the Four Cornerstones, have gone to the edge, and have asked 'So What Now' as we are on the journey down the 'New Road,' how does life play out? What is a Human Angel transitioning on Earth and how does that look? What is a Divine Human Angel? Will it seem we are playing multiple roles for a time, the old and the new? If so, will we be confused?

A GARDENER ATTENDING THE COMPOST A HUMAN ANGEL IN TRANSITION

Life is moving along, but somehow, it seems so different. There seem to be so many physical bumps in the road and so many cosmic potholes that appear to be traveling together somehow. We know that change is upon us as consciousness is changing. We hear and feel that New is the order of the day, but what does that really mean? How are we really playing, and can we begin to grasp a little of our story (part) in this process? Is it even possible to clearly see it as we so often feel so scrambled, and our life experiences just don't lend themselves to our intellect as they used to?

Are we participating in realms outside of 3D linear reality in designing a new template for Earth and all universes? It seems like the answer to this is yes, and we are being intuitively told that it is now time to bring the new human energy template into the physical realms of Earth. Therefore, perhaps the big thing left to do is the demolition process because the old space is also the ground for the new.

Thus, the story (journey) begins. The old is not to just be bulldozed in but is to be resolved and made ready for reuse. Energetically, it is to be transfigured back into the Love that is its immaculate conception from the beginning. As Human Angels, we are the gardeners of the Now. Sometimes, we are planting seeds, but much of the time in this Now, it feels we are making Divine-Human, Human-Divine Heavenly Compost. This is the preparation of the old for it to be utilized in growing new, but there is an added dimension or new formula here.

As compost builders, now our piles are not always balanced, so sometimes, they are burning too hot—we are in a physical emotional pain. Sometimes, they are not burning enough—we are depressed or feel alone, lifeless. Or sometimes, the mix is just totally out of balance and there is a big stink—anger or drama playing out. We could even be struggling with the compost container or 'Divine Right Space' according to the mind. We could be overly attached to the 'old need for a certain structure.' When it is not cooking, divinity and humanity are not balanced, but remember, we are the tenders of the pile.

Wow, we are realizing that as Light workers or Human Angels, this heavenly composting is big business! Therefore, we must immediately (in time) give up all resistances to being an entrepreneur because it feels we have just been appointed as the CEO (**C**onsciously **E**volving **O**fficer), over millions—not people, but compost piles! We are not just raking up leaves and grass clippings off our own yards and throwing in our own scraps; instead, the universe is our market! There is a demand for us as stuff from all over is being shipped to us quicker than 2nd-day air. There aren't very many of us, but somehow, we seem to be easy to find and everything imaginable is coming! Another one of our big challenges seems to be that we are being shipped the **SHIT** (**S**tuff **H**ot **I**n **T**ime) with not much mediating mix. So, what **<u>TO DO</u>** becomes the next **<u>MIND</u>** asked questions. We have a big job here so we must do something fast to generate enough balance and get these piles burning properly.

Surprisingly enough, the element of the heart is fire. Sounds to me like this could be the Love fire that could be a beneficial potential for the mix in the SHIT if used in a proper ratio. **<u>INTUITION</u>** is telling me this as the tender of the piles, but the **MIND is** still **RACING** around looking for the answer as it is becoming quite frantic, believing that if it doesn't act quickly, we will be completely covered with just the current supply of Stuff Hot in Time. Without a doubt, a new huge shipment will be arriving tomorrow if the **PAST** points of reference can have any truth for the future. We must do something quickly! Nothing to this magnitude has ever happened before so we can't go to the files and find an answer, but if we don't find one soon, in a week or less, we will literally be facing our own death by being suffocated under deep, deep, piles of SHIT. Uhm ... death by suffocation from Stuff Hot in Time—is this hell? And the mind goes on and on.

Meanwhile, back at the unloading DOCK (**D**estination **of** **C**alibrated **K**nowledge) the message of the Heart Fire is still quite audible even though it continues to be quite obvious that not all are hearing as **minds are racing** and **DRAMA is building.** In fact, tonight at 7 PM, there is a special race scheduled. All minds are asked to check in early as a big crowd is expected. The race will probably be the last one, at least for a while, and maybe forever, because the race track is the sight of the dumping of the next big shipment of that hot stuff! As we reported earlier, it will probably be here tomorrow, which is indicating we have to hurry and rally up this big race tonight! Because of the seriousness of timing and situations, instead of the usual 50-100 mind racers of a usual race, thousands are coming to be a part of this possible last race.

Energy is pumping, or is it anger is boiling? Tonight, I will go the fastest I have ever gone, and I am determined to not let anyone or anything stand in my way. With thousands participating, this is the only way I will have any room to move—to knock them out of my way. I'm ready! I'm really ready! Let's get going! I may not live through it, but I will go out racing, doing what I love, and I will not go out being buried by SHIT!

Consequently, the event forms as the Drama continues, all as a result of not being able to figure it out and to find an answer to balance the compost piles so they will burn properly! Another big issue here is, who appointed me CEO anyway, or am I really the CEO or do I just think I AM?

Meanwhile, back at the Dock (Destination of Calibrated Knowledge)

Now who is that guy standing over there beside the filled-up loading Dock? I don't know him at all. He only looks familiar because I have seen him around ever since these shipments have been coming in, but I know nothing about him. He is so quiet. He seems to have nothing to say even though he is always present. Funny, in looking closer, I am not even sure if the person is a male or female. At any rate, it seems there is no real threat here, so I will just let him/her be and not spend the time to see what he/she is about, and I will not chase the person away.

Back to the Races (**R**unning **A**round **C**lueless **E**scaping **S**igns).

I have a big event to get underway! And tomorrow, if there is a tomorrow, I have to figure out what to do with all of these compost piles. One potential is that I could just leave in the night after the big race and not come back. If I do that, then it would be someone else's problem. I think I will do that! If I live through tonight, I'm out of here, and I will just start over. I don't know where, but not here. I no longer know what to do here. I have failed and will probably be fired anyway. Therefore, I will leave before I am exposed for all to see that I really am not as forceful as I think I AM.

Now at the Dock …

Sitting here at the Dock as the CEO Human Angel in charge of Divine operation for the proper heat for the burning of the compost piles, some choices are up for decisions. What does the situation look like, and how do I really feel about it? Well, I guess I had better just sat and breathe into this for a while. This is so awesome as these huge piles of shit are here with more coming. How did I manifest all of this abundance, as it seems it just showed up? I'm not clear or sure at all where I am as all of these others racing around here do not feel familiar to me even though they do look familiar somehow. I sure can't and seemingly couldn't if I wanted to participate in their big event tonight. I have no resonance with it so I am just going to stay here in the warmth of this hot stuff while they gather for the race. I will breathe while they race!

Nighttime—I so love the nighttime. I love the black of the night. In this blackness, I feel so much closer to the presence of the void which to me is the **UNIFIED FIELD OF GOD** or whatever else it is called. I love it when I see the same thing whether my eyes are open or shut, and I don't even have a conscious awareness of knowing if they are open or shut. This is the closest I can, or have thus far, been able to experience the real feel of **ONENESS**. Here in pure blackness, I can put my hand in front of my face and not even see it. I have such a sense of not being a form as there is no form visible to my sight anywhere. I get so exhilarated in this space! I can see no difference being made by my being in form, but I feel air touching my body as though it were the very breath of life itself. I take a big breath to take it all in! This is such **PEACE**! I feel so joyful and loved—another big breath! Awesome, this truly is life—I really can't put it into words, but I certainly can feel It. I just want **TO BE** here!

Back to the Races …

Lights, get them all on. We have to be able to clearly see around every part of the track as there will be thousands of racers. There is a booth where you can buy earplugs because the noise will more than likely be deafening! It is already so loud here that you can't even talk to the person next to you, and there is no time to text! There are more spectators here to watch the races than there are racing participants. I think all feel the urgency of the moment which feels like an explosive mix of fear, anger, hopelessness, blended with the desire to live with the occasional tainted thought that even suicide would be acceptable.

All are now lined up and ready to go! The start is signaled by all of the track lights being turned off for one minute. This pure blackness deepens the panic as no one can see anything, and they feel all alone. This electrifies the explosiveness of emotions as the **INTELLECTUAL**

MASTER MIND comes over the loudspeaker and shouts, "It's okay, we will now turn the lights on where all can be seen," and the Race is on! Lights on, breath that was held is released, and the race is on full force. Everyone is tensed up, either watching or participating—intently wondering—will there be a winner, will I be the winner, so drawn into the action at hand that they hardly dare to even take a breath!

Back at the Dock...

I am having such a peaceful sleep. In the **knowingness** of this completely nurturing rest, **every cell** of my **BEING** expresses **conscious awareness** of how **SAFE** I feel even in this **UNKNOWN** place with all of those **slightly familiar** others who seem to be **PLAYING** different kinds of **GAMES**! It just registered to me that I said I was in a peaceful sleep. I am not sure if **I AM** asleep or awake! Oh well, either way, I know I'm safe here and that feels so good!

Back to the Races ...

Race over—lights out—all gone! Race over, wreckers come and gone, ambulances come and gone, congratulations exchanged, fistfights subsided, tired crying children quieted, bone-weary people retiring to home while at a soul level still wondering what all that had really been about. As the adrenaline stopped pumping and the spirit seemed to crash, shallow breathing began feeding the body again. The Mind reflected for only another short moment with seemingly no recognition of awareness or understanding of the happenings of the day before looking to tomorrow's agenda!

Oh, wait—Lights are out—I was going to leave. I can leave in the night when no one can see me. I really don't want to go, but I must because I have no answer for resolving the hot compost piles problem. I do see the reality of destruction, even perhaps, as I said before, death here is in the making. You see this Stuff Hot in Time is not just my imagination; it is right here in front of me in real plain sight. I see it, I smell it, and if I choose to step in it, I could even touch it! I am really feeling afraid! It is like it sees me, smells me, and is touching me! What is this? I have to get out of here! Where will I go? It feels like wherever I go, this shit will always know where I am and can come to me again. How can I ever be safe again? If I stay, I don't have enough money to hire enough dump trucks to haul this off as quickly as it is arriving, and besides, where would I have them take it anyway? Right now, I see no value in it. It is just a rapidly increasing problem so there is no time to find any research on a possible value or to even seek out physics to see why shit happens.

Well, the sun's coming up. I'm still here! Am I staying or going? I must decide quickly. It seems as though in the past, I would have known what to do. Now I don't seem to be able to grasp any of those once useful tools or reasonings. Oh my, I wonder if I will be of any value in the future—am I really losing my mind as I feel sometimes like my very essence is going away! I feel like all of those wrecked cars after the Mind Racer's event. Some cars were a little broken, some a lot broken, many mangled together, some dripping human blood, some leaking oil, some with broken gas tanks with gas seeping out just waiting for a spark from something, someone, or somewhere to give it a reason to explode. My soul asks, "Did it have value?" STOP—I can't go there. Life must go on! Am I going or staying?

What? I can't believe what I am seeing—yes, it is real because I am seeing it with my own eyes. That person, whom I still cannot decide if it is a male or female, is what appears to be, either again or still, sound asleep as he/she is all quiet and curled up right on top of the biggest hot pile. What is this thing? I have never heard it utter a word. It obviously must be an escapee from a mental institution who wandered into our area and has no place to go! I understand some about being crazy, but I absolutely cannot wrap my brain around any conceivable level of sanity or insanity that would cause or allow one to crawl up on a pile of shit intentionally and go to sleep! But because I have seen it with my own eyes, then I must be willing to formulate the hypothesis that some things must be beyond my realm of understanding. With this one, I wouldn't, once again, even know where to go to do the research to find the answer!

If I stay, I will probably have to deal with that person, but my first priority would be to get the race track cleared off because the night for our routine scheduled race is just three nights away. That one will go on as planned if the track isn't covered by then. My, if I could see into the future and see that I wasn't going to be able to save the field from future shipments, I would just not bother cleaning it up. I would let the compost just cover up the current mess and deal with it at such a time that I knew what I was going to do with all of that hot stuff.

I'm very tired. I guess I am staying! So, guess I will go home and sleep for a few hours, and then see what I can **DO**. At least I have a home to go to. Even though I want a better one, I don't have to sleep on top of a hot pile of Shit. Some people! Oh well, I guess life could be worse!

Now at the Dock—remember, Destination of Calibrated Knowledge

Wow, the sun is just getting up good. Stretching, I feel so alive, alert, and rested. Wiggling out of my warm, cozy, spontaneously-made bed of last night, I sit up and begin breathing in the sunrise. This is such a beautiful, as well as powerful, time of day as it is one of the two times that yin and yang—male and female energetic characteristics of the whole—are in balance. I really love breathing this in as it just makes me feel so loved, nurtured, and inspired to the point that my passion for the day seems to just gently, but powerfully, move about to get going into the day at hand. At this precious moment of sunrise, and after taking it into me for creating, I almost feel like "I'm off to the races" with my plan in my hip pocket, and I won't read it until I get there wherever there might be. It is so exciting! I feel like a little kid getting on my two-wheel bike for the first time, and I wonder what the training wheels are for because I just know I am ready to ride without them, and even if I do fall, I'll just roll around and feel myself on the Earth. There is nothing to be afraid of! I AM safe!

Anyway, it is Now, and this day seems to have had a beginning as was signaled by the sun. Still feeling such joy, peace, and love, I take a breath. This always seems to bring something to me that somehow makes me feel I'm right where I am supposed **to be**. It also appears somehow that if there is some action that I am **to do**, I just see or feel what that is, and then as if by some miracle, I find myself involved in creation. Well, this didn't fail me on this particular morning! I knew it was morning because of the sun and the light. I like the light too, but it is a different experience than that of the pure dark where all forms appear formless. Oneness, for me, feels different when all, or many, forms are visible.

Anyway, back to this Now. I just knew it was appropriate to make something out of these piles of abundance. All of this Stuff Hot in Time just came to me for transmutation to a new potential use. Breathing into this, I recognized the Hot as being the heat from the Fire of the Heart. However, there was an imbalance here which just meant it had yet to receive some loving, heartfelt gratitude for all that the old had been as it was coming along for the New Journey. It was showing up for a new conversion preparing it to be a new mixture as it entered into transfiguring back to pure love energetics to play new and not used up. This, in combination with some passionate heart-felt love from the imagination for the New Earth, together, they would have a properly burning combination for the creation of many new potentials for the use of all Mankind as well as for Mother Earth. This would be the new composted soil! Wow, I just experienced a fading memory here telling me that I was a Gardener!

Wow, what a dream I had last night! I truly seemed to experience myself as a part of the Old Mass Consciousness mix in the compost while at the same time, I was also experiencing myself as a part of the imagination, and already manifested reality for the newly transfigured Love ready for the collective in and as the ONE. This newly transfigured Love version is to bring into manifested reality a New Mass Consciousness for All that IS playing out everywhere and in everything that is visible and not visible.

The End

Written by Norma Ervin

Having now, in some way explored/experienced a composting scenario, what does compost really mean? In one version of Webster's Dictionaries, it is defined as:

1. A mixture of decayed organic matter used as fertilizer (noun)
2. A compound: mixture (noun)
3. To fertilize with compost (vt)
4. To convert (some matter) to compost (vt)

The definition of compound is to combine to form a whole: MIX.

Stopping to reflect a moment on this Gardener's dream, how does all of this apply to 'So What Now' in our reality and the **Bold-Faced Message** at the end of that poem? Perhaps, we collectively are making up the whole of the ONE humanity mixture. In the beginning of our immaculate conception from the Image of our Creator, we were from organic essence energetically transitioned into an organic matter as human form. We as a collective, through the free choice we were given from the beginning, messed up the organic part and became alive in a decaying mass consciousness. In this current change, we are at a perfect time to rise up out of the old mess and convert what now is playing out in horrific ways, not of love to a resurrection and restoration version of our original organic immaculately conceived Creation. It seems we as gone-astray mass consciousness energetics players are the **S**tuff **H**ot **in Time** showing up for change. There is still an organic essence to us that is not decayed and is still guiding us to awaken and get back on the road to heaven all around us which is including on Earth. We are also being guided to release the heat of hell as we believe it to be, which really is just the absence of Love, that we also walk in a lot. Our Immaculate Design was that Love is all there is; consequently, we must realize that everything is expressing Love or looking for, searching for, longing for, or yearning for Love! Ultimately, we as the Unity/ONE/Whole collective represent all facets of the Stuff Hot in Time. The components are the decayed matter (old energy going away) and the organic aspects (original essence) still inside us guiding us to a resurrected-restored way. These two are joining as a compound (restored mix) to fertilize a New Mass Consciousness which is being converted by LOVE and is the breath of All That IS and that is the Immaculate Concept Design!

Through Free Choice, what do you (we) choose as you (we) remember there is no right or wrong answer? Or are you (we) playing a little bit in two worlds right now as we are making new meanings, new expressions for many changing aspects in our current reality? Choices are, the **Dock**—**D**estination **O**f **C**alibrated **K**nowingness or the **Races**— **R**unning **A**round **C**lueless **E**scaping **S**igns.

The **Bold-Faced Message** seems to be the Human Angel's Transitioning on Earth's understanding which fits right in with understanding the truth of Love and putting it into the mix in the proper proportions for bringing about a balance of, for, from, and as the Divine Human Being.

The Bold-Faced Message

Out of this
Even now
I know.
I feel
Even in as all of this
Expanded.
Now, as a Human Angel transitioning on Earth

I AM
LOVE!

LIVE AND LEARN
PART 1
SPIDER'S UNEXPECTED MESSAGE

Have you ever had one of those days that from the very 'get go' you felt totally out of sorts? On this particular morning, I felt so stressed around life in general that it seemed from deep inside I was grasping in every direction for just some semblance of an answer. When what to my wondering eyes should appear . . .

Itsy Bitsy

While unconsciously staring into outdoor space,
A very small form appeared right before my face!
"Hard" was the current presenting feeling of the day,
As Itsy-Bitsy spider was awkwardly wiggling with something
    to say!

Now with focused attention on this flailing speck in the air,
At first, all I could do was just wonder and stare.
You amaze me for so very, very small you are,
I watch as all your legs move like you had been too long at
    the bar!

Look, just like me, you are grabbing for a hold,
A support out of reach, still swinging, you are so bold!
A place to land is so close, but seems not to be so,
As in mid-air, you seem to remain, with no planned place to go!

Is this my life I am seeing,
Being shown to me in this tiny Being?
Today, feeling I am desperate, grasping in space,
This little life shows me the world as a safe place!

For you see, in mid-air, Itsy Bitsy was not flailing,
But from a delicately created web string, she was sailing!
It was so very fine and transparent, I did not see
She was not grasping for a hold, but swinging free!

Itsy Bitsy has no creations of an illusionary life,
So there is no other reality to cause her strife!
Her life tool truly comes from inside to out
For home, food, family, travel—her web is about.

So Itsy Bitsy today to me does innocently say,
"In the vastness of all that is, new attention you must pay
To your perceptions of what appears for you to see,
I feel, I believe, therefore, I AM is no formula to BE!

A web you too have which is more transparent than mine,
It goes everywhere, gives and receives as needed, with nothing
        out of line
So could your perceived flailing, translated fear invading
Also be known as free sailing, so hang on celebrating?

If there were no used theories waiting to make your life better,
Would you still grab ahold to define them to the letter?
Perhaps, whole worlds await to show you what yet to live
So what directive to your web of life will you give?

Today, my illusion seemed huge with no alternate choice,
As the truth slipped in when Itsy Bitsy appeared with a voice!
When your world appears scary and upside down,
Your web can always bring some "Itsy Bitsy" around!

Poem by Norma Ervin

On the practical side of life, these little creatures serve a very important function for us as well. They are a vital part of nature's natural pest control. Spiders are the most important insect-eating species and are, therefore, responsible for holding down the insect population.

They are fascinating little creatures from the way their body is formed and functions to the webs they weave. They have a two-part body: a cephalothorax (a fused head and thorax) and an abdomen. The cephalothoraxes have a pair of chelicerae (jaws with fangs that spring out and inject venom), a pair of pedipalps used for touching, walking, tasting, and manipulating prey, and four pairs of walking legs. The abdomen part of their body contains the spinnerets, usually six of them, used for producing the web, also referred to as silk. Their eyesight is not very good even though they have eight small eyes toward the front of their cephalothoraxes. The spider's sight is enhanced by their legs which are covered with numerous long stiff hairs that are sensitive to vibrations. The type of web they weave helps to identify their family in the species.

They cannot eat solid food so they have a unique system for getting the nutrition from their prey. When movement is detected in their web, they quickly move in and wrap the victim in silk. The spider then injects venom into the insect which at first paralyzes it. Along with other injected juices, the insect's internal body begins to break down. The spider then sucks out the nutrients and discards the inedible exoskeleton.

**Let the small wonders of life speak to you
as they play their unique role in the
rhythm of Mother Earth!**

LIVE AND LEARN
PART 2

Life's journey seems to have a series of polarity-appearing characteristics, with the seemingly regular ups and downs being one such pair that we all experience!

THE SWING

Oh, how do you like to go up in the air?
Up in the air so high . . .
I have felt my life move as the pendulum swings.
I have felt the heights of all,
Happy—Excited—Elated!
Truly every question answered,
Every dream within possibilities,
I have soared with the eagles,
Flown into Heaven itself!
Celebrated with the Angels,
Sat at the right hand of God!
This is real—this is Truth!
Trust—Why Not?

Oh, how do you like to swing . . .
I have felt my life move as the pendulum swings,
I have felt the depth of all,
Hopeless, Depressed—to the bottom of the deepest spaces!
No answer offered any life I would choose,
No dream was present—let alone possible!

I crawled lower than the creatures in the deepest bowel of the
    darkness,
I fell into Hell itself!
I AM with no one and nothing!
This is real—this is my Truth!
Trust—Why?

Does this Heaven help us,
Or there's no way in Hell?
Possible answer: Yes, No, Maybe.

So, how do you like to swing?
What's Up, what's Down?
What's in Between?
What is Real?
What is Truth?
Why?
TRUST!

Do the ups and downs in life that seem to be a given part of, or pattern in, our life journey have anything to do with helping us learn to 'Live in the Now' and to become more acquainted with the reality of 'We Don't Know What We Don't Know'?

Let's see….

SAND BLASTING

I once watched this program on the travel channel or one of those out-of-ordinary channels that was called Sand Blasting. I was totally fascinated by it because for me, it portrayed a scenario for an explanation as to how my current life felt. Here is how the game went: It was a beach activity that took place somewhere that I am not recalling now, but it is my understanding that these are summer events in various beach places around the world.

There are teams of sand sculptors that gather somewhat in competition mode, but there is much more than just competing involved. The larger piece being, at least to me, the luck-of-the-draw is a type of fate. The playing field is prepared ahead of time with huge sand piles that are already dampened so the sand will stick together. Each team has their hill of sand, much like an easel with a canvas ready for painting. Another factor of these playing fields is that they are somehow electronically wired. Each site is electronically attached to a central power station of some kind. Each site is also randomly set up with a specific number and a specific timing before any of the sculptor teams choose, or are assigned, to their location. Each team has at least two intricately drawn designs for sand sculptures that they are prepared to sculpt.

The dynamics of the game are that all teams begin sculpting fast and furiously as a time clock starts. At certain intervals during the course of the day, one of the sites will be randomly picked and blown up, and a plan B, less complicated design immediately starts. The goal of the game for the players is to hopefully make it all the way to the end without being blown up. If their sculpture is blown up, the best-case scenario is to have it be one of the earlier blow-ups because then, there is more time to create another sculpture before time is up.

In the end, the judging is done in two categories, one being on the ones that were the original design and were not blown up along the way. The other category is all of the restarts factoring in time as to how far along they got depending on the time they got blown up, earlier or later. Another big piece along the way for everyone is keeping the sand wet enough so that all designs, curves, bends, etc. stick together and don't collapse. Now at the end of the game, all blow-ups over, all sculptures complete or completed to a point, and the judging done, the winners chosen, the awards of whatever kind given out, the astonishing happens! The entire field is blown up! The beauty of all the creations is only enjoyed for a brief moment in time!

So, how was this relating to me? It was as though this threw out a whole box of puzzle pieces in front of me. One side of the pieces, when put together, formed a picture of me with situations in my day in the play while the other side had words. These words were seemingly in pairs; attachment-experience, can-can't, accept-resist, allow-deny, trust-doubt. For in this now (summer 2008 or 2009), I have (had) created my life in such a way that I do not (did not) have a job outside my living space nor did I have any obligations that pulled me in directions that I didn't want to go. Speaking as of that time, I am, seem to be, fully immersed in the energy of the changing times. I feel as though the mere existence of my sustaining energy has restructured putting new not-so-well-known results right in front of me. My resonance with the sandblasting game, play, happening, moment, or whatever else it could be called, is that whatever I get up with in the morning as my chosen design for the day, which includes my doing-ness, my emotional state, and my blowups, if any etc., I will play it out in some way before going to sleep that night.

I then, in some reality not well known to me, see that my day is blown up, completed in some way, and not up for replaying or redoing. Consequently, I virtually and in reality, start over a new day the next day, one that I have never lived before and will never relive the same. I wake up, feel the day, access what appears real for me in that now, and start from there. I move on to design my agenda for the day, play it out in the medium of my choice, accept that it may get blown up along the course of the designated path and time frame, and then move on to the end of the day.

Not understanding how it works or what is happening, not knowing what I don't know, is it like all of the creative energy utilized in the current day is brought back (recycled back) to create substance particles in preparation for tomorrow's play out? What today's sculpture was may have no bearing on what tomorrow's will be. If that is a fact, is life not about attachments rather just experiences for us to express through and then move on to next?

The following few paragraphs are an interjection from my 2019 timeframe as I was recognizing that I wrote the Sand Blasting scenario followed by my comments in 2008 or 2009. I now feel the answer to that last question could be Yes, No, and Maybe just depending on if our current polarity is swinging up or down, riding high or low, or pushing or pulling. What is the energetic cosmic pattern in the cycle of a day? How much of the truth of all that is taking place in the field of 'we don't know what we don't know' as we walk thinking, believing we know far more than we do?

When the sun comes up, the light brings with it something from the dark. The light comes in gradually, runs its full gamut of rays, and gradually returns to the dark allowing all 3D agendas to return to the dark creative substance of creation for re-creation. Is this what is happening? If so, this appears to be a natural occurrence operating on a very succinct rhythm within a dynamic smooth-running complex system that has the appearance of simplicity in its receptiveness. The whole process is so unobtrusive and non-invasive that we don't even recognize it as a real player or a piece of the truth here and now. Rather, we have the perception that we as the human being are the dominant Being here, and that our intellectually created 'doings' are pieces of absolute truth at some level. Following that concept, the mentally designed doing creations are used by us as measuring devices of our individual value.

Now returning to the Sand Blasting way of living life; every day, I 'do' something representing symbolically building (sculpting) my sculpture which is demolished at the end of the day from a place and by a force/source that I don't hold in full awareness within my consciousness. My subconsciousness may have more clarity. I don't know. However, I do know I am open enough and accepting enough of this 'Life Sand Blasting' way of living life in this now time of tremendously changing times, that I will flow with it to the best of my ability. Frequently, it feels like this is the most challenging, as well as unknown, way of living that I have ever experienced! Scenarios happen that feel real and that they are taking us somewhere of value, and then they just stop, blowup, or disappear without taking us anywhere, so starting over seems to be the answer!

A multiple days' journal from my written Book of Life might actually portray some of the challenges in this craziness of the Sand Blasting way of life. These were written in the time frame of my first knowing of the Sand Blasting.

Day 1—I awakened fairly early this morning. The sun was up enough for me to see that it was a clear day. I really didn't want to get up. My ego-mind immediately jumped in with its list of To Do's as the agenda for the day. In other words, it was offering up its blueprint of the sculpture for the day. I wasn't feeling any motivation for anything, let alone doing the items on the agenda. Continuing to lay in bed, I closed my eyes and attempted to go to a space where I couldn't hear the voice of my ego-mind rattling off its choices. Being somewhat successful, I listened to a different space and heard the birds singing-chirping their morning greetings to each other while they were being joined by the full-body cooing of the dove's morning routine. I heard the wind blowing some, as well as the sound of the cars on the road a short distance away. For a few moments, I slid into a space inside of me that is always so peaceful, safe, whole, and complete wherein it seems I can do anything I want or choose to do, or nothing at all! There were no loud-speaker directives for me here to hear. Oh my goodness, why would I even think about, let alone want to, get up and leave this space? After what was probably only a minute max in this space, but what seemed much longer, I dozed off.

I slept for only five or ten minutes, but it was enough time to rewire something which consequently redirected my subconscious mind's directives. Now when I awakened, my conscious mind was experiencing an entirely different beginning for the day. I stretched, got up, and stretched some more before going to the window and breathing in the beauty of the day! Inside of me, I really felt a chapter of my book unfolding, and simultaneously, I felt the urge to pick up pen and paper and write. I quickly dressed (I don't feel productive or maximized for expressing while in my pajamas), made my bed (an absolute first agenda item instilled in me from childhood), made me a cup of green tea (green tea is a good antioxidant, and tea time, according to my perceived assumption, is a fun time), and settled in with pen and paper ready for the creative writing to begin its flow of words for my transcription. This was my sculpture design for the day!

The creative chamber within me seemed like an underground spring today that I kept flowing with as a continual stream of book thoughts and words which I gathered and recorded until I literally could write no more! I felt so good, uplifted, fulfilled, productive, joyful, and thrilled with the progress of the book! Even in this inner excitement, I was experiencing deep awe of how the universe works. I was giving thanks for being alive on Earth in this now so I could explore, experience, and express so much more while living life! I went to sleep that night excited and looking forward to a new day tomorrow so I could continue with more of the same.

Day 2—I awakened around 3:30 AM and could not go back to sleep. I wasn't necessarily stressing anything; I was just wide awake. So, what now? I endeavored to reconnect with the (my) creative space. No connection, nothing flowing! I tried getting back in touch with all of the wonderful feelings of the night before when I went to bed. Nothing there for feeling, only words for remembering. Sometime in the course of a few hours, my sculpture had been blown up! It seemed that one more time, what was left was the composted substance/fertilizer for building something new, yet one more time! Why can't anything last? Why can't I actually get to a place where I don't have to feel like I am on a perpetual teeter-tatter, or like I am a virtual reality swinging pendulum? Consequently, there in the middle of the night, my own components for blowing up, i.e. doubt, lack of trust, feeling hopeless, etc. began as the pendulum swung to the opposite end of the experienced previous day.

After what was literally hours, I did finally go back to sleep to awaken to the day several hours later. I didn't linger in bed but got right up to get on with whatever was going to appear. I felt sluggish but not really tired. I had no mental chatter residue from the night's happenings other than a remembrance that it happened. Checking in, I heard nothing from the creation mode of ego-mind. With no compelled directives, I felt my two main options were: 1) go back to bed, or 2) do something. Number 1 seemed to be vying the hardest for my attention, while number 2 seemed to be the most prudent choice. While pondering my options and noticing how I was feeling, I reflected on the memory of yesterday as I pondered who I was then as that person seemed so absent now! Did we, do we (we being yesterday's me and today's me), even know each other? Sitting here with all of this, I feel somewhat disoriented and slightly crazy—insane!

So now back to the situation at hand, what is my choice for today's sculpture? I guess it will be one of simple doing. Therefore, after doing the given first agenda item of any day, making my bed instead of crawling back into it, I moved on with domestic household duties with a non-charged-for-creation energy present. I just moved because that was the thing to do, and these maintenance chores were necessary for my well-being. Life didn't have much spark, but I did experience being somewhat balanced as I did not go into a depression-type feeling or fall completely down the rabbit hole! At the end of the day, I went to bed feeling somewhat tired but mostly very restless with subliminal anxiety making its presence known.

I had no expectations of tomorrow for a good day or fear of a bad day. I just knew it would be another day. Still unable to go to sleep, I put on some relaxing music, and at some point, I did fall asleep. Nothing in this day I wanted to hold on to! I didn't consciously connect with the seemingly truth factor that sometimes between night dark and daylight, this day's sculpture will also blow up!

So, how is your life like a swing with the seemingly patterned ups and downs within the Sand Blasting way of life? What are we to do with this as we factor it into our journey as a piece that has some kind of value to us that is a part of "we don't know what we don't know" and even as we will continually learn more, there is some that we will never know? What are natural creation tools, and what are our individual blow-up tools? What is the value of polarity? What is polarity?

LIVE AND LEARN
PART 3

A NOTE IN THE DARK

In the lush blackness behind closed eyelids
I hear beautiful clear higher tones sounding,
I open my eyes and see your silence like snow falling onto
    cotton,
But in my memory, your tone lingers!

I hear you say, "I am one of many, but this toned sound is just
    for you,
Please, let me tell you my story. Singing for you is my Glory!
Listen for me in the wind as it blows through the trees.
Listen for my joyful note in a raindrop as hundreds fall upon
    your head.

Listen for me as the clear tone sounding from the melody of
    the bird's song.
Listen for me greeting you as one single note in the orchestra
    of the ocean wave
Listen for me in the laughter of the children playing at the
    playground.
Listen for me in the honking of the geese flying overhead.

Listen for me in the after-tone of the chiming of the church
    bells.
Listen for me in the babbling of the mountain brook flowing.

Listen for me in the choir of the tree frog's serene night songs.
You may even hear me in the dog barking, cat purring, horse
   neighing, or bee buzzing.

Listen for me in the crackling of lightning and clapping of
   thunder as Father Sky energizes Mother Earth.
Listen for me as the sun heats the Earth after the moon time.
If you listen closely enough, you can even hear me in the corn
   growing, the flower bud opening, the butterfly flying,
For you see, at conception, all living creatures received a
   signature note which collectively makes up all sounds in
   the Universe!

I am your Note
In the darkness of the void of Creation!
Together, we gave birth as ONE!
I am your Note from the dark.
I am you participating as the voice of all that gives sound,
Listen for me in all of creation, and you will experience life
   more fully!
I am always present.
I tone more clearly when you are listening!
                                        Author Norma Ervin 1/20/05

Experience the Dark and Black
1/2/04 Early AM

As the Earth moves away from the sun at night, all forms, trees,
buildings, vehicles, and more appear as black until all, or most, light is
gone, and then they are not seen. As I sat quietly with mother nature as
light diminished, I felt as one of the black forms of the just IS. Looking
down at my clothing of red sweats and a colored shirt, I had no colored
clothing or flesh-colored skin. I was one with the dark and was black, but
it was different than the known color of black. It wasn't black as one of
the colors, but black as a natural component of the dark. This dark is not
just the opposite of light.

Upon going to bed after switching off all lights and unplugging all other night lights, and with some window blinds up, but most down, I again experienced the dark. In this, I didn't have black of the dark. I had dark which was black. No form was seen even when moving my hand in front of my face. It was not visible, and yet I had a knowingness of its existence as well as a sense (knowingness) of all forms around me. In letting go mentally of all that, I was consciously aware of what was around me, but I could not see. I allowed myself to be as One with the presence of the dark, not a separate something from it. I realized that I would see the same nothing whether my eyes were open or shut. In playing with this for a while, I really lost the awareness of if they were even open or shut because all immediate environment was reflecting the same—visibly nothing. My mind had a stored (remembered) vision of what was present, and there really was something present, but I saw nothing.

So what is Black within the dark, or dark within black or dark and black as components of each other with no separation? In surrendering all and allowing a space where nothing could be seen and becoming one with it, the Peace and the Power of the connections for me at that moment in time were of great magnitude! Was this as near to the physical appearance, or lack thereof, as we can get to in Being at, in, as, and from One with the recognizable presence of the Unified Field that holds all that we are and yet has so much to it that we will never see and never know? The Unified Field around us and in us, is a major aspect of the Creator's design that is, was, and always will be. Is the reason we have eyelids is so that we can physically, at any moment, be in the dark and experience a flash in time of a closer reality of our presence as the Image of God that we were designed as from the very beginning of humankind?

It was amazing to me the next morning to see all the forms that were around me. I saw it so much differently than I had ever seen or perceived it before. I was like, "Wow, look at what all is here with all of its shapes and colors and even my body with its shapes and colors and movements." In this very spot, just ex numbers of hours earlier, the absolute truth was none of this was appearing as visible. Also, in the night dark black as the breeze came in my slightly opened window and gently touched my whole body that was not covered, I had such an awareness of the Presence. I then took in big breaths knowing that my breath and the air touching me was (is) the way the Presence physically feels to us. It touches us on the outside as we feel it, and it sustains us in our very alive existence as we breathe it in. Our breath is the essence of life as air being given to us. It is God's out-breath as it is our in-breathe. This is the movement—the aliveness within the deep dark black.

In the formation of duality, this space has been one set up to be feared. Be afraid of the dark. Buggy men get you in the dark. Always have a night light or something on so the kids won't be afraid of the dark. Thieves come in the dark. If we are not in absolute complete awareness of all form of energy that is in our immediate environment, we don't feel safe or secure. I can truthfully say my experience was one of the most secure and safe, peaceful, and loving than I could ever have had.

We have eyelids not just so we can cover our eyeballs during sleep. That is a physical function they serve, but by no means their only function. How often do we close our eyes when we want to disassociate with something? In our conscious or subconscious space, we are doing this to separate us from something we don't want to 'see' or to be a part of. Perhaps we have used it as a tool to pull back and regroup without knowing what we truly are doing. Could it be that we have the ability with the closing of the eyes to instantly be in the Void, Unified Field, Presence as/of God, and not only feel it but see into the dark and/or black of it? With this understanding, it truly is a regrouping tool to come back together, and not an escape tool, used to separate from.

Therefore, black is not just a color to see. It is the representation of all when there is nothing to see. What is winter? The going inside to the dark black or the black dark to the recognition of what that is. The leaves leave the branches of the trees, eliminating the beauty of part of their existence for a cycle in time, called a season, but the tree is not dead even though it visibly looks like it is. Deep in the ground, in the dark, as we would define the space, the tree is very much alive, just regrouping for another cycle of leaves!

What are some potentials for our use of the dark black or the black dark? Could they be, to be willing and not afraid to go into that dark black or black dark space-presence for recognition of what that is, after recognition, then go even deeper to the experience of what that is, then reap the gift, which is the knowingness of who you are? Within all of these, always remember, know, that we as a current mass conscious co-created collective over eons of time have put forth some false truths that have been presented as truths! One such miscreation could be, and in my opinion is, found in the various beliefs or definitions of dark and/ or black. These two words are very often associated with the power of the devil and evil as ultimately being the master and agenda of the path to hell. If Love is all there is, how does that fit? Everything is expressing Love or searching for Love! It is mankind, through free choice that has messed up the truth. God has not assigned an entity to treat us in a way not of Love. We have created some energetic systems on our own that have served as our design outside of the Intended Love. The gift of these to us is that we have been allowed, again through free choice, to create whatever we choose that is not appearing as Love with the purpose being for our journey to finding Ourselves and All That Is as the Image of God that was our creation model. We have many opportunities to see what Love isn't as we journey to find what it IS—Who I AM—Who You Are—Who We Are—What Oneness IS and how LOVE IS ALL! We were all conceived from the same Image of God and there is no place that the Love of God is not present! We are the ones that have gone away. God never changed or left. No Devil picked us up and brought us to evil. Turn these words around and they become Evil-LIVE and Devil-LIVED

What is, and where is, the dark of winter? What is the purpose of the cycle of seasons? How did those cycles come to us? How do we as a Tribe of Humanity honor the cycles or just take them for granted? How do Humanity and Divinity walk together to be as ONE not separate in our conscious awareness? What is our Human Physical participation in this connection?

WINTER

All seems finished and categorized in books on the shelf,
I've read all and experienced many looking for myself.
I feel completed yes, but finished NO,
So, where else does this life go?

Winter, yes winter, an answer may give
As Mother Earth's rhythm turns inward to live.
Winter shows the tree naked with its' color gone,
As it turns to its depths for renewal to move on.

Winter is so versatile and amazing,
And so very excellent for stargazing
The dark sky is present more, you know
As winter offers its compliment, the snow.

The stars in the darkness are us shining from above,
As the millions of diamonds in the snow beam us back to
        Love.
No other season offers such love-beauty blend,
So, from the very depths "Thanksgiving" I send!

As I am sealed into the inner world listening, being,
At first glance, it feels like structure is keeping me from seeing,
But wait, no hard structure is in place,
As the designing of a cocoon is forming with such grace.

It truly feels like me as Creator creating inside a worldwide but
        personal womb
The dynamics feel so very vital, yet volatile so what is
        happening in this room?
When I am birthed anew as spring's rhythm is up for review,
Who will I be, and how will I express myself as the new?

Who will I be outside the structure of the trunk of the tree,
Exploring more of my expanded self for me and others to see?

Will I be walking with all of my feet on the ground,
Or will I be using my wings to carry me around?

Either way, winter has supplied her gift
As the season has a special way to give all a lift!
I AM that I AM with all being LOVE
As Humanity and Divinity are ONE on Earth and Above!

Author Norma Ervin 1/19/05

LIVE AND LEARN
PART 4

Recall . . . I am still in the 18 years of learning and letting go of all that does not serve me anymore. What this really means is, I am not just cleaning house or remodeling. I am studying and/or becoming aware of New Life Plans for me to pick and choose from as I prepare to build New from New plans with New tools, all of which I have to be open to finding as all are pretty much unknown. What was is becoming not only obsolete, but instead, not even energetically available as a higher vibration reality. The bottom line of all of this for us in human form is this: We are traveling a journey that is just leading us to know more of who we really are! This is a good thing, a grand thing, even when the process is not always peaceful and joyful and we are not always comfortable! There are a lot of layers to be peeled away for us to experience our True-Truth Core! We must journey through our miscreations as a mass consciousness with divine guidance and genuine understanding before we can resolve and dissolve them. Saying Yes to Beyond gives us a guiding hand to doing our part in Becoming a New Earthling on a New Earth. Following is something more I want to share with you on this 18-year journey of learning and letting go.

December 29, 2003

Today, I felt led to write what came to me and through me.

The Journey is just you doing what you told yourself you would do. The cosmic two-by-four all the way to gentle nudges are you doing what you have to do to get yourself awake and moving and do what you said you would do when you are (were) in a space of awareness before entering your body and traveling here in form.

In utilizing intuitions, it is important to know what it is. Intuition is different degrees of consciousness carrying within it the capability of the Human Angel to hear the communication from their non-human dynamics. It is not someone or something else talking to us. It is our Higher Self. Higher only means more of us; therefore, it could be also appropriately called our 'More Informed' self or our Bigger self. Big and little do not denote duality because we are already an essential piece of All That Is, and we have never been anything less than the concepts within our Higher Self. Intuition is the uploading of information—upgrading previous system—the body system that can then hold and utilize more. The upload is going to a place where we have more of us available and is integrating it with the present amount of IS (Infinite Source) for utilization in each Now.

We have lived here on Earth with a veil (an invisible covering) around us. This we have seen as the distance between and density of the space between us and Heaven as we have defined it. We formulate and define Heaven as a place of reality where we can go and all the good stuff is. Sometimes, it appears many want to go to Heaven to get away from here and what we don't want. We have seen this Heaven as far away and unreachable for its total benefits until we die. Therefore, at a subconscious level, death, which is our most feared thing, actually becomes the doorway to the potential of our greatest reward.

If one carries the concept that, I am as this here (on Earth) in this now, but I will be more there (Heaven), this shows an awareness of the fact that this is not all that we are. There is more of our Truth somewhere else where our Higher, Bigger, or More Informed Self is wanting, needing to connect with us. Intuition is a line of communication. Maybe, or maybe not, it is a cyberspace connection, but more.

As the energy of the Earth and the grids have changed, it is now possible and appropriate for us to have easier availability to more of the Truth of who we are. Our perception of the space and denseness between us and heaven or hell has changed. Heaven is our perception of all the good; as suffering, pain, and struggle free, prosperous, loving, kind, all as a Being in a free life that we know inside of us is who we see we are. We have to already know this about ourselves or we could never have a sense of or definition of a Heaven. Hell is the same kind of creation. It is just a place where we have defined and felt all of the dark—perceived evil, feeling lost, searching for Love as we play unlike Love—side of ourselves. This is also a part of who we are that has been experienced over and over many times as we are on this journey of learning what Love isn't as we are searching for what Love is, and where we fit in all of this, All that IS!

In duality, we then have a Heaven—all good beyond what which we believe we have ever experienced, ruled by a man, Jesus, with the primary ingredient being Love. We know we are more than what we are experiencing as a member of the tribe of humanity. The other end of this scenario is Hell. This is made up of every kind of bad and evil the mind can possibly conjure up. This is the point of complete separation from Love and is the eternal punishment controlled by fear. In ending duality, we cannot separate Heaven and Hell. We cannot separate ourselves from the concept that eternal bliss or eternal punishment are our gifts of death. Being made in the likeness and Image of God, that Divine Essence did not, cannot, and will not create this model!

Heaven then is all of our potential for a good guided by Love being defined and looked forward to because we don't believe we have the capability to have it now. Heaven is our future projection to get us all that we want because the past has shown us we can't have it here and Now. Hell is all of our potential for bad and is the ultimate payoff of fear. Consequently, Hell defined and carried out, is creating a perceived true wall as a separation from the Truth of Creation—LOVE!

Love IS the Image and Likeness of God! The Essence as the Presence in and as the Void, which is the formless dynamic of all that is, all that has ever been, all the potential for all that will ever be, as well as all potential for that which will never be, is actively alive and moving, and never will be stagnant. There is nothing, no thought, no possibility, and more that this Essential Presence is not. This Essential cannot even be labeled with a word because it is beyond words and our understanding. The closest we can come to using is LOVE and we are still learning more of what that word really means beyond it just being an intimate emotion. Therefore, LOVE is All there is, ever has been, and ever will be or ever will not be. With this being the Truth, there can be no intentional lasting or real separation that is subjected, projected upon us by the God that designed us. The Universal Creator, Universal Spirit, God, or whatever is chosen as a title IS Love and never pulled away from us in any fashion or faction. Mankind is the one that walked away and created a false belief.

As we, the tribe of humanity, are going on the journey of self-discovery, we are just endeavoring to get more of who we really are into a much larger understanding. From here, we gain an expanding way of viewing ourselves as well as the ONE that we are all as a collective. Love is All there IS, but All there IS has not been realized or expressed! The entire 'trip of duality' was (is) a tool that was created so we could see what Love really is. Through and within the duality 3D journey, we can see how much more we really are capable of as Love gives us freedom of choice so nothing is off-limits. Our good or less than good (according to us as the judge) outcomes are our choice results on the journey of learning. They are not our Creator of All Creation punishing or rewarding us!

As life changes in our current life cycle and concept of family trees of generations, generation by generation, things change. The Essence as Love also expresses more of what it is by potentials being brought to the experience. In the invisible undefined, structureless, no-play-reality realm of purity, time does not exist; therefore, it just IS—flow and movement is ever-present. We have created time as a linear measurement tool so we can see the results of our choices. Therefore, I entertain the thought that I get to be a player more than one time. Just as the cosmic system of life is made up of cycles, isn't it possible that I am (you are) a human cycle of beginnings and endings, birth and death, within the system of creation of All that IS? My cycle has a definite divine purpose in, as, and to the whole (ONE). There is a constant movement within but never breaking away from—a separation from the pure Essence of Creation itself! It is impossible. What we (you) see is not all that is visible. To learn all I can and Be all that I was originally intended to Be, it feels there is no way I could complete that journey or purpose in one lifetime on Earth. I even have had flashing remembrances of other times of being here not as who I am now. The capabilities of the dynamics of life itself are so far beyond us that we will never know of, or understand much of it, but what an adventure to take a place in the Divine Human Being role.

December 30, 2003

The momentary flow of bliss—spaces where Love is all empowering, not just overpowering, and all is right with us and the world, as all of our potentials are being felt. We want to capture this and feel this way all of the time. It has come into us from a space outside of time as a piece of our potential for what is up for us to experience. It carries no concept of hanging around forever. It is ours in expansion, just is as all that is in the moment we receive it. We then pull it into time, which then puts it in the vibration of the environment. It feels we have it, then we don't as we rubber band it in and out. Perhaps, when we quit playing with rubber bands, we will be free! When we have the empowering Love, we can expand within the expansion. It is our grasping to hang on to the moment and hold it still so we can make it a permanent part of our life that takes it away from us. The nature of the Essence (essential) that comes to us in potential elements is movement, never stagnation. There is constant flow because at that level, there is no form. Consequently, we can Become the gift (realized potential), but we can't have the gift 'to have and hold from this day forward' taking it out of the flow.

The moment of bliss really came to me when I was outside of time also in a different realm—maybe that of my Higher Self. It didn't come inside time for a second to give of itself. I was drawn outside of time within a linear definition of time, be it a nanosecond, minute, hour, etc. to receive it. It never came and went; I did. It never changed spatial realities to reach me. I went outside a perceived spatial reality, duality, to receive it.

December 31, 2003

The silence vs silent place (place is structure)—Silence is without noise. I experienced moments (hours) around sunrise in the winter where there is complete silence in the physical world around me. No birds, no wind, nothing appearing to be moving except the air being felt as it touches my skin as the breath of God kissing or touching me. This truly is how close God is and what God is—Breath of Life! In these moments, there also was no noise in my head. My mind chatter was not just turned down; it was turned off!

While I sat observing in awe of this presence and how it felt, I could stay in it as long as I was in a feeling as one with it, but when I went into description without feeling, I heard, "You can't think" in here. It was as if there was a directive resonating out within the space stating, "No Thinking Inside!" Once I went into thinking, I found myself in a different space with an automatic internal monitor revealing to me what was happening and what I had done. There was no indicated judgment of right or wrong for the thinking or me. No one stood in judgment of me for doing something wrong and pulled me out of the good place as a punishment. Literally, within the silent space, I was in an experience of potential around me that was bliss. Thinking altered the bliss, and awareness was simultaneously present for the recognition of the alteration. No duality. When I went into thinking, perhaps I shifted from Being a Presence (One with) in the invisible energetic dynamic, to pulling away to give definition. This could take some empowerment out of the potential of the One Presence as it pertains to me when I then put it into a structure. This changes all sense of the whole as it then felt to me. Now in Truth and Pure Reality, the Presence was not really altered, but it was for me because my perception saw a different reality. The thinker is a perception changer! It needs structure to support the definition. The structure could be time—past and present to a projection to the future. The silent space has no structure (form) or time measurement.

When we are trying to go to the silent space, we must go through the silence. This is where we often stop thinking we are there. Silence quiet can be the absence of conscious choices of everyday noise—TV, radio, music off, kids or others out of the room, house or whatever, earplugs in so outdoor sounds are not so audible. With this done now, we deal with the mind chatter. At this point, the mind is going to whip up really good because as an energetic player in and of itself, it knows it too is going to be asked to disappear. Consequently, it turns up the amplifier and rapidly brings in as many players as it can. Now in the quiet going to silence (without mind chatter), one may find accelerated mind chatter. Much energy is expended to get above this. This can cause one to want to scream 'SHUT UP!'

The Thinker (Mind Master) hears this and 'thinks,' "Wow, okay, she/he just wants me to shut up, not disappear! I can do that, and at some point, the volume is turned down so low it is not consciously heard for a while, or if it is heard a little, it is so much better than it was that it is not tuned into with so much energy leading to possible anger and/or high frustration. Finally, there is silence. This is great! A possible down side here is that 30 minutes was allowed for the quiet time for rejuvenation and all of this took up to 25 minutes!

A 2019 comment. What is the value for us here, what have we learned? Could it be that the Thinker Master Mind is very empowered and is very used to being in charge? That position must be changed as the Yes to Beyond journey begins and progresses. In order to be successful as a Divine Human Being implementing the purpose of the New Earthling, there has to be a balance of our Divinity and our Humanity in order for the New to function as it was (is) designed by the Master Creator of Creation itself. The Thinker is trained in the noise, the visible, and structure. It is important, even necessary, that our Divine Human Being has a constant awareness of, and access to, the silence, the invisible, and the boundless in order to be a functioning balanced Earth character for the changes of this time.

LIVE AND LEARN
PART 5
LOVING MOTHER NATURE

I am an absolute lover of Mother Nature! Mother Nature is my very best friend! She is my regenerating strength. Through her, I am stabilized and revitalized. Whenever I am completely out-of-balance and stressed out, or when I am feeling really good and just want to be with the love that I am feeling inside, either scenario, I go to the energy of Mother Earth. From there, I feel I belong on Earth and am truly at home in Her Presence.

As every one's life journey takes them to the energy of the Earth in some way, each one experiences it either very consciously in some way, or utilizes it as a part of the environment of the planet that forms the structure that we play in, and just accepts it as that with no special connection.

From my path of feeling, there is much value to us in appreciating and being with Mother Nature from and in our heart. I am going to share with you a poem I have written that pertained to a place of nature that I have loved since the mid-1960s. That place is Big Thompson Canyon which is the Canyon that leads into Estes Park, CO which then goes on into Rocky Mountain National Park. I just loved being in that canyon, went there as often as I could, and spent as much time as I could just parked beside the water and felt a part of all that the hill sides had to offer, from trees to birds, rocky walls, and more! Over the years, there have been two major floods in that canyon which caused major damage. As I recall, the first one was in the later 1970s. At the time of this one, I lived with my family in a fairly close town of Eaton, CO. My husband at that time and I were leaders of the youth group at our church. A number of the churches in the region were gathering their youth together and were taking a larger group up the canyon to do projects that we were capable of doing with some professional guidance. We took a group from our church to be a part of this.

What our mission was, was to help tear down the main office part that led into some other rooms of a motel that had been completely flooded and destroyed beyond use. We literally started from the roof down. We were told that there was no way of knowing yet if there were any bodies in there or not and that it was necessary for us to be aware of that ahead of time. As we progressed with the project, at a point, there was a very strong awful smell that was very present as some structure had been removed. The group was called together as collectively, we prepared for what we may be facing. Fortunately, what we did find, was not a body. It was a deep freeze full of meat and other things that had thawed.

The destruction to the canyon that we saw coming and going from our project sight was horrific. There were pieces of cars and other things hanging in the trees. There were all kinds of pieces of dishes and other materials in the attic of the place we were breaking down. The river had changed its course. The highway was gone in many places. We had a special truck that took us to our destination on a make-shift bridge that was temporarily put across the river at that point. This was my experience with the first flood, and my heart was so hurting for my beloved canyon.

The second flood was in 2013. This one was not as destructive to the magnitude of that first one, but it did bring about a lot of change to the land and river of the canyon. After the road into Big Thompson was reopened, which was months later, I heard it was open and I felt a strong internal urge to go see my beloved Mother Earth after all of her repairing surgeries so-to-speak. As you can see, by the time in years that these two happened, there were many years in-between, and much had changed in my life too. I had actually traveled that canyon much more as I had actually fulfilled a long-time wish of mine and had lived in Estes Park for a short period of time. That canyon road was my route to and from home every time I left Estes Park. I also went to a favorite spot up the canyon later and spent hours writing. Having shared some background, here is a poem I wrote the day after I went into the canyon the first time after the road was partially open.

THE FLOODED CANYON

My Soul's calling brought me to you today.
Approaching your entrance, I felt unsettled in some way!
Driving on, I immediately felt your loving Canyon walls
  merge with me!
Loving you as I always have, I knew I was again where I
  wanted to be!

Slowly moving on, a flood of tears began washing my face,
So many changes had happened in our most sacred together
  space!
Some of the paved roads was familiar and miraculously
  repaired as it led me on,
With every glance out my window, and with the feeling of my
  every heartbeat, I knew and felt so much was gone!

Entire hillsides were drastically changed with the remnants of
  houses hanging in their wake!
The course of the river had left so many old routes and cut so
  many new ones, it felt it wasn't sure which paths to take!
Many physical earth angels were on duty everywhere all along
  the way as some functionality was returning through
  their skills and grace!
They could be identified by wearing bright green, yellow, or
  orange work outfits and hard hats as they appeared in
  various places.

In some places, what used to be the flowing river bed, is now
  a parking lot for the large equipment that is so much
  needed.

The divine human angels in bright colors and exercising their various skills, equipment, and grace were there as heeded!

What do you do when there is an entire rooftop in the water, when there is a horizontal bridge standing vertically, when there are boulders larger than the trucks blocking driveways, when houses are sliding off the hillsides, when crying hearts are needing help in cleaning what they have left—or not, to name a few?

My heart began to show my eyes' potentials for experiencing further insight!

Within what I first experienced as tragedy, can there be a glimpse of delight?

Can I release the concept of mass destruction,

To allow it to show up as divine reconstruction?

I merged with the Love of the canyon as I drove into her space,

What Love connected translation serves the highest good as to what has happened in this place?

While driving on—my heart-felt heavy feeling of tragedy softens as I begin to feel compassion from and as the greater part of my Being!

Now, riding on in compassion, my heart song resounded for me to create a new now feeling for what my eyes were seeing!

Having gone from experiencing tragedy hard to compassion soft, am I too now a divine human angel dancing for a new functionality as all landscapes change even though my uniform doesn't glow?

Turning around at the end of Big Thompson Canyon, I start back through to explore what more is up for me to know!

YES TO BEYOND

Together, in these words, between these lines, on these pages, we have shared and perhaps resonated with each other from within our own life journey. We have explored Unusual Experiences, A New Road, Life's Four Corner Stones—Relationships, Abundance, Health, Self-Esteem, going to the Edge, and jumping or not, and then stopping to contemplate on So What Now. All of these bring us to what's next—who AM I really and how big is my reality beyond just what I see as a human being in form and all around me in structure form of some kind? Early on in these Yes to Beyond pages, the information of how we, as humans, and the cosmos are in a cycle of change was further explained. This change is focused on a 36-year cycle of time from 1994-2030 with the first 18 years being of leaving—recognizing, resolving, and composting back to Love all that has been miscreated as being our truth. That first period of time was from 1994 to a globally known date of 12/21/12, December 21, 2012. All of this extended chapter in time is to purge an old mass consciousness and create a new mass consciousness. Every one of us as an individual is a major part of the change whether we know it or not. It is not a role that we play where we just sit down and put our intellectual mind to work and come up with a new (altered) plan for some fraction of what is already presenting as our reality.

The emphasis of the journey that we have already shared in these beginning pages are ones of exploring, experiencing, and expressing in the first 18-year period of this 36-year duration. Within our own individual journeys, as we review, replay, and relive emotions of all kinds, we come in touch with what we are finished with, what we are now resolving, or what we have already resolved, as we also get in-sights to more of our 'designed to be' magnificence. Through the free choice that we were given as a birth right, what does Yes to Beyond mean and what choice do we as an individual make as we play our part in the collective as ONE? There is no right or wrong choice as no one else really knows all the ins and outs of our internal story that we are reflecting as our outside self. The following are some more breadcrumbs (tidbits) from my own experience that I am choosing to share with you as we spend some time together on these pages.

It is amazing what comes through our thoughts to us from an intuitive place or source, or whatever one feels to call it. One morning in June of 2017 (it is now 2019), I was sitting on the edge of my bed focusing on starting the day as I was tuning in to what that looked like. I usually do, read, or listen to something or just be in trance-like quiet as I come into my day after the night. On this particular day, as I was feeling into what felt best for me in this transitioning moment, I was thinking to reread something I had previously read that had really resonated with me. At that moment, I heard, **"Read your own written words!"** This led me to a notebook that I picked out of many that I had written years back. I began exploring to see what I might like to share from this particular book, not knowing if anything would feel relevant in this now. I followed my guidance, and to my amazement, this is what I found. I knew immediately why I had been led here as I was in the 'now' of really getting this book out for sharing with those who might feel to read between the lines in their own story. Right now, we are in these expansive ever-changing times which are intuitively speaking to us that we as individuals are also a major part of the larger change.

What I am going to share now are words that I wrote in 2005 which in this now time is 14 years ago. The amazing part to me is that the words that I wrote or channeled then are very true statements for my continued process of this now in 2019. As I was rereading here and now, I just kept saying to myself, "Wow, really did I say that and hear that?" However, I knew I did as it was all in my handwriting as well as following the paths that my life had taken since then as well.

I am going to share with you just as I had written it then, and again, I give the reminder that all of our stories are different. Therefore, I am asking that you feel with or resonate with (or not at all) what is being told knowing it is in no way suggesting what your story or path should be. We are all changing in dynamic ways, and just know we are not alone when we feel so odd and different. Perhaps, we don't know what to do with that as we are dancing, or even dangling, in the world between the worlds. I am going to date my original time of writing these just as a point of timed steps in my process of letting go of a lot and learning much at that time, which I was not aware of in my then reality.

At the time of all of these dates in this chapter, I was participating in a class that met once or twice a month for six months, if my memory serves me correctly. It was a very deep class and our homework required us to dig into finding more of who we were in order to manifest a different or new life for ourselves, one that we could add to a new collective of others to create a new mass consciousness. Recalling these words were written in 2005, and we are in 2019, it is easy for me to see that we were being prepared, groomed, for what our mission is now in these extremely changing times. I know there is much more to explore, experience, and express from this now, but it is comforting to me to get a look at a window of time and have the insight to see how far we have come, and not just see it as magic where someone or something beyond us did it for us or to us. We were, and had to be fully involved!

February 14, 2005

This was our first class. I feel what I am going to share here was directly from the class, and not experiential insights perpetuated by our homework. Thus, points embodied from class number one:

1. Manifestation is a real, actually designed process. It is not just a randomly given selection.
2. All is ultimately Love manifesting as expression. Courage, contentment, abundance, joy, laughter, health, and many more are all some aspects of Love.

3. There are three places to manifest from which determine the difficulty of the process and the outcome. They are the Heart, the Head-mind (the intellectual brain-mind playing as the heart), the Solar Plexus. How they each can be identified:

Heart—the heart opens to freedom spaces and uses Love components right away. This is the least painful and least forced. This uses power, not force. Feel it in. Totally above fear!

Head-Mind—This is to intellectually strategize—make a plan, work the plan, apply force. May get there, but it is much harder; an old energy way, some power, but lots of force.

Solar Plexus—This is generated from a place of need with very little, if any power present, and not a lot of available energy for force either. The push is fear.

February 27, 2005

Much clarity came this morning. I see where the original book I was writing was to be written for the New Energy Library. (A 2019 comment on New Energy Library meaning that in 2005, it was not time for it yet. The right timing for 'New Energy Library might have meant sometime after 2012.) I have been wondering why I quit writing when I have so clearly heard, **"Your job is to write this book!"** That was happening very intensely until I went to put it on the computer, and nothing would take form. Then I would just quit being in the process. It was as though the energy for it was no longer present. I see now where I was writing the book in a time when the mass consciousness was not ready for it yet. It doesn't feel as though I won't write a book here, but this initial one was for the New Earth Library. This insight is very freeing to me. I now know this is not just one more thing I 'didn't finish'!

I have such a much more integrated feeling of old and new and am able much more of the time to see where I am, and how it is All One. I recognize how my body is still, so to speak, upgrading, and it (body) really feels challenged at times. With Divine guidance, I have been able to go to other dimensions much more readily and really be there. My body is needing to do accelerated changes to accommodate this exploring and experiencing. I am wondering from both old and new how I am going to be able to function in confined space and time serving at the clinic. (This was a contracted job that had come to me as an opportunity to serve with the skills I had). I know this was brought to me, so I am seeing it as the stream to the river or perhaps the river to the ocean. As I write this, the bioenergetics (clinic) feels like the stream to the river, and the teaching, the river to the ocean. I will allow all of the gift to unfold as it came from grace!

Another insight (thought) is that those of us in human form or any life form as humans, animals, plants, minerals, etc. are the filled test tubes in the experiment of changing the earth. The earth (planet) and all of its connected parts, galaxies, other planets, the Universe, etc. all make up the laboratory. At this exact moment, I see more clearly than I ever have before, how I am energetically creating in both worlds through the depths of some insights on how the workings of humanity, i.e., bodies, thoughts, feelings, situations, emotions, etc. actually work, and how I experience what is New and then express it too. I see these teachings as a vital part of the curriculum in the process of Oneness! This is seen more clearly to me, and I am honored in knowing that much more of me.

March 23, 2005

This writing was a result of an experience I had while traveling to and from the city to the funeral of a dear friend and client of mine when I had my bookkeeping service in Denver, CO and lived in Littleton, CO, a suburb of Denver. I had not lived in the city for a number of years, and I got totally lost and confused. In the extreme uncomfortableness of it all, I learned a lot about myself and the 'stumps to jump' that I was encountering in my life journey! I am leaving out a lot of the details here and just putting in the, to me, major insights that change furnishes.

Now the journey and the insights begin...

Going to the funeral brought me to, or past, all of these places for reflection and insights. I now know another kind of compassion—a deep one for myself. In experiencing many different aspects of my past pain and fear in Littleton, I witnessed myself here now. I saw these fears and pains now in a time and space to the extent I couldn't/didn't see them when they were actually happening. When turning onto a road with a well-known name to me, I literally had a very scattered vision of what roads, places, etc. were ahead of me. I knew that I knew them because I had lived there and this was my way home, but I had no conscious recall of where anything was or how to even get to where I had lived. Going to the funeral put me there. I went past the courthouse where my divorce had been finalized, past the quiet park where I used to walk to regain peace, and many streets I had explored as I expanded to 'live in the city.' Moving on, I went past the mortuary where mom was taken and then transferred to Durango. I don't even remember doing that process, but I know I did. I don't remember where the hospital was that I went to where she was when she died. I didn't even remember the address of the house where I had lived when I was married, but it showed up on my 'day's lost journey' path.

All in all, what I experienced was a Norma that had functioned so completely consumed in fear, pain, and a subtle discomfort that life just nudged me along as my soul was saying, "Let's just stay alive here somehow!" I witnessed hurting people, particularly my sons, and I was deeply hurt by others.

I gave such thanks that I survived, and I felt such tremendous compassion for my every action and thought as I witnessed those days from the Now! I was amazed at how much I had truly closed out. I know I operated as best I could. From this compassion for myself, and really seeing me then, I am experiencing a deeper knowingness and appreciation of Oneness. There really is no place that I am just me and not you. Every breath I breathe, all have breathed and exhaled their essence as well. All aspects of myself that shattered into multiples have been, or were, intermingled with all multiples or aspects of all others. I have a sense of that now that I didn't have in my most recent conscious memory. Therefore, my compassion is more truly real for All That Is!

The continually getting lost and crying out stating literally, "I am lost and cannot see in the dark" was so fact, and yet so much more! I had enough knowledge of the area to keep moving to something else vaguely familiar. Traffic too thick, my vision so factually unclear, and I was ungrounded enough that I couldn't change lanes in time to be where I needed to be to turn. My most extraordinary was when I ended circling in the parking lot of the Pepsi Center trying to get out and didn't even really know how I had even gotten there! I stopped and asked questions multiple times during the day. After dark, when I was so turned around that I had no sense of direction, I could not even encode what I was being told! This was not a dream state—I was experiencing this in and as my reality—totally lost inside of me and outside of me!

Insights: As I am Being more and more outside of mass consciousness and duality, I do exist differently. However, I am still consciously looking for 'familiar roadways.' I go in familiar directions to known roadways and am 'bumped off course' multiple times. In those situations, I don't have the focus or clarity on how to get back on the old path even though I know it has to be close.

It feels as though the Master of Creation is telling us that in working with us as co-creators (co-workers), there is a closing of old trenches so we couldn't run into them anymore. In this light, I did truly go through an experience of being in a place of remembered reality to me, giving the appearance to me of what I thought I knew to be the way just wasn't getting me anywhere but lost. After it got dark, I actually had to stop yet again and ask a guy where I was—I truly did not know! Four hours later, I got home in Fort, Collins, CO, and in exhaustion, but humble gratitude, I went right to bed to be in warmth, cozy safety, and peaceful quiet time! In this space, I went to the way that I know how to communicate with the Creator and ask for guidance on understanding what the whole day's experience was for me to embody. For the next four to six hours, I was in multiple scenarios of awareness experiencing great love, fears, and changes with some feeling more individual than others, as my body was doing twitches, and having big bursts of energy in various parts of my body. At various times, I would cry and then be at peace.

After probably two to three hours of actual sleep, I awakened into a new day feeling like a person I didn't know so well. Upon awakening,

I really resisted getting up. My main directive that was being heard was, **"Keep moving, define nothing, wrap around nothing!"** Stepping beyond resistance, I got up and walked into the day. It was uneventful as the integration of all from the day before continued. Who I AM had no definition. Who I AM not, based upon who I was (knew myself as), before whatever changed, also had no defined aspects.

It is all of those 'familiar' roads we take in duality that give us our energy. We know how to mix, match, and switch to join with others to create new (different) energy paths along the old lay lines that we have functioned in for millenniums. At this Now, I am experiencing a sense of/for expressing that I am no longer a copy of a copy with some items either added or deleted over time!

Moving on now to another avenue in the class previously mentioned, it appears that we had an assignment for between classes to commit to a 'Yes to Beyond' scenario where we were to experience ourselves as various aspects of our whole, and not just as one player. Seems like this was mainly to bring an awareness of our 'NO' aspects and our 'Leader' aspect.

In rereading my pages, it appears that we were to do this for an extended period of time. In this now, 2019, I don't remember all of the assignment particulars, but I do see value in how I recorded my journey with the assignment. I will not put in all of the days, but I will enter the date and which day of the journey it was.

The 'Yes to Beyond' journey begins...

April 2, 2005—Yes to Beyond—Day 1

My journal indicates that I did my 'yes' role play on that day to a friend of mine via email, and since that has been so long ago, I am not finding it, and this person has since passed away. The only note I left in my writing was me saying, "I don't really know why I so willingly did it as it was (is) my heart and guts and is not up for discussion. I really have nothing to hide!" I would really love to know what I revealed to her, but oh well, it just was! On with the journey of getting acquainted with my aspects as me.

April 3, 2005—Yes to Beyond—Day 2

Earlier today, through unplanned settings, I had the opportunity to visit with both of my sons in separate conversations. In the first conversation, that son represents so much to me in various ways. I felt the test of the old being presented to me. I felt its sting but didn't completely fall into the clutches of fear. I felt my true self standing stronger! Yeah! Also, from my heart, I felt a good connection with him. It was not just an attachment but a heartfelt connection. To me, there is a difference. Insight here: Lessening of family hypnosis.

Interestingly, my other son reached out to me today as well. I feel his dynamics so strongly sometimes. He made a statement around a trying situation in the life of his friend saying, "It just makes me want to be in the 5th grade again when school is out so there is nothing to worry about then you just go play ball and know everything is going to be okay!" Deep inside, I cry for his pain. 5th grade is when we divorced, and I left him with his father. Insight here: There is more family hypnosis here that I don't feel as free from, but it was up for my viewing today. I was also aware of deep feelings around mass conscious creations of sadness as he was also sharing sad stories around his friends. I do have these almost overwhelming feelings when I just say, "How can I live life with any quality when I feel these so intensely?" However, I do see these intense feelings are not all my creations, and I can see and experience the difference.

Here is what I embodied as my **Leader** self when I sat with God and the Divine Helper Beings today as a response to one of my **"NO" aspects** that seemed to keep shouting, "I can't have what I want!" This was a subtle scream that was going on deep inside of me that was adamantly expressing from the depth of my concerns over my financial status at that time. At some level, it was presented as a small child throwing a fit reacting by: 'no, this isn't how life is supposed to be,' and getting the attention of my Leader self. In dropping my concerns momentarily, quieting my mind chatter enough to listen after asking for Divine Help (bringing me in as Leader aspect), this is what I heard:

"Your picture of desires does not have to change. That which you have created out of Love is yours to keep. We are not here to take away from, dictate, control, and recreate your life. We are here to enhance what we are doing together and with your free choice permission. With this connection, there is a more vital part of your 'self-correct' mechanism as we see more clearly aspects that you do not see. We are not the dad and some who tore up the business school papers and said you can't be and do what you want, but must be and do who and what we (parents) want. This permission you gave us through free choice was not for that."

Wow, I feel like at least four of my **"NO" aspects** were loved today!

Right now, while writing this, I (the **Leader**) keep wanting to address—So what am I really going to do about my finances, now that the situation was brought up today?" Even now at this moment, I am not in a real 'truth' space worrying about it so I see that 'Out of Habit,' I need to have some saga playing in my life. Therefore, to the best of my ability, right now, I STOP the saga! This is a control action through consciously-actively participating. Another potential would be to step back and observe by allowing the saga to play out on its own with no audience, and it will leave the stage! (Here, the **Leader** was guided to some pretty good insights that could bring about a difference in the Worry Play of Habitual Saga!)

Again, in quiet space, I go to the Master Creator, and All help that is in All That Is and from my heart express, "I invite and expect you to be with me dynamically and clearly present each and every day! I am so ready for 'Beyond' showing up at this present stage! Thank you to all who are with me in this process. I truly love you!"

In 2019, I am adding this small footnote here. My 2005 response here seems to be quite long. All I can clearly state is that it came to me intuitively, and I took dictation so-to-speak. I feel this is a form of channeling, and if that is an unknown thing to you, or something your belief system does not embrace, I ask you to just read through it and get what you get out of it, or not.

What came to me: **The truth of creation doesn't answer or recognize the ego mind so it is useless to have the dialogue. That dialog is an ego-mind-brain directive exchange. Therefore, when you keep asking the questions, you are demanding the ego-mind-brain to give an answer. This catalyst no longer has a source to pull from so it cannot give an answer. Thus, you are left with no real answer and feel really frustrated and even afraid sometimes. The mind-brain will try to formulate something based on past points of reference, but these are not working for you anymore. Because you cannot get an answer, it doesn't mean there isn't an answer. This is the precise point for trust. Trust is the answer. We/you embodied together and are going beyond anything your ego-mind-brain has ever done or even recognized to exist. Therefore, allow us to go there! You are safe!** I as Leader (or maybe not) respond, "Worst case scenario, I come to the complete end of my rope; I sometimes feel to kill myself and start over!"

Intuitive response: Know that this is the pattern of old energy duality life.

It is like we are calling and leaving a message but there is no way to return the call. It is not a flaw in the system that can be fixed. The system no longer exists, and there is nothing we can do about it, so just stop calling. Old energy duality no longer provides the answers because in other realms or dimensions, it is not present. The Old Energy duality cell phone isn't aware of higher cyberspace. Just because Source can be everywhere doesn't mean everywhere can be with the Source. From this perspective, have I (we) just gone from limited to limitless? Also from this perspective, what is the answer to any question I might have? Could it truly be, "It is anything you want it to be and believe it can be as long as it does not negatively affect anyone or anything?"

A 2019 comment: Is that projected answer a component of free choice, one that we have chosen to help us out on our mission of finding our true selves that never disappeared? We are the ones that went away.

As for the cyberspace calls brought up for review here in 2005, I have since then become aware that the really deep desire questions are from a place, a space, that is above the frequency of the 3D linear reality, but we interpret them as being from that space; therefore, when we call out for an answer, we are calling into a system that is above where the problem/situation was created, and we are waiting for the intellectual mind-brain to give us an answer that still fits into the 3D linear duality reality that we are used to and where we are somewhat comfortable and familiar.

How many times have we had to come to the realization that as an individual, we have been on the journey of awakening to something higher in frequency than what we have always known. Much is appearing before us as well as for us. Within these new awakening experiences, there are many that just have no resonance with us at all. It is not that they are wrong or bad or that we are right; it is just an example that there is a higher frequency reality that is showing up, and not all are presently recognizing it. Could this be higher than the cyberspace that is yet to be normalized? The higher frequency of the Universal God is not going to give us a diluted answer to fit our old way of thinking and believing.

I feel these thoughts do correspond with what is being stated above, and hopefully, add a little more clarity. In addition, we are always known by the Universal Creator wherever we are, but we are known by the energetic essence of what we are resonating out as a Human Being, not what we are reflecting in manifested play-out reality like a Human Doing. What our life journey is about is finding us as a true Being and allowing that Being to direct the Doing. However, in the Old Energy way of living, as a collective mass consciousness, we have designed our normal way of living to be that of human doings, with no, or very little awareness of what part of our species named as a 'being' even factors in. In these intense changing times, we truly are not looking for flaws in the system that can be fixed. We are finding a way to move on to a much more loving and productive way of life that creates Unity of all as ONE and puts the All into a circle. This eliminates all of the defining boxes that have been used as separators for eons of time! **End of 2019 comment—back to 2005.**

I am feeling I am getting too wordy and intellectual now. Is my imagination being too chatty? (This was a question from the 2005 writing.)

Response, **"Let your mind go—Let it be out-of-control!"** At this moment, it was like I had 1000 thoughts come flooding in all at once. I just knew I could not make any kind of sense out of any of it. I felt there was no reason to even try! I realized (felt) my frequently experienced anxious moments when I couldn't 'get my ducks in a row' (couldn't control). I couldn't get my intellectual tidbits focused enough to chew on them in order to have any kind of control of anything!

Returning to my financial reality still calling for an answer: Do I have an option? Can I move back into the duality range and receive a duality answer to review?

Response I heard: **"Any old energy duality answer will have some component of fear. There is no way fear can be resolved in the old duality energy because the basis, basic creative component, of the duality creation is fear. There is no way it will have any resonance with resolving fear. This truly means annihilating itself. Therefore, it battles to not self-destruct.**

I now more clearly see that when I focus on my financial picture from a strictly 3D viewpoint with this Now (2005) strongly set within time, it is appearing that there is no way anything but fear can be reflected back to me. There is no way duality structure can factor in anything from outside the box to change the facts that are presented as a reality portraying as truth within the box. When none of the normal or rational that is beyond the box is happening within the box dimension structure, all it can reflect back to me is, "You're done. Be afraid because it is (you are) near the end." It has no resources to tell me anything else. It doesn't matter how much I cry, plead, or pray for a different response. In the old energy, as long as I haven't or won't take a job, and there is no money flowing in, all of which is in the guidelines of the structure within the box, I will never get a different response from strictly 3D duality. It has no place else from which to speak. It is limited. Duality, I helped create it utilizing false conceptions as truth, but it did not create me ultimately.

It has programmed me over time, but it did not create me originally. Therefore, when I fall into 3D mode and go to my finance picture, there is absolutely no way I can be fed anything but fear! When all else fails, and nothing else is presented to manipulate the picture, it can show me no other than that which it is.

A 2019 comment: At the time I took this class, I was really wanting to be a teacher in changing mass consciousness and was feeling into what my path would be as I wasn't really sure of myself enough yet to just jump out there. Also, as you can see, financially, my situation was not the best. This next comment that was heard on Day 2 of Yes to Beyond still gives me chills 14 years later! **End of 2019 comment.**

I heard this: **Rushing to teach this isn't what is going to be your salvation—knowing it is your salvation if you still feel you need one!**

April 4, 2005—Yes to Beyond—Day 3

Within the observations and awareness of this Going Beyond process, I consciously call in all who are with me in the process in this Now. I truly want to walk this outside of my ego-mind-brain (my intellect).

I feel I heard, "**Trust is the bridge out of the box of duality. Trust leads beyond definitions. We are not asking for change just inside duality, but for allowance and acceptance outside duality where definitions don't rule. The ego-mind isn't the shovel. There are new tools.**"

I feel this is still my mind working. Please help me here!

Clearly heard, "**Observe—You are (I AM) adjusting pieces to form a new picture. That is okay as you are searching for the key that will throw you out of the pictures to the artist's way once again. Be patient with the process. We work with none other than what is. What you are doing is what you're thinking is. There is no right or wrong here, only movement, expanding and changing what is presented. Keep melding and participating in creating something.**

Walk ahead (beyond) the doubt and limitations. Travel seeing it all as a good manifestation."

I am feeling very vulnerable and somewhat shaky physically. I do not want to just crawl under the covers, cover my head, and stay there.

Heard: **"It is still not about Bioenergetics for you. It is about staying out there for you. You simply can't retreat into the comfort zone of the inner self and have what you have created to pull through. There is so much ready for you, go claim it!"**

Here are the steps that I feel I have created as my cycle:

1. I have a dream
2. Then state I can't do what it takes to get it done by judging my belief systems
3. Cry because I don't have it
4. Give up
5. Dream again
6. Start the cycle over

Response: **"You can't receive when you are holding on to so much!"**

April 5, 2005—Yes to Beyond—Day 4

The night hours were very volatile—high winds and every aspect of every one of my lifetimes was presently whirling around. I was experiencing fear to panic toward guarding against death as the ultimate control. I experienced mass confusion not being able to grasp ahold of anything. I couldn't completely let go to be with the wind even though it did bring some comfort. However, I could find no point at which I could be in peace. I experienced myself with millions of others as a very fast spinning, tightly spun tornado like a vortex in the ocean. These (we) were all individual vortexes! It felt like all of mankind was here. It was all-consuming and scary! It seems all I wanted to do was just stop spinning, but I didn't know what would happen if it did. I then experienced for a short time a spinning vortex on top of this one but in the air. During all of this, I had some awareness that all of the aspects flying around were illusions, but I couldn't dismiss them!

I was feeling great fear for my son who was flying out today in a blizzard and fearing for him even getting to the airport safely. At one point, I even just let him die in a plane crash. He represents to me all aspects that I know I have consciously birthed and have made a conscious agreement to 'keep' (control) in the guise of family dynamics. Perhaps, or I might be making this up, but I did have deep feelings around his safety, and they went past just Now in time.

I had various dreams mixed in all of this that had some keys which I remembered. In one, some guy was saying how life was so right, and he was so free I could tell. I asked or commented on how did he get there, like above it all? His response was, "There was not above it all. There was nothing to be above. He experienced none of the illusions as reality, and just lived from that place!" In other dreams, I was building a big new home, and my family was participating. A motor home was in this dream, and my one son and his family were enjoying time together. The motor home was on snowy roads.

Upon awakening, I went into role-playing with my aspects (as the Leader). Talk about stepping out of reality into some other dimension or realm!

Light and Dark, White and Black. I am the one of trust. I am the one that has to get us through! I am the one, the only one that can do it! I saw that we were having some rocky times and many cards were slipping back and pulling me and others in. Even the whites were turning gray. With me whirling with them, no one was in charge! So I must recognize and execute my role as it is still so absolutely necessary that we successfully made the New Energy Crossover!

As the leader, the communication with my aspects was recorded as follows:

> "Okay all, listen up. I can clearly see and feel that we
> have just gone through what felt like a 'A battle for survival!'
> I feel the unsureness in each one of you as you are wondering
> how we are going to make it. All you want to do is just go

back, or better yet, just lay down and go to sleep and forget the whole thing, but rest won't come!"

Many heads are nodding yes as they felt I knew how they were feeling as I was feeling with them. This made me feel stronger as I knew we had connected at that moment.

I continued, "I know last night I was flailing with you, but I gained much insight so now I can stand here before you and be a Leader. I ask you right up front in this journey to trust me. I now know more of what that means. I am out of duality energy out of the time, but because it has been so recent in my playing, I go, could go, back in easily. As your Leader, I must not allow myself to go back and forth. I made a commitment to you as we agreed to yes—yes, to move beyond. I will lead you by moving with the YES forward, not dancing with yes, no, yes, no—not doing that two-step dance. I now more clearly see what trust is, and what I want from you as I represent it to myself as well."

Eyes are opening, heads are raising, and I know I have their attention! I can feel their anxiety and/or lethargic feelings eagerly wanting the truth or at least something new that resonates with them. This seems to be the pattern felt in all black, white, and also some gray. It doesn't appear that any blacks are moving to whites, same with the grays, but some whites are definitely in doubt, therefore, turning gray! I hear several voices speaking for most saying, "Please go on—you were saying…"

Me as Leader continuing, "At this time, would everyone please join hands? As best as you can, mix, intermingle, or alternate blacks with whites so we have more of a balance. Thank you, nicely done! We have now formed a connection as a group. This ends us as individuals on our own and will reinforce our Oneness as all on a single mission. Consequently, we will less and less feel that we are separate or out there by ourselves. This is very important. From now on, be very conscious of holding hands or touching each other through some contact. If someone drops out of contact for whatever reason, please someone else move in and bring them back into the ONE. Can we do that for each other?" Many yeses were heard and more heads were nodding yes.

"So how does this feel as we all hold hands?"

Multiple responses are expressed out loud for all to hear. "Great, not so scary! Mission is possible. More secure. Less threatening. Many with us. Black, white, and gray intermingled. It is not us and them, good and bad, or better and lesser. This is good. I have help. I am a part of the whole. We are together. I feel love flowing to me and out of me. I feel loved. I feel I AM Love!"

Leader—"Magnificent! As we explore trust more together, as your Leader, I am going to share some more concepts. I see it is not helpful or appropriate when I go back into duality as an energetic player. Therefore, from this Now forward, I stand strong at the Trust Post which is located outside of duality—outside the old—outside the energy structure we are leaving. The Trust Post is where we are standing right now, where we are safe, and where whatever is next will show up. Now I know, just by the nature of the beast so-to-speak, many of you will slip back into duality before you have any direct conscious knowingness that it even happened. This is not a moment for judgment of self or projected blaming onto anyone or anything else. It just is and is a part of our process, and it will, and must, happen until all is cleared. When you find yourself there, try to remember several things:

1. Quickly see if you are still holding hands as others may have come with you.
2. Know you are never alone so allow the presence of our newly made connection to reach you. This connection that we have formed right here and right now is a part of our Being-ness and is alive in and as a part of every cell of us individually and as a whole. It cannot be diminished or taken away. Take a moment right now and just let that flow in as a vital component of our truth." After a pause.
3. As your Leader, only until you are your own Leader, I will be with you here as well, but I promise to only be observing you, not playing in your story that you are there playing out to let go. Feel my presence and know we are still on track, and you are not just being swallowed back into the darkness of the whale's belly with no way out.

Perhaps, this is enough information shared for now. Please know that we are ONE Being and Doing together so you are never alone as we have all agreed to 'Yes to Beyond.' Consequently, you are never playing by yourself. Love is all there is, and we had a remembrance of that as we experienced our Oneness when we were feeling into holding hands. Rest now as all seems peaceful."

As I look out over all Now, all seems peaceful as some quiet conversations are going on, some are asleep but present, and many are sitting in quiet space and still holding hands. Before my eyes appear a form that has engulfed All. It appears as a big diamond ring with a bigger diamond in the center surrounded by a circle of smaller but connected diamonds. I know in my heart that this circle is us! As I looked closer, I saw this diamond configuration sitting as the top stone mounted to a golden ring! Looking straight on, the configuration seemed to be all there was, but viewing it from another perspective, it was formed in a circle of life. It was like the shining lighthouse for us to see who we are as we are connected in a circle of our 'Yes to Beyond' journey. In that frame of knowing, I also knew that the spinning vortexes of last night's experiences were communications of birth as they appeared in the water! I truly embodied the essence of this received wisdom as I instantly became a better Leader! At this point, I also recalled having seen the King and Queen of hearts cards in my last night's dreams as I felt the love of home, and knew the completely balanced love of male-female energies had flowed into us and through our circle!

2019 comment: Who AM I here really? It is projected that the Leader is coming from another realm outside of Old Energy duality, and yet, the comment about the experiences in last night's dreams was not defined as the Leader's dreams. Me as a human being was having the dream. Is this a tiny, but real, beginning example of a multidimensional situation that I had in 2005 as Old Energy was up for review for being removed, and we were walking through the gate to the new? Is this a clear call for us to Watch and be Amazed as we travel the huge journey of change and give a new voice to what we see and play out differently beyond our learned limitations in our 3D limited reality appearing as our real Truth? What is the definition of a Divine Human Being? **End of 2019 comment. Moving on with the Leader!**

ALARM SOUNDING! Someone has found themselves back in the duality quicksand, and is definitely not there voluntarily! I am now going to them as a **witness-observer** of the happening and how it is being experienced. I move to the involved One's side as I view the situation presenting and then just listen. This is what I see and hear; an email has been read which pushes buttons of emotions and projections of blame. I hear, "I am very scared here if this correspondence is not handled properly, and it has not been! What am I to do, etc.?"

Observing perception—the good guy just became a bad guy (projection), the situation is escalating rapidly, all adrenaline is flowing, fear rushes in full force, panic moves to anger, aspect feels betrayed, victimized perhaps or at least needing of other's authority! Further emails sent! Then **aspect** stops drama to feel, to check into self and surroundings. In this, aspect noticed she wasn't holding hands so she grabbed a hand in the circle. After doing this, she noticed the presence of the **Leader** as a **supporting energy, not a player** in the situation. We will reveal more when we communicate at the Trust Post.

What I saw from the observation point was, I did fully experience myself as the observer, but I also was so aware of a **Presence supporting the observer who was supporting the aspect.** This was my first experience of that. It was cool! I then saw, had an awareness of, some light pieces that were activating energetic potentials manifested that were just hanging out at the Trust Point. I got the clarity that they were not down in duality so they were not playing this or that, good or bad, feel good or bad. There were some whites floating to the picture as the situation was presented, but I didn't observe them as present until the aspect grabbed a hand to reconnect. I also clearly actually felt as the aspect as I clearly experienced the same intense feelings, but at the same time, I was present and experiencing as the observer. Again, I feel as a more qualified Leader!

What is this Trust Point where we regather? It feels like a very stable place outside of duality and on our road to 'Yes to Beyond. As an evolving Leader, I am so grateful for its energy. It seems to have no definitions for anything but is allowing of everything. It is such a wonderful place to gather as everyone feels respected as well as truly loved and honored. It is like 'who I AM, you are also' kind of feeling. It is not a diffusion point or a fix-it point—it is just so all-encompassing and completely safe! It seems to appear outside of duality in placement, but its presence is felt inside of duality as well. It isn't an active presence but neither is it passive. It is more just like an essence as essential as the air we breathe. Maybe it is somehow!

"Now that we are all gathered at the Trust Point Aspect, do you have anything you want to share?"

"Yes, I do. Yes, I sure do!" When I was so all consumed by the situation and emotion, I was feeling out of control in many ways, but at the same time, totally controlled by the dynamics playing out as the drama. Because my emotions were activated, I was 'off and running full force' as though this was my concrete reality! It felt awful! In the playing out of all of this, there was a fleeting pause where I remembered to grab a hand. There was one right there that was reaching to me and was still connected to others. I immediately felt a calmness to some degree come over me and through me. I very consciously recognized how differently I felt and even commented WOW to myself. I then checked in for more and quickly recognized the Leader had kept her promise and was present! This too registered as supportive as I shifted a little more out of this disturbing reality. I don't know if I am all cleared yet or if I will slip back, but I don't feel trapped in that reality spinning fruitlessly. I experienced a truth for a way out!

Thank you and you are honored so much for a job so well done! Your experience has also helped build me into a better Leader. This is how we work together!

These next few comments are ones that I actually wrote at the end of that day in 2005. It has been fun and beneficial writing today. How will this integrate with 'out there'? When will I experience them (my Leader aspect self and my other aspects) as balanced and not so separated? What is this new tool? I think I am beginning to feel it! May tomorrow bring more Oneness and insights!

2019 comment: As I reconnect with the flow of clarity that had come to me 14 years ago, I am truly amazed at all of the answers and directives I was given even that far back that are still very true answers or insights to the many questions that I have continued to ask over the years as though I had no clue of the answer or the way to walk the path of progress. Reconnecting with this information in this now is literally, for me, like looking back to the future in some way. I have (had) already been given the answers and the directions.

In this now with so much more going on than was even happening in 2005, we are reminded that the pace of change to move beyond so many of these horrifically destructive happenings that mankind as a mass consciousness is still playing, will be slow. Therefore, we are told to practice patience and endurance because the process for good is happening. It doesn't go at jet speed; it isn't a fairytale that can turn out beautiful by just waving a wand. To bring about the changes that are up for our mission now, it is a matter of changing mass consciousness which is the one we have created collectively over thousands of years. This mass consciousness is an energetically structured form because of all of the dynamics that humanity has programmed into it declaring it as our Truth over such a long period of time, it is not just a product of the knowledge of the intellectual mind that can be changed just by shifting around a few thoughts, processes, or things. A new mass consciousness is a whole new ball of energetic responders and human being generators that require changing the energy insert to something new that we are not familiar with at this time, this Now. That change happens to a large degree within the body of each and every human in form playing on Earth right now!

Therefore, going back to the information that the process is a slow train so-to-speak, and knowing that the humanoid is one of the main factors in the change, that means that we (I) have to play more intently in remembering (discovering) who we were originally when we had the knowingness that Love is the key. Love is the essence of all that is, and that we are (I AM) a vital part in restoring us to that pure Love beginning and Being that person. This is a huge process, and we have layers and layers of cleaning up and clearing out to do before we can even create a new foundation that is not just the old one shined up or painted over. In clearing up my layers and layers of miscreations that are not honoring Love, and knowing it is a slow process (which I am not always at peace with), why should I be surprised that I have been playing a role that is lesser than who I AM for these 14 years, and who knows how much longer?

As we continue to do our part in co-creating the re-creating of the New Earth to One of Living Love Consciously, may we be willing to hold hands at the level that we know ourselves to be until we are different and know ourselves to be more, and then more, and then more as evolution continues as we recognize that no label other than Love truly defines us! We are just playing our role and doing our purpose for the good of All That IS (Infinite Source) as we play in many productions on the Human Stage of Life!

Consequently, it seems I got the answers in 2005 and cleared up one or more layers and then moved on to the next layers seemingly forgetting many of my answers as I had not fully embodied them yet. Thus, in shoveling into another up-for-clearing layer, I must have started the cycle of clearing over and over again until I got (get) it and become the change that I want to see! I am feeling my next big request is "please help me be a faster learner as sometimes, I am very tired! At times, I feel I don't even want to move up from wherever I AM to be more of Who I AM. I just want to be on vacation enjoying all of the Love I know how to give, receive, and integrate inside and outside me while operating in complete freedom, beyond all limits! Anyone else interested? **End of 2019 comment.**

April 10, 2005—Yes to Beyond—Day 9

Today, Mother Nature is doing a wild dance with her Earth. There is a big 'Country Swing' going on. At one point, a beautiful magpie walked right up to my full-length glass doors and stopped. He/she just stayed there looking all around. I quietly and slowly walked from the inside to the door to within a foot of the bird. I had never seen how beautiful they really were. I had seen the black and white feathers but not the magnificent iridescent deep blue-greenish feathers. I told her how beautiful she was as she turned and then looked at me. I started talking to her about the storm. "Are you lost? Is it too hard for you to fly? Where is your nest? I know how the storms of life feel. You keep looking all around, what are you looking for?"

At this point, she turned directly facing me and the door and walked right up to the door. I wanted to let her in but did not open the door at that time. Face to face, I said to her, "This is not a storm to hurt you. You are safe; fly home." She turned and walked away from my view. I opened the door to see where she went and she was gone. I then saw I was not to save her from her dilemma but to tell her the truth. Also, my nest was not her nest so putting her in my world would have stressed her even more, but I felt our communication had merit for both of us.

As I am writing this, facing a window and watching the storm, a magpie was flying with difficulty in the wind and lands on a fence top within my view. Seemingly struggling to hang on, I hear what seems like frantic chirps of distress. Was this the same magpie I had seen and talked with previously? Is this mirroring to me the fight through the storm on the way to 'Yes to Beyond' or the panic of feeling lost in the storm for those still not ready to say yes? Does it really matter as storms are storms, players are players, hearts are hearts, and outcomes are outcomes? My path isn't your path unless you see it to be, and your path isn't my path unless I see it to be. Why is the precious magpie flailing in the storm appearing to have forgotten even where home is?

What is a fence? A fence is a place to land and perhaps sit for a while. It appears safe and solid enough to maintain some support. It can appear as a place of separation and/or boundary as it presents its facade. It can help us hold judgment or it can be just a spot to sit as we check out our potentials. Both sides of any fence are the same—potentials to be created, experienced, and expressed.

Random wonderings-wanderings. I think I was just asking these questions about me to me, but outside of me somehow. However, while sitting in the silence of these moments, I was hearing responses to my questions. Maybe this was a conversation involving some of my aspects that I didn't have to be a part of as their Leader. Whoever and whatever was involved, good information was delivered!

1. When can I really love you? **When I don't need to in order to be whole myself.**
2. When can I really share my heart with you from its deepest chambers? **When I require nothing back from you in return.**
3. When can I truly and freely receive what your heart is offering? **When I can fully dance with you in celebration of you and me as/in togetherness, and I can still, at any moment, fully dance the same celebration of life by myself and for myself needing no partner or audience.**
4. How do I know I am ready to venture through Love's gate? **When I am totally vulnerable—be out there with no illusionary armor of protection needed.**
5. How do I get 'out there' when I can't seem to get out of my multilayered inner to outer cave? **Accept your ascension and claim It! There is nothing more of value to see in the deep, dark, damp spaces. Go from deep to inter-dimensional, from the darkness of divinity to where that card blends with light, and go from damp to where water was to where water is fully present, abundant, and facilitating creation.**
6. How can I function here when I can't seem to focus on anything for any length of time? **Embrace it All!**

   I am lying here watching a pretty active spring storm, but I am warm, cozy, and fairly content. Is the storm from one dimension and me in another, and there is another observing me and so on? Can I look through the storm and see it for what it is? Is it neither good, bad, major, drastic, sensational, or malicious in intent? It just IS! It is Mother Nature doing what she does as she waters the Earth, her child, in the spring. The magpie and I have the opportunity to respond. It then plays into our reality however we choose while always remembering it is our choice!

The storm is! My ascension is! The Titanic sunk—my duality broke apart and all structure fell into the ocean. I have experienced hate, jealousy, unfulfillment, dreams, ego, knowledge, a little happiness, sadness, devastation, struggle, panic, truth, deception, disappointment, fear, trust, kept and broken promises, and expressed hopes and loves all the way from births to deaths that life had to offer me. All that remains is who I AM as a result of All of it with the key to all of the picture being the Love that remained a part of me as my heart experiences more. That was real, that was the truth, that was (is) my fulfilled promise to myself. There is the part now that wants to find more, to experience more of itself so I can express more of what God is through who I AM as I know myself!

Seems like the previous conversation between the aspects continues. In the reality of me as a whole with all aspects playing their parts to make up the whole, I know in some fashion these are conversations with me talking to me! Feels like the mix could be a part of the Divine Human Being interacting. Moving on . . .

How do I live now that the boat (ship) has sunk and all is in the water? I know I have asked this repeatedly.

Yes, you have wound around all kinds of scenarios today, just as you have so many times before, and you have come to the same place and the same questions. Guess what, the answer is also still the same! Allow, trust, and don't keep circling back for the answers. That won't work. Don't question why 'the Titanic' sunk and/or what could have been done differently, and how do you rebuild. You have lost nothing, and you aren't rebuilding anything! There is nothing to repair or redo! You can write all day and philosophize all day if it makes you feel better, but the answer to you Now will not change. Play all the games you need to, see your energy as you choose, but Now is Now, and it didn't change just because you went on a search of clarification for what is. You want the answer and have beautifully stated it several times. Perhaps, you are playing a numbers game! If it serves you, go ahead.

I am feeling reprimanded!

Feel as you feel. Sometimes, Love appears as tough Love and is experienced as tough Love feels. You are still using the shovel to dig into empty spaces. You are still digging in the shit (Stuff Hot in Time) to find the pony! The shit is an illusion as there never was a pony there! There never was and never will be a pot of gold at the end of the rainbow! This means nothing other than, "Stop digging for your salvation and all substantiating records why you can't find it and/ or have it! Plain and simple, you don't need a salvation—you have nothing to be saved from other than your own creation of a prison! You have defined it yourself when indicating a noose is around your neck, keys locking your heart, and shackles on your hands and feet with the ego-mind running the systems! We will never fully claim life from the heart space as it has been created by anyone to keep feeling, viewing into, to learn what Love isn't in order to define what it is. It isn't the opposite of anything! You want to be wrapped up enough in your own rick-rack that naked isn't real! Did you strike out or did you hit a home run? Are you still alive on the Earth or not? What is your perception as to whether the game was won or if your batting stats were good or bad as you reflect on your life?

I truly feel naked with nowhere to hide! I feel everything has been stripped away, and I have nothing to put on, and no words to express to reflect who I AM to you or to me! **The Water Embraces it All!**

Where is the Love in this? **Love isn't fluff! Don't you see in all of your 'dug-up' substantiating records, so-to-speak, you're portraying a 'this vs that' theme? However, be it as thought or matter—Source IS!**

I have just experienced the ultimate criticism! That part of me that comes closest to expressing my God aspect has been posted as 'suggested trash!' Do I trust what I hear? I am not going to lick perceived wounds here! I am just going to sit on the fence for a while. (Here, remember what the positive qualities of a fence could be. A fence is a place to land and perhaps sit for a while. It appears safe and solid enough to maintain some support. It can be just a place to sit as we check out our potentials. Both sides of any fence are the same—for potentials to be created, experienced, and expressed.) While I am sitting here, please quit yelling at me! I have put myself in time-out! Now saying to myself while I am sitting here, I am making the choice to trust this is valid and helpful.

Coming from a new voice and tone being heard inside of me:

> **My Dear, Dear One, you are never alone and you are loved, honored, and celebrated right now in this very Now moment and that will never stop! If you could just see all of the angels and support you have around you now, you would know I speak the truth. If you could just see all of the angels and support you have around you now including I, Tobias, you would know I speak the truth. Take a moment and feel into our presence. Yes, to answer your question, I, Adamas, am with you also and love you also. I, Adamas, say to you, "Oh beautiful one, everything you experienced and felt in your heart today and then expressed on paper is beautiful and of such service to All. I just want you to know that you gave me permission to enter as I did through some of your thoughts and feelings. That is what this demonstration of mine was about. You were giving permission to see where you are stuck, and it was clarity on your habit of looping; in going around and around the same thing over and over! Thank you for joining us on a new playing field where you don't have to swing at what comes your way, and then be marked by whether you hit or miss! Here, we don't keep score. There are no sides chosen, or competition displayed! WELCOME!**

A 2019 note: Pertaining to the last part of the above communication, a point to really contemplate could be, to be more conscious of what we are giving permission for as we ask for answers, and then be able to see the gifts and/or answers in what we are experiencing. A seemingly bad situation just might be a 'play out on stage' for us to recognize something inside of us that is not serving us in a higher way that we have given permission to be shown to us.

April 13, 2005—Yes to Beyond—Day 12

This has been the least dynamic day of the 'Yes to Beyond.' I feel I am moving from Spiritual and Ignorant which probably keeps me hypnotized. I can listen to these CDs and they speak to me somehow on being outside the box, outside of mass consciousness. I still don't know the value of today, but I hear to not need it to have to be one in the old box. I just ask that I stay awake and alert and not miss a clue for an opportunity or understanding (insights). **Allow and trust! Maybe just sit and experience yourself as Bridget Leigh and feel new.** (At some point several years back, I gave myself a new name, and it was Bridget Leigh Thomas.)

Well, it wasn't an uneventful day after all! Ultimately, it seemed all of my aspects have shown up for attention. It seemed Norma wasn't able to connect as Bridget. It was like everything was all tangled up and there was no integrated stability present. **Trust and Love Yourself!**

April 15, 2005—Yes to Beyond—Day 14

I am sitting here in my office with nothing to do. **Then sit and do nothing for at least 15 minutes!** I am still tangled! Good information I did find today. (I don't remember if I read this or intuitively heard it.

The good news about fear:

1. Fear is a naturally learned response that comes from the Love of ourselves and is designed to protect us from pain and danger. Fear kicks into gear whenever it recognizes a situation that is similar to what might have caused us pain or stress in the past. It alerts us when we are not sure of an outcome in a new situation.
2. Because initially, fear comes from Love of ourselves, we know that it does not indicate we are self-hating, wrong, or have low

self-esteem The feeling of fear comes from a natural response to protecting ourselves.

3. The presence of fear signals "Get ready, be alert, growth, and dreams are coming forward and based on past points of reference. You may need some protection!

Fear pulls me out of the moment and into a future perceived bad outcome.

April 16, 2005—Yes to Beyond—Day 15

As Leader today, I created a gathering inviting and allowing all aspects to come. The black (dark), white (light), and gray came. Here is how it went:

Standing there before them, I begin addressing them, "I realize and truly feel the turmoil all of us have been in these past few days. Please come, and welcome, all of you are invited to be here and know you belong here. We are in this agreement of 'Yes' together."

I view the room and see all darks are on one side and all lights are on the other side. Interesting view here. I am feeling darks to my right and lights to my left as I am energetically present with them. The left feels more present, and the right less present. However, as I am facing them and calling them forth, their position seemed to be reversed. The darks were to the left and the lights to the right; therefore, there really is nothing stated here and there that holds solid. Either way, they are still standing separated no matter from which perspective they are viewed. In looking at them more closely, I do see there is a line of whites and a line of blacks, but after the shift of movement where they seemed to have changed sides, what they actually did was form an X. In observing them further, I see stirring amongst them with quiet conversations and many nodding heads acknowledging the intensity of the turmoil of the last few days.

Leader—"We have felt very tangled up and seem to stay bewildered and separated from our truth and vision. Remember how in the beginning we were connected by holding hands?" Heads nod, yeses heard. "Let's do that now and form a circle." They hold hands from where they were so that meant that only in a few places were black and white, (light and dark) holding hands; consequently, we still have a very dominant light-dark configuration.

Many speak out, "This doesn't feel much better!" Others confirm.

"Ok, so drop hands, close your eyes, take four steps in any direction, turn around in a circle two times, and take four more steps, all the time keeping your eyes closed so you can't see and judge where you are going. Do this four times." In watching this, I see the first two times though there is still some felt recognition of where they are, but in the last two, they have to let go and are more allowing the unfamiliar!

"Now open your eyes and look around. We are now intermingled and cannot easily get tangled with our like-minded brothers and sisters in our familiar stories. Now take the hand of the two nearest you and reform our circle. How does that feel?"

Different, freer, lighter, strange, unfamiliar, scary, exciting were some of the responses called out.

"Do you like it?" Various answers—No, Yes, I'm not sure, and What is this about?

"Now I am going to turn on some music, and we are going to dance—dancing two times with two different aspects (partners). For the first dance, your partner will be the person to your right. For your second dance, you choose your partner. The first dance will be the Tango, not the tangle, and the second dance will be the Waltz. Then if you like this experience, we can do some line dancing where you can, each one just be in rhythm with the other without a partner. Now, here we go. Remember to Tango. Your partner is the one to your right, and for the Waltz, your partner is one of your choices."

Observing: This intermingling is creating much more integration as light-dark connections were showing up, and we did two-line dances! In continuing to observe the room now, there are many out-of-breath aspects sitting on the floor with some talking amongst themselves and others just being—some smiles on their faces. I see that there is no clear separation of black and white. I wait a minute to just let this 'now' be fully present and experienced before moving on.

"How was that?" Multiple answers, but all affirming good!

"Just sitting where you are, let's visit and share some. Having just experienced yourselves as an integrated participant with everyone here actively playing, the separation boundaries are somewhat diminished. Do you feel that and agree?" Many voiced yes, and more heads nodded.

From this 'Now" which is much more, of or as, our truth, feel into the energy of our intensely tangled days. In doing this, state an intention to just go to the core for the main driver(s) or instigator(s) perpetuating the tangled-up dynamics; and don't, absolutely don't, stop along the way to play in the muck! This isn't about playing with all of the story characters; it is about tapping into the motivation of the play writer or artist. What was the driving force? That is the core. Let's take some deep breaths together to facilitate us in by-passing the muck and bringing forth the core. In observing the setting, I see much good cooperation and participation happening.

"Now let us sit in this 'now' for a few moments of meaningful silence."

After a while, "Begin to really be fully embodied and present here and now! In answering about the core, what did you find?" Here, I did not know whether to have the whites answer as a group and the blacks as a group also, or just let the integrated group answer as it would. Viewing the group before having clearly decided, I was really surprised to see some grays in the mix. Had these just emerged? I had not seen them before. This truly is a sign of integration. This is good!

To the group as ONE, "So what did you find?" In unison, all spoke at once, and I heard two distinct responses—Fear and Confusion!

"Wow, how powerful was your energy in that response! I clearly hear us speaking as One saying fear and confusion, expressing to me, give us more clarity! This is fantastic, and we are making great strides with our Yes to Beyond commitment and/or agreement; therefore, let's keep going! In our tangled-up days, we seemed to be separately tangled and tying two big knots, one white (light) and the other black (dark), and yet I hear a common core! Now let's feel into fear a little more and see what was its driving force.' For this, lights (whites) together, look into your fear and blacks (darks) together, look into your fear and grays, be together for your response. We will take a few moments here."

"Okay, are we ready now?" Heads nod. "Okay, blacks (darks), what was your driving force?"

Dark's responding to Fear: "We were/are afraid of losing everything we had/have and absolutely didn't/don't know how we will continue to exist. There is a Fear of the ultimate death where all is taken away, and we go out in disgrace and complete failure of all aspects of our life. We scrambled and scrambled to the point of force and then panicked to find something to hold onto (old) or grab ahold of (new and/or old) just to assure our existence! We would grasp for the light but it seemed to clearly elude us, to be beyond our reach just enough that it couldn't help! We are somewhat unsure, and we see no outcomes, but we are feeling much more peaceful."

Thank you so much! We truly feel compassion for your process and so, clearly hear your words spoken from your heart! We are Love with you!

Whites responding to Fear: Yes, we were (are) also really, really afraid. We are so afraid all the wonderful potentials we want to manifest as a new life for experiencing, truly is never going to happen. We see and feel it so clearly. Sometimes, we really believe it is going to happen, and then we hear screams from the dark ones so loudly calling out that it shakes our whole being. We then feel we are slammed back to or way below square one. The light then goes out, and the dark appears as the presenting reality! We are so afraid we will never be able to birth (co-create) the life we truly desire! We really feel we are far more vulnerable to the dark than they are to us!"

"Thank you so much too! Again, we truly feel your heart as it is expressed, and there is such compassion for all of you and your process. We are Love with you also!"

"So, Grays, what is your response?"

"Confusion. We feel absolute confusion at times! Here we are seeing and feeling all characteristics of both our black and white (light and dark) aspects. We were you, and we are you changing! What we see is fear regardless of how it is playing out so we are standing in confusion somewhere in-between 'birth and death' desiring a different creation to experience and are confused as to how to get there. We seem to be in a space where everything has no potential or is being canceled out even though everything still seems quite possible. We seem to see the 'has beens' fading with dark fear, evading much beyond their own playing field, just trying to hold on. While the lights, on the other hand, are saying, "This too is a way to experience and express. Let's go and build new." The dark doesn't want to go, and the light doesn't want to stay so now, it feels like a war is going on! We feel like we are in the space/place where the fighting has stopped as there is no move active battling. We are the assimilation of the energy essences of the slain warriors from the battle. The battlefield is dark. All swords and torches have been deemed useless. All spirits are tired and wonder what just happened but know somehow life is different. We now are the Grays determined to stay alive on Earth, but are totally uncertain as to what that even looks like!"

2019 comment: Yet again, recognizing that these words were written as intuitively delivered through me in 2005, 14 years ago, and from the 'watch and be amazed directive' given earlier, I am amazed! I am amazed at how this word play, if you will, came to Earth through a human as a simple perhaps but a powerful metaphoric tool. It is for us to utilize in understanding these times of extremely tangled and potent energy changes in humanly scripted and designed playouts as the dark fights for its very survival. The dark is playing as a stick stirrer stirring up and magnifying everything in the current mass consciousness that needs to be seen even though it doesn't recognize what it is doing. All that it is doing needs to be seen. The light has, or is, consciously and actively moving beyond as a reality for truth. The space of time between when these words came in for me (14 years ago) until now is just proof to me that many people who are open to being the change that is up for the co-created New Version of life have been being trained and groomed for an unknown period in order for us to be more ready for our part now. I don't have a clear memory of how I embodied these at the time, but I certainly do breathe in the breath of their truth Now. It is really another one of those in 'going back to the future' for being given insights and awareness for answers as we are asking for clarity in walking as or preparing for being New Divine-Human Beings on a currently newly changing planet Earth. These changes are even for a bigger space than just our planet Earth.

At this present time in 2019, I am adding a reality clarification as a personal note to my real-life situation in that time of 2005. I was experiencing a financial challenge and was engaged with it as a battle with life itself. I had all kinds of light and dark battles going on inside of me as well as their reflection outside me. Consequently, this Yes to Beyond journey that was coming to me, through me, was very much clarifying my life to me by giving me new tools and different roles to play on my then battlefield. The amazing part to me was how I saw what the truth of my battle was for, and that was to show me how aspects of myself, light, dark, and gray (black, white, or gray) play out the scripts we have scripted as humans in a form involving all kinds of people as characters in our stage play as well as we accept all kinds of roles in another form of people's plays.

In the Yes to Beyond personal scenario, we are not fighting others with real war weapons and being killed or killing others through the energy of hate when it is just our personal-in-form circumstances. We are Divine Human Beings on Earth in the form to play out our own evolution through all kinds of human doing plays that restore us to the

Love that we are. Therefore, Yes to Beyond is a pathway that leads us to all that is there for us for our use and understanding of how to recognize all of the available gifts that are not of people-biological-visible form, but our invisible essence aspects that are beyond the form intellect. Yes to Beyond integrates, melds us with more understanding and use of the Divine part of our Divine Human Being.

Moving on now to Yes to Beyond…

April 17, 2005—Yes to Beyond—Day 16

Blacks and whites are merging, and all are going Gray in preparation of stepping into the energy of what feels like the final door—one month of money left and no current flow. No seen, felt, or known way of how life on Earth past that time frame can even possibly BE!

Blacks and whites have seen they are not separate. They no longer need to fight or resist each other. Black talking to white, "We are not afraid of dying without you. We felt we had to die because of you. We were on one hand pushing you and your dreams away while at the same time trying to hold on to you and keep you securely tied in our world. For a long time, thousands of years or even more, we were able to do that easily, and our system became a more and more perfected goal over time. Recently, however, things began to change. It seemed you became less and less content and began to try to look beyond us for answers. We had to jump in here and really gear up to protect you as we felt you were going to 'no man's land' and we couldn't take care of you there. Well, this battle has gone on for so long and seems to be getting too hard so we release you, and lay down to die—choice to make—if we must."

"We no longer fight for you and against you at the same time—for you, in protecting you from the unknown so we have to keep you in our folds, and fighting against you because you keep dreaming and wanting to go somewhere else which feels beyond us and that is our death! This is our surrender, not to you because we have no desire to be you but surrender in playing our known roles. We can no longer play. We no longer have the energy for it mostly because all of what used to work the way we could depend on, no longer works, and the perfection of our system seems to have stopped. For reasons that must be beyond us, if these are even answers, we are surrendering our lives as we created them because it seems there is nothing more we can do and we no longer have the energy to keep fighting. It feels like fear has, or least is, lessening its grip on us."

All is quiet as every aspect is just in awe and silence around the voice of the black that has just been heard. No judgment is expressed, no argument for or against is voiced or even felt. There just seems to be a melding of all energies with a subtle understanding which flows into all feeling as being One of Love.

From this space, another black (dark) voice is heard which again comes up as one voice for all black. "Something really is happening here, and I know you all feel it. We just surrendered to one part of our existence, but there is more; there is much, much more to see! We had to protect you, the whites (lights). We had to from the beginning of your journey's existence outside of the space of the perfection of All That Is. You didn't ask us to, but you allowed us to. You were so shattered after coming out of your kingdom of pure Love that your sense of being was so distorted and unknown and you appeared completely unable to function at all! This was your birth into expanding Love and expressing itself in a way to be seen and understood. This was such a big undertaking that you literally fell all to pieces. This totally unknown feeling had to be given a name so it was called Suffering and Pain and was interpreted as extremely bad because it was so unlikely, opposite of any experiences that had ever been expressed up to then in time."

Taking a breath and continuing, "As Creation is eternal and always in motion, the shattered energy wasn't dead or dying, only different, and still knowing there was a purpose for this and a way to continue. As there really is NO space even in what appears to be a place/space with nothing present, we were potentials just hanging out. We had not been a potential for any intention up to the point. Human creation was pretty virgin and not a lot had happened up to that point! We caught the knowingness of a purpose, continued, and rushed out to embrace as many pieces of you as we could. With each one, we embraced your completeness at that moment as it flowed into us and became our heart. We became one with you and could feel all of you. The extremely strong all-encompassing Love that you had just passed out of was still very present in you. The energy that was evolving as a result of the shattering appeared to be keeping you, and now us, severed from the Original, Divinely felt, powerful Love space. This mixture had to be separated so the Love could be out to find and know itself as the That it IS!"

Taking another deep breath, a short breath, and then continuing, "Our purpose then became one for you, one where we were to protect you, to take away when we could and minimize when we couldn't, your pain. You didn't ask us to do this at that point in time. You allowed us to do that, and you just trusted that this is what was to be as you had no handle to grasp and no awareness of the existence of such a thing! You didn't know we even existed, but the ultimate of Creation through the Master Creator did. Consequently, our relationship with you began at the beginning of time outside of what you knew as Home! We don't hate you. We love you and always have. We have loved you always as your love did become our heart and thus, our love too."

Again, there was complete silence, tears, and a very strongly felt energy shift in all as the true essence of what had just been heard had also been embodied into all present. It was hard to remember that the sword had even existed, that there had ever been perceived opposing sides as at the same time surrender felt like the pathway of a peaceful re-entry to the Now expanded Love that we all together had evolved.

I looked around the room and there were Now no completely black (dark) aspects. Fear's grip no longer had force or perceived power in them or from them. Its energy may still be felt from time to time but certainly not reinforced. Many whites are looking on in awe and feeling deeply stirred with compassion. They were feeling they also wanted to give voice so they just sat in the quiet pregnancy space allowing words to come.

Whites speak, "First off, thank you! Thank you from a place way deeper and purer from the bottom of my, our, heart! You, from the very beginning, continued creation by consciously taking us in, (embodying) us, when we were in a state of not being able to make a choice and really didn't even know what that was. We just knew we were where we had never been before and what we were experiencing felt like we would never BE again. However, we were still something as we were experiencing, but could pull in nothing to work with! Everything was out of control! Thank you for putting us back together enough to move on. I feel a resonance, and I am sure, a partial understanding of our beginnings, but I feel there is more as we have evolved to this Now. I feel us coming more completely integrated as One, and fear is definitely presenting differently, but there is still something dividing us; still some separation presenting!"

Pausing a moment to see and take in the facial expressions of both whites and blacks, White continues, "It has something to do with who we, the light Ones, are in the space outside the box of duality as well as our part regarding the dreams we have imagined for the manifestation of a different life experience here on Earth Now. We want to understand more, and we Love you Now too! Therefore, I feel we are still in process here as we continue to evolve. As One now, we are more on the same side—not opposing each other at the 3D level—as we see we never were opposites in the beginning. This perception wrote its own definition over time."

Whites sharing continues, "Now we are returning to the truth and know we were working together all along in some seemingly hidden way. Now how do we do that in a beneficial, visible way? You have surrendered and energetically are allowing death (finished, completion), tired, can't go on, feeling no source of energy, and there not being any path to walk with a purpose. At the 3D linear, or some realm that affects the 3D, you released us to our dreams indicating that you are no longer an opposing force. You lovingly say you are no longer playing. You are not fighting us; there is no anger that we no longer need you. You still don't see where we are going or how we are going to get there without your help and protection, but you fully realize you no longer have the resources to help us and don't have any new sources or tools immediately available. You appear to feel that you are done and are laying down to return to the ultimate potential pool where you were when you found and connected with us."

Pausing again to swallow and take a breath, "Somehow, this isn't resolved within us. We desire what we want! We are not willing to throw away our dreams as un-manifestable and just say, 'Oh well, maybe next time.' Rather in moving forward and continuing in form, we are not sure we have to, or want to, leave you out of our present creations, even though at times, we did dream big dreams and did many visualizations just so we could have opposite experiences to the dark to express when changing times were presenting as really difficult. We weren't and aren't in form existing to just be dreamers, but to sometimes agitate you, and/or do battle with you, for the purpose of helping some see what they want more clearly by seeing it for what it isn't, in the dark. We are not enemies. We have put down our swords and torches. The war is over after all of these millenniums, and there is no more energy for battle. There is no argument so there is no argument to win. We are One Love as you so beautifully told us of our beginnings, so how can we still be together? Please help us here because this seems so very important!"

Something came to the Light in/as an immediate flash creating not only a short pause but also a very interesting facial expression which was noticed by all. As the observer at this point, I was also curious as the Light one continued.

"Could it be as simple as it is Now our turn to embrace you? Could you allow this to happen when you have just left all you have known and feel you have no awareness of any options? Would you be open to death (ending) and birth (beginning) in the same process?"

A pause for reflection; I am feeling no answer, but I know this seed was planted and has a good possibility for germination and potential blooming or harvesting!

Continuing expressing after the big flash was received by the light. "It feels like there is another big portal or vortex close that we are to walk through, and it feels that we aren't just the questioning white lights or the momentarily checked out dark blacks, or even the consideration of including the neutralized gray one. Rather, it is All of Us must go through as ONE!"

A 2019 Comment: As I re-read this Dark Black and White Light episode, I had to stop and ponder it a bit. This is what I came up with for some possible clearer vision by putting some of the pieces together in this now. It is known from previous Yes to Beyond that I was literally under a financial stress at that time. In the conversations involving Leader, Observer, and Black, White, and Gray aspects with all of them expressing a part of a given reality at the moment, and as reflections of the past, all of them are aspects of me being with and as me, as I am finding more of who I AM and my truth! There are challenging times when we are in a situation of perceived lack, or whatever is up for us as an individual in a particular period, that is really a false reality that mankind has created through not knowing and being the Love that is not only intended for us but IS us! I feel here that I am saying Yes to Beyond with a part of that being to go beyond the lack part by having a piece of LUCK, meaning **L**iving **U**nderstanding **C**orrect **K**nowledge. Consequently, all of my aspects are joining together as a whole to aid me in my process, and I know more about who they are and how they work together. I am learning how to be a Leader, an Observer, and a Listener to myself when black, white, and/or gray aspects of me are playing in conflict or balanced, harmonious connections. This lets me live in peace inside and outside and not in conflict or drama, with feelings of failure and all feelings that come in that show me the blinds are pulled down on my Love. Consequently, all of my aspects are joining together as a whole to aid me in my Life Journey of resurrecting and restoring myself to my true SELF and living as my I AM Presence that I AM, not as the mass consciousness of the miscreations have programmed us to believe is our truth! **End of comment 2019.**

Now, back to the portal that light, dark, gray, Leader, Observer, and Listener are all going through together as One—ME. The energetic portal is right in front of me. The energy of a different creation is felt as ALL the ONE, step through, and the situation is stated including the Intention. It goes like this: "I want to continue living in form on Earth Now exploring, experiencing, and expressing in dignity made possible in part by flowing and receiving Grand, and I mean GRAND Abundance.

A solid one has to stand at this threshold in order for the transition to be of my choice—a complete expression of freedom on Earth flowed in and as the Truth and Love of all there IS and for ALL that IS. This is my visioned Life Creation of Giving and Receiving Love in, as, and with every Breath I Breath, Every Step I Walk, and every Beat my Heart Beats through the manifestation of my Intention Vision of Living Love Consciously!

I feel I can't do this with any aspect of me dormant, doubting, worrying, or in fear. I know I can't bribe, trick, or play games with any aspect but must allow and trust. This is my surrender: I surrender everything I hung on to in beliefs, control, perceived light to save me from the dark (perceived dark), games, false systems, everything known and unknown to me that is in-between me as a piece of God as my ultimate truth and me as not God presenting as my truth! With my aspects divided, this is hard, but as One, this is easier and life Just IS. I walk the freedom, and at this juncture of change, I know I have choices. I now have a greater awareness of my wholeness than I ever have had. I am becoming the Divine Human Being placing me on Earth with a primal spark and a divine energetic essence as I yearn for my place with my tribe of humanity, my visible partners, and my out-of-form, invisible essentials as my Divinity.

From this place, through Divine Grace and guided wisdom, I am capable of manifesting dreams that are my preferences (benevolent choices) as to how I desire to actually create the New Life that I desire to Live. From here, I can also choose to do this in perfect health, lack of suffering of any kind, and in freedom and knowing I need No Salvation as we came to learn through Love and not to ever be abandoned from Love. I know the freedom I will, and am, experiencing is and will be, from Who I AM as more of my God Self. Much more understanding and awareness I have already manifested, and for this, I am truly grateful!

At this moment, I feel neither stress, forcing or pleading with fear to let me out of its grip or any feeling to catapult me out of Now! I no longer feel, in this now, that I need to fight for what I want or be afraid I can't have it, and I no longer need to convince God or any known or unknown deities or entities that I want it, deserve it, or anything.

YES TO BEYOND
THERE IS NO LIMIT AS TO
HOW FAR ONE CAN GO!
KNOW YOU ARE FAR MORE
THAN YOU PERCEIVE YOU ARE!!

Moving forward in 'Yes to Beyond,' Where is there some nourishment? How about some soup?

THE SOUP

SOUP—Source **O**ffering **U**niversal **P**resence! What do we as humans call a soup and why do we even have such a thing? Possible answers might be a soup is a variety of ingredients mixed according to the desire for a particular taste with the reason being to receive satisfaction or nourishment. Could that explanation not also be expanded to being **S**ource **O**ffering **U**niversal **P**resence? Would that not be the ultimate nourishment with all of the ingredients for any kind of mixture always there just for the selection? Here within these two different perhaps, but somewhat similar concepts of 'soup,' we have a soup for the biological body and a soup for the soul. They meld with each other to nourish our humanity and our divinity as we become our New Earthling Divine-Human Being.

This morning in the early hours before the rising of the sun, I was awakened with what felt like a massive mixture churning inside of me. I am in those hours now writing these words as I am saying to myself, "I know within me and as me, there is an awareness or an answer to something on my life journey as a reason for, or as a result of, this churning within me." As I am now beginning to write to investigate my inner discomfort, I am experiencing it more as 'dry heaves' within me. It is like there is nothing more to come up and out, but the impulse to keep upchucking is still actively pursuing. (I am using metaphors here, but the deep feelings are real.) Therefore, this active upchucking impulse is creating the churning within me. There is no apparent nourishment or comfort in this internal storm, and I can't seem to get out of it! I can't outrun it; I can't find a place to hide; I can't convince myself that it isn't really happening, that it is just my imagination, and I seem to have no clue as to what to do about it! I want to just observe, but somehow, I am not able to disengage enough to just stand behind the short wall and watch. It seems the only thing I can do is be in it without an agenda or definition. Upon getting up to write, the first word that came to me was 'soup' so I am going to go to the soup for the soul and listen for what I can pick up for nourishment.

In this time of the new beginning with the old ways that used to work, not working or not even being present for trying any more (dry heaves), what would give my spirit comfort and nourishment this day? I hear, "**Dear one, remember, remember right now that you are not now, and never will be, and never can be alone!**" Is this the beginning of my soup for the day? Is this **S**ource **O**ffering **U**niversal **P**resence to me? I know I am not alone but it seems I need to look at that more closely at the beginning of this day. I know there are many Spirits—Angelic Helpers, within the Source that are with me, but I am not always so clear of my connections with my human spiritual family. As the new appears before me, and I embrace my choice for my new life, which is birthing within me and as me now, who are my spiritual co-creating partners? I am consciously aware of some as new friends are being made for various purposes for connections. I am being led to look beyond that which I think I know. I do know there is a New Menu somewhere for me.

How do we see that which we haven't been able to see because it is outside of the realm of the vision of our imagination and any points of reference with our experienced and perceived reality? I must find the way here as I am so finished with what was, all that has been finished, as it is not even available for further investigation, or manipulation for remodeling life.

In my gathering nourishing ingredients for my Soup for today, I am (was) drawn once again to the book 'Solutions for a Small Planet, Volume One, Gaia Speaks Through Pepper Lewis." These words further clarify for me the truth of never being alone. The points I am going to share from this book come from a section called 'Searching for Your Spiritual Family.' Following are quotes:

"A spiritual family is like a point in the universe, and it has a very specific frequency—one that is attuned with yours. And it has a beacon, and it has an understanding, and you are drawn to it magnetically. But it is not always that you are drawn simply to gather family members together."

"You are due to discover one another; you are due to retrieve from one another what is necessary. You are due to incorporate the frequency of being-ness that will make you whole. Because it is not the other person, it is not the family member who will make you whole. It is you, your beingness, your desire to become whole. However, there are those who fulfill your ability to understand yourself. Each of these beings who make up your family is as mirrors; when you look upon that mirror, you understand one more aspect of self. You understand one more aspect of Source."

"Some of these family members will stay in your life longer than others. Some will come and some will go. Some will share themselves with you for a moment and some for eternity. Some you will not recognize at all. And these are perhaps the greatest teachers. Again, I say to you that a spiritual family is an act of Oneness of Source. It is not numbered. It is not ordered. It is geometry. It is a progression. It is an understanding of where you find yourself. And what support you need, you will encounter, and what you do not need, you will not manifest. You are well-supported by Spirit in the form that Spirit supports you, and that perhaps you have integrated more than you can now imagine."

So, what now for This Day? I am going to make a Soup from a recipe in my Source Offering Universal Presence recipe book I am going to consciously select my ingredients from the recipes and menus offered. It feels my soup will be mostly of the broth nature today for my biological body nourishment with the main Soul ingredient being the expansion of my awareness of my 'aloneness' feelings being experienced on my new journey. I am not just remodeling my life in the new. I am building brand New. Therefore, I am 'viewing for construction' the basics of my New Foundation. I am nourished by experiencing more of my Oneness with and as the Source (the broth of Life). This experience gives me a bigger view of what it is to be whole which is essential in my new life foundation. Today, it is not for me to add a lot of other ingredients because the broth has to fully integrate its full flavor for it to be a perfect base for the rest.

My New Life is about me finding me, all of me, for me to live as the whole/holy aspect of the One that I AM. Through experiencing more of me and receiving more of an awareness of my connections with my spiritual family (visible and invisible), aka spiritual co-creators, I can more easily let people and experiences come and go as divine design progress and not need to form attachments and formulate new definitions. I do feel nurtured and more comfortable at this moment. I am not having the intense impulse to upchuck from the dry heaves! The old is not there, so there is nothing to come up for manipulation for remodeling. The new menu, blueprint, is not clearly seen yet, but the viewing is available, the door is open, and the tools for new construction (recipes for new soup) are all in place and ready to go! I can now more readily relax and allow my new journey to continue without resistance (to the best of my now ability) even though I am not totally comfortable. Can I more fully recognize that I AM a piece of the peace, and to be whole means who I am looking for is the whole of myself?

As is our practice in connecting, please read these words as you will, and then read between the lines as you are led to do. Pause to recognize if you find (found) any ingredients for, or in, your SOUP!

MAY YOU FIND YOUR NOURISHMENT

A 2019 comment: Again, it seems these are 'back to the future' words of the Soup. I actually wrote this in the fall of 2012, close to the ending (12/21/12) of the 18-year part of releasing the old and moving on to the new. On the morning of February 18, 2019, I awakened with the very same churning going on inside me, and in my quiet moment, I heard the words **The Soup** multiple times. I wrote this at a time I was doing blogs and because of having written it at one time, I knew what the words meant as I heard them. The Soup perfectly fits my emotional mixture of the current day going on seven years after the initial writing and feelings! Even though the wisdom of the words that were revealed once again brought the same information, and I was doing a similar churning inside, I was involved in a different layer inside of me than I was at the original writing. Much has been cleared since then leaving me without the familiar and floating in the unknown. Right now, in this current time of 2019, my energetic generator if you will is finally writing this book and getting a manuscript ready to present for publishing. As you may have noticed in various ways through these pages, there has been a mention of the intention for the book that was there, but the actuality of it happening was not flowing. I have been amazed at how the Soup for the Soul part of the Source Offering Universal Presence has been right beside me and actively present inside of me every moment in this now 'book manifesting divine right timing' process!

Once again, this is proof that this purging of the old and birthing of the new is happening in layers one at a time. It is not an intellectual mind creation that happens with complete understanding overnight in Cinderella fashion. Breathe into the dynamics of our new spiritual family and how we play somewhat differently with them than we did in our most recent reality. Let's keep moving forward on our Yes to Beyond journey even when sometimes, it feels like we are just crawling and can't seem to pull ourselves up to anything yet, or anymore!

YES TO BEYOND
A NEW VERSION OF LIFE

One day, when I was driving a short distance from one town to another and looking around at all of the farm fields with various crops in various stages of growth, I was also glancing at many of the various styles of farmhouses. I began to feel something very different not only inside of me but a huge difference in how I was recognizing the world around me. As I continued driving this familiar road, I began to consciously notice that nothing I was looking at had any meaning of purpose or any definition as to what it really was! It just was! I became fascinated by the feeling of this and how it, whatever was happening, was changing what and how my eyes were seeing or translating what was being seen. I really chose to consciously be with this new way of viewing my outside world as I continued my journey through the countryside on my way to the bigger town where I was headed with a specific purpose once I arrived there.

I saw electricity poles in the ground just as something presenting in a vertical position. I didn't consciously state the word vertical, but in sharing these experiences, I have to use some descriptive words. I saw all kinds of trees, and to me, they were just there in various shapes or heights with different leaves or needles, and they were various shades of green. They, like the poles, were just a part of what was present in that (this for me) now. Tractors were just sitting on the ground in multiple places where the dirt was appearing abundantly and not encumbered. Multiple kinds of buildings of all kinds of models—houses, barns, garages, etc. were there to be seen just because they were there, and I saw them. I saw fences as just shorter poles with wire between them placed in different places and around different things. At one moment in time, I looked up ahead of me and saw magnificent mountains with a few patches of snow still appearing at their highest tips. When my eyes encountered them, I did have a heart flutter of a resonance that I did consciously recognize, and in some way, I did embrace it as a piece of peace and love connection with Mother Earth (mother nature)!

When I went through the small town before getting to the bigger town, again, how I saw and felt the town inside and outside of me was different. Unlike in the country, things were not just randomly placed like they were in the countryside. Instead, they were all lined up or placed into some kind of predetermined designs, around buildings, along straight-line roads, etc. Reading the signs of the buildings was like I read the words, but they did not offer up within me any definitions as to what that meant, what it meant, or what went on in a particular building, place, or action directive. Towns as structures designed for bringing some things together were certainly a different feeling presentation than the more open spaces.

The last step in this different way of exploring my surroundings was when I arrived in the bigger town. This seemed to shatter my senses all at once somehow. This was just too much to take in for me to even sort it out to grasp what anything was. There was so much to see, and everything was moving at a fast pace doing something, going somewhere! The huge part here was traffic! There were all these different sizes and shapes of vehicles that were propelling around on wheels with someone inside at the steering wheel. They were going at different speeds, in all kinds of different directions, in somewhat of an orderly way. The only familiarity that I resonated with them was that they all had to have someone at the wheel who had some idea of where they were going and why. After all, here I was in one of those mobile vehicles, sitting at the wheel stirring my transportation model to take me to this bigger town to buy supplies for a printer and get more paper so I could continue creating this book. Consequently, in a small surreal way, I knew, or resonated in some way, with all these drivers. As to what their mission was and what all these other people were doing in their vehicles didn't even register for me to consider. It just was!

All these were a part of my viewing without any stories, definitions, replays, or mental judgments, to mention a few. I resonated with the green of the fields and the trees and lawns. I noticed other colors as they were on buildings of various sizes and shapes designed for multiple purposes. I noticed groups of color being presented as flowers and/or other landscape components. I did have a deeper felt feeling, heart flutter of some kind, any time I passed water, be it a small pond as a piece of a designed landscape, or a lake or a stream flowing to a river. These were all so magnetic to me that I just wanted to pull over, park, and stay awhile.

After arriving in/at the dashing and clashing of the bigger town which was my destination for the accomplishments of the various parts of my mission, I immediately realized that I was so ungrounded, so out-of-reality with the world in that current time. I recognized I needed to be experiencing myself present, visible, and feel myself back into a reality involving a realm of definitions and predetermined wheres and whats! In other words, perhaps, it was necessary for me to engage with my "should-to's without any yah-buts (yes, but) excuses." I came with a mission! Get it done! Do what it takes!

Following my own orders, I went to Best Buy first, as I needed ink cartridges. I had made the mental and emotional recognition that I needed to re-enter the reality so-to-speak, but just because I had the recognition of that certainly did not mean I had done it! I was consciously made aware of that fact very quickly. Immediately, upon entering the store, I was so overwhelmed and dizzily unbalanced that I felt I had to really get a grip somehow, from somewhere, or I was going to faint right then and there! I turned around and started to walk back outside, but I knew I really needed the cartridge.

Walking on a little further and just stopping and doing a wide overall scope of the store while consciously taking a deep breath helped calm me down and ground me some. As I found myself just being the observer in those few moments and not the customer, which was obviously me still in my other reality mode as I was when traveling here, I viewed a world that was very foreign to me! There was all this noise from every counter and every conversation on the sales floor, and among the large crowd of people that was in there. From the reality that I was in for those moments, I was aware that the noise was present, but it wasn't affecting me as somehow, I wasn't actually experiencing and hearing it.

Still as the observer, I did a wide visual scope of the whole store while standing close to the front door in order to have a good view of the space itself. I got a picture again from an 'other-world' view of what was in front of me. I saw hundreds of all kinds of technological devices all the way from every kind of present-day computer devises, I-Pads, I-This, and I-that much of which was way beyond my knowledge of operation. Smart devises for whatever that is all about, to printers, to all kinds of cellphone covers, and rows and rows of gadgets for choice of expression in this new technology age, that I was clueless as to what they even were! All of this was present and much more! There was a store salesperson standing within every 5 feet of space to engage you as an answering person or as one to encourage you to buy this or that. You certainly did not need to look for one for helping or guidance. In viewing all of this, I seemed to be internally asking, "Was this a good thing on the one hand, or a designed part of marketing and sales on the other hand?

However, another thing I observed was the crowds of people looking at all this stuff to find what they needed to define them and what they needed in the latest and greatest inventions so they could keep up with the fast pace of change and be on top of what is out there. I had the internal awareness that I was not just a foreigner in that store; I was (am) an alien of some kind to this version of life. What am I doing here? How and where do I belong? Somewhere, within that big scan of the store, I returned to really being present there as I was now somewhat calmed down and put back together. Maybe what brought me back was while in the other realm, or state-of-mind, or whatever one wants to call it, as I ask the question, "What am I doing here?" an answer came. The answer could have been as simple as, "In and all of these store dynamics, you came here as a writer to buy an ink cartridge!"

Shaking my head somewhat, glancing around and knowing I was clueless as to where to look for the cartridge, and certainly didn't want to do a search through the store to find it, I found a salesperson who was standing waiting for their next opportunity just a few feet in front me. Connecting with him brought me to the location of my sought-after item. I picked up my cartridge and headed for the cashier glad to be getting out of there. At the cash register, the cashier kept asking me for my phone number and email so I could be known in their system. This did not set well with me today because I am (was) experiencing myself as an individual of some kind in a new reality of some kind. I don't have that new puzzle all put together yet. All I wanted from that store was just to buy an ink cartridge. Consequently, I responded by not giving him any further information and just saying that all I wanted to do was buy the cartridge.

In furthering my day's mission, I went to several other stores, and to a lesser degree, experienced the same 'out-of-present reality.' I went to the library to continue writing this book. As I was copying words into the manuscript from pages that I had already previously written on paper, the words began to feel of no value. All my energy for any of it just dumped—stopped! Feeling depleted and beginning to go into somewhat of a panic, I left the library and went to a favorite lake of mine where I have (had) been able to align with nature and water, and I have been very 'loved in' there. Upon getting there, I hardly had the energy to even get out of the car but did because it was very hot in the car, and I didn't want to keep the car running just for the air conditioner. I got out to do my usual walk around the lake and be with the seagulls, pelicans, and other nature life as well as watching all the people there enjoying themselves in a multitude of ways in being with the water.

In watching the people, I resonated with nothing and no one. I just saw various kinds of people moving about in various scenarios be it swimming, boating, picnicking, or whatever. In looking out over the lake as I usually do I experience it as my own water pool of All that IS where I see All melding and All is unfolding beautifully giving me the feeling, and/or knowing, that All is Well, I saw and felt nothing. I just had the recognition that it was a big body of water.

At this point, I had sunk into the depths of despair. I literally almost didn't even have the strength or energy to walk back to my car even though I had not ventured very far away. Still being too hot to sit in the car, I sat on a bench beside the lake being thankful that I had my sunglasses on as I began to have tears coming. It may have been appropriate for me to sit in the hot car as it felt I was sinking into the pits of hell on earth! I continued asking all kinds of questions to God as I know and experience that Divine Essence. I also continued going deeper and deeper into an abyss that it felt I would never find the bottom and when, or if, I did, I would never get out! In the perceived muck of all these, there was an exposed glimpse of the earlier part of my day when I had played out a short role of seeing and being in a whole different reality and experiencing it in a whole different way than my currently familiar reality. However, sometimes, I had the momentary conscious flashes of awareness of me experiencing the reality as a mixture of the familiar and the unfamiliar, which left a feeling of confusion and discomfort. I wondered, wanted to know, what the truth or connection with that different reality had to do with what was happening to me now. Nothing in my whole day after arriving in the bigger town had looked the same to me or had been experienced the same by me. I wanted answers because I wanted to climb up my emotional ladder and not continue going down it deeper to the point of no return.

WOW! There in the question was my answer delivered to me from the Presence that I was calling upon. I have been in my own way, through my own way of understanding my life and asking for my guidance from the core of my own gained wisdom. I have been consciously living or navigating toward a 'Yes to Beyond' life for several years. Millions and maybe billions of us are doing this with our journey being individually designed as ours with no two alike. Each individual player also has their own perception of what 'Beyond" means to them and how big or expansive the 'Yes' is within their perception for a new reality. All intentional choices are acceptable as long as there is no real harm intended to oneself or others or any of the creations of plants, animals, and Mother Earth herself.

Returning to my own human stage of reality sitting on this bench beside the lake, I am experiencing deep despair metaphorically flailing around (because I can't swim) in a huge pool of nothing that I can feel or resonate with inside me or really even identify with outside of me. I am in an emotional state of feeling defeated, depleted, hopeless, helpless, with no way out so I just need to keep digging until there is no more ground for digging and then all that is left is to just quit and die! However, just as deep as the water, equally as high as the sky, is my knowingness that I want to Live—to Stay Alive—to Live Beyond—so where am I and why is everything presenting as it is today? I was experiencing all these as I just wanted to stop screaming inside and just cry! It was as though I was simultaneously experiencing my ultimate Yes, Stay Alive, and my ultimate No to Die, all in one expression of what I was experiencing! Because I ask, and because I am known by God and perhaps other invisible players, and because I was not in victim self-pity mode, I was asking into a Yes to Beyond realm where there would be clarity that I could receive that would be beyond what we have already experienced as the only reality orchestrated by our old mass consciousness,

Here is what was revealed to me pertaining to the whole day:

Stepping out of one reality was for the bigger understanding of moving beyond the world where most, or much, of it is set up in a system of definitions as to why for everything and every action, labels of existence for every visible structure, identities-personalities-ego for every human's doing life agenda, and so goes the rules and regulations presenting our perceived truth as human existence! All these need to be understood and interpreted in some universal way that fits into, and unspoken perhaps, but an expected set of rules and regulating directives for all to follow. All of this and much more is what we have created as life here on planet Earth, and how we do this is called 'living' that life. We designed these over thousands of years of time or more.

I clearly saw and got it that going to Yes to Beyond meant it would be beneficial for me to see how it felt to be in a reality that is 'naked' from all or any of those old judgments, definitions, and set in stone realities. From here, I could truly see more clearly who I AM as I have already within my free choice Intention stepped beyond much of this and I desire to go even further! Actually, seeing how differently so much was to my vision even though I was seeing with the same set of human eyes in my head, it was like a lens inside of my outside eyes had somehow shifted or come in new in some way. I was clearly informed that I did consciously explore and experience playing within reality from a different realm thoroughly enough that I got a good taste of it. This experience facilitated me in gaining an insight into what stepping out of what was (the old), and moving into what the beyond is forming to be (the New) is going to change reality as it leaves much of what 'was' finished out of the picture.

Even though my short experience was more with things, and not people and their thoughts, I still got a big taste of more about what pure means in any kind of existence when it is not already defined and programmed by the masses. I also know how different I felt inside as I was viewing out from that other realm. It felt really good to just see what was there presenting, just being present in the space of what was presented in my immediate space without me giving or feeling any story about anything. I was just driving along as a spirit from somewhere, wearing a human body as my primary vehicle, which did have identity clothes on, driving a car as my secondary vehicle, seeing all kinds of things that are present for being seen with that changing every few blocks or a mile that I moved on. In recognizing this as I was driving and seeing myself as a spirit in form, I had a chuckling moment when I wondered when, where, and how I had learned to drive!

What was my stress really revealing to me other than the seeming reality of all the negative aspects that I fell into battling with? I was shown (reminded) that I had already made much progress on my Yes to Beyond path, that I had learned much and had become different already as a result of my intention and the allowance and acceptance of my guidance coming as it was asked for. Many times on this Beyond path, I don't always feel to ask for guidance as it just feels like there is no need to ask, as we, the visible and the invisible, are already playing co-creation. These changes we are facing are being carried out in a field of unification with many participating partners, visible and invisible, appropriately doing their piece of the dynamics in the One, as the One, on the One stage of life which is made up of many mini-stages. However, when I am in a less confident place, feeling less powerful, and have lost vision of who I remember myself to be and what my part of creation really is beyond what was, I fall into a deep, dark, muddy hole of misconceptions. In this hole, my false witnesses are presenting to me a current in-the-moment reality flooding me with false definitions that I need to recognize for me to find my truth. I get as much of the false as I need until I blank out everything that is not in alignment with the energy the false wants me to feel as true!

As I fall into that trap, I plummet into the grip of it to the point that I then define myself and my life in that way too. In some way, I seem to void within me every good, positive, or just truth that defines me all the way from what is known to me and what is unknown in me and about me. When I am sane, I am totally aware that I am far more magnificent and valuable than I even have the conscious ability to catch more than a glimpse of that reality! When I am battling insanity, I can readily turn all situations into some lesser story until I am a worrier battling every demon I have ever known and using every weapon I have available to me in my old artillery closet. From this state of mind, I march out to face death through defending myself until I feel there is nothing to defend because I have no answers of anything different leaving the ultimate answer as "What's the Use, DIE." That becomes my surrender mantra! This may be a little exaggerated, but we all know what the black-dark battle feels like deep inside of us when it overtakes us.

Clarity continued to come while I was sitting on the bench beside the lake. However, it did not come in with all these words. It was just like a flash of lightning that stuck me and my intuitive mind did the translation and presented it to me quickly as a big gulp of understanding. The bottom line, the message was telling me that I was misinterpreting what was being offered to me, as it was a positive piece in the path on the road to Beyond. Obviously to me, this certainly needed more explanation because, in my current emotional state of insanity and false witnesses appearing, I couldn't grasp a positive perspective here! Recall one of the statements I had made when I was feeling desperate for an answer or guidance of some kind. That statement was, "I wanted answers as I want to climb up my emotional ladder and not continue going down it to the point of no return!"

Well, my clarification delivered here was:

> **"The main intention of this particularly intense internal battle that seemed to keep pulling, and/or pushing, me further and further down the hole (whole) of despair was accomplishing exactly what it was designed to do! I was aiding the perceived battle/fire by continually putting old logs on the fire (by defining all my feelings with old definitions) on the already out-of-control fire/ battle. These false-acting-real fears were coming in from all directions, and the intensity of the battle and the fire escalated until I was ready to, but didn't really want to, give up! Allowing emotional pains of discord to be felt and go to the very depth of their domain is a tool to melt fear down to where it loses its old identity and hold onto us to the point of no return! We can't heal and/or release that which we don't even see or feel for the true reality it is playing out in our life. If not healed or released in some way, it just keeps visiting us as a False Energy Appearing Real (FEAR) reality. This keeps us from experiencing our True Self and our Truth as it was intended from the original immaculate concept of our human creation."**

For me, I was shown that I was endeavoring to dismiss, dilute, or fix my perceived negative and discomfort to devastating emotionally reactive feelings by processing them back through my old energy system of understanding which was an imprinted and programmed way of being that was governed by false reality concepts. In fact, exactly what was supposed to be happening was happening. Therefore, in having set intention for the Yes to Beyond journey, I had (have) consciously set out to remove these false realities and to release all negative reactions I had (have) given to them to surrender myself to the new version of life. That new version is One that is of freedom that is beyond the influence set forth by the old.

As all this freeing energy just flashed into me without all these words, I did have a new feeling flood me that again put out the fire and stopped the internal and external battle. I didn't feel like screaming anymore, but I did experience an even stronger feeling to cry. I got up from the bench and felt that maybe if I walked a little more, I would gain more of a sense of each that would disperse this welling up of tears. Again, thankful for the sunglasses to hide my eyes, I checked my pockets for available Kleenex just in case and returned to the walking path around the lake. I didn't get very far before a flood of tears came so fast and fiercely that I had to look for the closest bench I could see as a place for me to sit as my vision was becoming too blurry for me to continue walking. I just let the flood come as it would without giving myself any definitions about any of it; without switching to any old replays of any stories of the past, or fears of outcomes in the future; without pulling out any previously used tools to stop it! I just allowed the flood to run its course, moving to slowing down on to a gentle rain, and then stopping.

I sat for a few moments just being in a quiet-to-silent space within me. While in that space, I did express a silent 'Thank You' stating that I was so thankful no one stopped to ask if they could help me. Inside of me, I knew this as my divinely planned part of this chapter in my journey. I knew it was just designed for 'me to me' and that was not to be disturbed in any way! I fairly quickly became very peaceful and felt complete with what was there to be resolved and released as it had been successfully done. I had done my part within the guidance of what had intuitively been with me and told to me.

I got up and went back to the car walking with much more strength and energy than I was experiencing when I arrived and could literally hardly get out of the car! I was feeling very grateful for the whole experience with all the insights of clarity that were given and with the opportunity for me to see and understand how it all fits into the bigger picture of change. As I was driving back to where I was currently staying, the benevolent outcome of it kept resonating inside of me as I kept hearing, "Watch and be Amazed!" I certainly was amazed at how much this whole day had offered up to me for my Yes to Beyond journey as I could feel that something was going more and more beyond it just being a journey.

I was recognizing myself as a new and different human being exploring, experiencing, and expressing in a new version of life through recognizing and understanding that what was is no more up for the basis of the truth for what is. Consequently, maybe we need to rewrite some definitions of our experiences as just maybe. The truth of them is that they are there for us to see beyond them. Could it be that what is appearing as negative is really co-creating with us to move us to see the opposite—the positive? Perhaps, we will be able to comprehend change more fully when, and as, we have a clear insight as to the dynamics of what is transitioning from false to true reflecting our truth to us as a New Way of Being!

We have been functioning as the tribe of humanity within a realm of dynamics that have been our perceived 3D linear reality relaying the human form of mankind is the most important and most intelligent of all life on earth. Within this perception, the human intellect, the brain, is the CEO of life's rules and regulations which can only be changed as mass consciousness changes. Up until now, that mass consciousness has continued to keep the design of false directives in play with the intention that not enough people will wake up to see and play any differently.

As this thought continued to linger in my mind and I was approaching the house, I had a clearer understanding of the information that I have recently and frequently heard pertaining to these horrific times we are going through globally. These horrific times are very much including our own country of The United States of America. That information was that we are in a time of a major battle between the dark and the light with outside appearances presenting a perception, based upon our old energy ways of playing and defining life, that the dark is winning. (As an aside here, go back into these pages to the discussion from the Note in the

Dark to review the Dark as a Love part of creation itself as opposed to the manmade definition and reality of dark which is the one that has been separated from Love.) This perception puts many into fear, into panic, into the worst upheavals inside of them that they have never experienced.

The known missing piece for a large factor of people is that this horrific layout is designed to be just as it is, not for the sake of fear, destruction, and mass killings. It has a divine purpose, and that divine purpose is for pushing everything that we are not as a human being soul to the surface to be seen and spoken to. In their own way, these horrific happenings will show us and facilitate our understanding of who we are moving to be by making it very visible and felt as to who we are not. Consequently, the light is winning as there is no way we can continue to play in this old script and continue to survive as a species when as a collective, the consciousness has so many flaws. We have to become aware of a different way of viewing ourselves, and the reality of life that we partake in referred to as 'living life on planet Earth.'

All governments, all economic systems, all religious belief congregations, all education systems, all schools and universities as education systems, all medical systems be they degreed medical doctors or trained certified alternative health practitioners, all places of incarceration, all participants of professional sports, and many more including every individual household and community of all family and friends all have at least two things in common. The first being, we are each an individual created in the image of the same and only God. Secondly, every system that the human being partakes in is made up of a collective of individuals who are individually, through free choice, living a uniquely created book of life! If we are not living that life through free choice, it is mankind who has taken away that free choice, not God.

From the perspective of many within whom it seems to be the truth that the light is destined to win, we had better be ready from all our heart, spirit, mind, and body to say Yes to Beyond! It is within our wisdom to follow the directives through our individual insights, whether we hear or see them, to understand and learn from the depths of our fears or other modes of feelings, emotions, or beliefs that have us locked into the destructive patterns which are being translated and foretold as our destiny for the end of times. As we play our part in the change within us, we will play as a changed new perspective in every collective in which we participate.

I recognize the whole day that I have just experienced and share the dynamics on paper, as a micro glimpse of me to me. It flowed all the way from stepping out of the macro reality that has offered all descriptions and reasons, to crying me a stream to flow into the lake as I wept for all that was done and released within me. Within the release, nothing had been termed by me as good, bad, or indifferent. However, at the same time, the flood was clearing the road for the new, I was also crying tears of joy and gratitude! I was willing within me to try out the viewing with different sight and hearing with a blank mind. I felt I was experiencing myself as an alien in a foreign land, or as a foreigner in a barely understood culture where I really didn't even know the language. This was so new, unusual, and unfamiliar to me that when I was caught in-between the worlds of the defined according to false beliefs and one of no definitions, all I could experience inside of me was uncomfortableness escalating to fear somehow of the unknown with the biggest being, "WHO am I and WHERE am I?"

This all really hit me when I was writing in the library and all energetic life force for that shut down. This certainly wasn't the first time that had happened, but this time was different because I thought I was really going to make it happen, sustaining the energy somehow to bringing in a real completed version of a real book this time as the flow had been good for a few days now. I initially crashed when I couldn't put any more words down. After the initial crash, and I couldn't get any comfort from the water while actually being there in the loving connecting space that had supported and lifted me multiple times before, I was energetically depleted as well as feeling defeated. From my explanation and perception, all this emotionally took me down to never return. However, the truth was that it was taking me to a place of no return, to and for, much that was no longer serving me. The divine purpose of these dynamic emotions of all of it was saving me, not killing me!

After the celebrating of 'me with me' as I had passed my test in my Learning of Life self-initiated course, I continued the route back to the house as it was just beginning to get dark. What a day it had been! All the way back, in driving down the road, I had an excellent view of the beautiful full moon which was to be full at 9 PM our time that very day in July. I believe in the pull and the push power of full moons. I just wonder how much this planet's moon cosmic energy had to do with the dynamics of my day as it too could have been a part of the push to the surface of everything I was at some level ready to see and release. Perhaps, the push then was experienced by me as a pull and helped me bring it all out resolved and up for release. All this was for positive changes for me for sure, as it positioned me for serving beyond my old ways as a different player in the Whole (One).

This has been my story shared with you. I am not sharing it for you to confirm to me job well done, or you're full of hooey, or whatever else may come up for you as an expression. I share it because we are each and every one Living a Book of Life whether it ever gets transferred into an actual book or not. In that life journey, we are never alone as we are guided to all kinds of things, experiences, people, and places along the way that have been divinely put in front of us for a purpose. If you are one who has been led to this book, I know there is something of value for you somewhere in it so be sure to feel in the space between the words or between the lines. You might be shown a piece of 'you to you' in your own Life Journey of Yes to Beyond experience.

Now for the final WATCH AND BE AMAZED aspect of this amazingly perfect day in my Yes to Beyond journey. The day ended with a synchronistic happening that I could never have planned. When getting up today, I didn't even know that all this was going to be a part of my day! Are you ready for this? After arriving back at the house just as it was getting dark, I walked down a few blocks to get a clearer view of the full moon beyond a row of houses. I found a place in the grass to sit beside the street to just view the moon. Unbeknown to me, I was just in time for a nearby celebration a few blocks away. It was a day or two before July 4th and this town was having their own fireworks in their own time frame. After sitting down on the grass, I was blessed with a beautiful 20-25-minute FIREWORKS CELEBRATION display a very short distance away! How was that for the divine right timing for me to me celebrating more of the whole of who I am becoming which brings me joy and more independence in a realm of more freedom?

At the same time, I am experiencing this as a personal celebration at the end of a powerful and beautiful day. I know it is guaranteed by the Creator of the change for all that my realized changes will go into the waters of creation as a ripple for all to receive whether they consciously recognize it or not. That is the truth for all of us! How we play it out in our book of life is our choice. The ripple is permanent and there for receiving until the light has won completely and our reality has changed to one of peace not war, love not hate, abundance not lack, to thriving as a way of life instead of fighting for surviving to be here, where all people are respected and honored for their beliefs in how they see and walk with and as the love for and of the One God however that resonance feels within their heart as it calls them forth for expression!

LIVE AND LEARN
PART 6

This is a blog that I wrote in the fall of 2012 at a time when I had my own website.

Wrapped in Cellophane

I often get messages early in the morning when I am first re-entering from the nighttime. My early morning message on the day was, "You are wrapped in cellophane!" What an unusual message to wake up to. My contemplation of this began immediately as I actually felt a clear warm wrapping around me. I lingered with the feeling and then went deeper inside for the insight or awareness that was surely available to me within the experience. This is where my inward journey took me.

Cellophane is clear whether it is of color or not. When something is wrapped with it, there is a protection of a type for the item that is wrapped. If the item(s) are not in a container or some kind of structure, the cellophane provides a container structure for them to be in even if only for a given period until it is time for the next function. Cellophane never hides what it has been wrapped around as the wrapped object is fully visible and ready for action for its designed process or destination. I continued feeling the presence of myself being wrapped in cellophane as my perceptions expanded.

Most windows in all structures are clear. They allow light in from the outside, but their bigger factor is utilized by what is transpiring inside the structure. I am sitting right now looking out the window at a beautiful view of a winter frozen lake still partially covered with snow. Because I am looking out of a 2nd story window, I have a broader overview of the lake. Also, from this higher place of viewing (2nd floor), I am looking through the leafless branches of a winter season tree that is just being a natural naked winter tree. From this viewing point as I see the human dwellings around the lake, I see more rooftops than I do house fronts. I don't have to look up so high to see the birds and geese as they go flying by and they seem closer somehow. From this vantage point, I have a glimpse of the world of other humans and their creations. In addition, I see the world of mother nature, all as a snapshot of our planet, its creations, and how it all coexists together somehow in a unified way. At least, that is my perception at this now moment.

All these reflections and perceptions of my actual viewing are happening inside of me while I am sitting on the inside space of the clearer window, with the actual 'what' I am viewing on the outside of the clear window. From the inside, I am warm and cozy. I can look around me and see all kinds of objects that suggest reflections of me and my creations in my created home environment. These reflections gave an insight into how my home space actually feels to me, and in what ways it is serving me or not in my physical and emotional state. This is the space where I can be in charge. However, neither the cellophane nor the window has any concept of an inside place or an outside space. They are just doing what they are designed to do. I am the one that utilizes them to serve my needs.

Now from a metaphorical perception, how is the clear window like clear cellophane?

- Both the cellophane and the window offer a type of protection.
- Both are clear—which means transparent—which in turn means permitting the passage of light.
- Both are positioned in such a way that inside space and an outside space are always visible one to the other for any circumstances and actions required if there is a perception that they operate separately.
- Both have a major purpose.

- Both predominantly serve the individual which eventually moves to be the masses as a collective whole.
- Both make life easier.

Why did I hear and then feel that I am wrapped in cellophane? Why did my contemplation of this take me to look out a window? Am I just a nutty writer who has a big imagination, or was this a true gift of a synchronistic for me that inspired me to go deeper for an expanded understanding of my own life? I choose to make the choice of this being an opportunity for an expanded understanding of my own life as well as that of the whole. Having declared that choice, what has been my expanded understanding as a result of experiencing a feeling of being wrapped in cellophane?

Here is my awareness for this now and for further embodiment as my truth and the benefit for the masses as a whole playing collectively. Basically, these are all just reminders.

- I am safe in this world. I am divinely protected, and there is more than one form of protection.
- I am warmly wrapped in a transparent wrap that permits all divine light to flow into me and permits all the light that I AM to flow out of me. At some level, it is as though there is no distinction between the direction; it is just light moving in and out as a cycle of life itself.
- I am reminded that from a higher space (2nd floor) or higher, I see a broader picture, and it is easier to see what is above the ground physically as well as experience it spiritually.
- I am reminded that I have a major purpose here on Earth as does everyone that is walking in physical form or spirit.
- I am reminded to see and feel that life is easier than I often experience it to be.
- I have a heart-felt-warm feeling reminder that my inner self and my outer self are always within sight of each other, and that they are always connected in any situation or actuality that is a part

of my unfolding. However, I know they can only play as big as I allow them to play.

- Within all this, I have a greater appreciation for the necessity of my inner self and outer self to be operating as unified partners and not functioning separately.

Now going beyond the form of cellophane and windows, what does clear mean when it is not referring to a thing? Clear is defined as cloudless, untroubled, serene, easily heard—easily visible, free from doubt, capable of sharp discernment, easily understood, and to give light to. I embrace these words to be characteristics of myself!

I am so very thankful for the experience of being wrapped in cellophane this day! I know why it happened. Last night upon going to bed, I was in a place of asking questions as my mind was beginning to doubt my ability to create my new life. I was having the feeling of sinking back into that space of old reality that I know is already resolved and gone for me. What do we do when there is no place to return to as we momentarily forget that the now holds all the potentials of our new; when we need to be reminded of the potential synchronistic messages along the way that will lead us to our highest intention as long as we continue to embrace the intention? My highest intent is for the freedom to be truly sovereign! I intend this for me and for every Divine Human Being walking on this Earth now as well as everyone that will ever walk this Earth in the future. Being wrapped in cellophane has brought me closer to my freedom; consequently, closer to my sovereignty!

As per usual, read between the lines here as much as you want, to see what speaks to your heart as you walk your journey while writing your individual book of life. Your story won't be my story, but our hearts can resonate!

**JOIN ME ON THE ROAD
TO FREEDOM**

LIVE AND LEARN
PART 7

2019 comment: The following was written by me as my self-proclaimed initiating words after completing a multiple-day Avatar class in 2001. This class actually brought me to a place of recognition that I was living a much smaller life than I was capable of living. I was crying to get out of the prison that I was in that I had built for myself. I was the one that had convicted myself to be a prisoner, and I had been there so long, it felt like I was serving a life sentence with no way out. My only freedom was to look out the window in-between the bars and dream. This was comparable to a totally trained house cat looking out the window watching the birds; wanting to go out but afraid to go when the opportunity arose.

I factor this realization into my mission at that time of learning more and letting go of that which no longer served me. This was a moment in time of expansion for me on my life journey as I was finding more of what it meant to be whole, at least certainly more than I knew myself to be. What does being a Divine Human Being really mean when the only way or the main way we (I) had experienced actually living our lives was as a human doing in a small world with some windows. The doing-ness gave me my value which was visible HERE. Regardless of how happy, unhappy, comfortable, or uncomfortable I was in my circumstantial life, it was familiar and seemed to be all my truth. It was what was seen and what was playing out as living life reflected by my external environment. I responded to this way through my actions, responses, or reactions. Consequently, there goes Life until a good view of the invisible THERE appears! I choose to further explore, experience, and express a to-do and to-be balanced and harmonized expanded version of myself that could be the unification of HERE—form and THERE—formless.

LIVING LIFE HERE AND THERE

I'm HERE—Living life seems hard!
I'm THERE—Life feels good, thank you for saving me from
    HERE!
But I must go back to HERE because I still live on Planet
    Earth.
As that is the place where I experienced birth.

I learn THERE can't be a substitute for HERE, so I won't be
    going THERE as much
That makes me feel very, very sad!
But thank you THERE for giving me another perspective on
    HERE.

I'm HERE—Living life seems confining and small because I
    am not going THERE.
THERE is so big—without limits and freeing…
I know that, but…
I can't go THERE because I am still presently living HERE
    trying to make a good life.

Time, explorations, and experiences tell me HERE and
    THERE are of the same space.
If so, I can now go back to experience the expansiveness of
    THERE,
As I now feel it isn't a substitute of HERE!
Wow, HERE is much bigger now too—Great Joy!

I'm HERE—Living life is good as THERE filters in!
I'm THERE—Being THERE is manifested differently
    because HERE filters in!
Can this be real?

Time, explorations, and experience tell me about 'The Bridge.'
The Bridge joins HERE and THERE. Wow, what a creation.
What is in-between HERE and THERE?
I am not sure, but they are still somewhat separated!

I simply Love the Bridge as I can freely run from HERE to
    THERE and THERE to HERE!
I'm HERE—Living life is good!
I'm THERE—Living life is good!
Now I know The Bridge is just joining Living and Being!

More time, exploration, and experience,
Why are HERE and THERE separate?
Why do Living and Being seem separate?

More time, exploration, and experience,
The I AM that I AM is The Bridge that joins Life and Being.
Life feels pretty good HERE.
Being seems pretty comfortable and somewhat Earthy
    THERE.

Spiritual Shift!
Wow! Where did the Bridge go?
My eyes are open; I am in a more real feeling world than I have
    ever experienced HERE before!
Thank you THERE for helping me see this kind of HERE!

Wait, Oh really!
What do I now know?
HERE is THERE and THERE is HERE!!
Living is from Being and Being is for Living!

Separation is gone!
ALL is a part of ALL That IS
That is my Primary with no secondaries!
More?

Time, exploration, experience,
A true profound gift awaits, or are there many?
Oh really, was it a gift to me, or Am I the Gift?
Primary: I AM a part of ALL That IS!

What?
Nothing . . . Everything . . . Nothing . . . Everything
Is this the Beginning or the Ending? See this as a circle not a
straight line.

OR

IT JUST IS!

Norma Ervin 2001

THE TO-BE, TO-DO
TRAIN

Right now, I am feeling pretty blank. There is a pretty big draw to just tuck back in and rejoin the day at a later time. I probably won't give into that because of the deep-running parallel, There (Here). There is a beautiful day Here up for the living. The birds are singing, the sun is still presenting a cool day, and the world still feels like the inviting fresh breath. I don't want to miss this time. I won't tuck back in. Yeah for me!

What train am I on today? The one going to the glory land, but not really. It is the one joyfully whistling down the track enjoying everything it sees with its agenda being just **To Be** going someplace, **To Be** moving and not be stuck at the train depot. There is no destination luring up somewhere as the ultimate day's goal. The little train is signaling it is ready for the day's journey, and it is now ready to take aboard passengers. Sometimes, the sparkling special engine goes down the track alone while other times, there are cozy loving passenger cars ready for service attached.

Today, I am not sure if I am the engine or if I am one of the passengers ready to hop in one of the cars and go for a ride. I see the train yards hold multiple engines and cars. It is quite an expansive place. It is definitely up for more exploring than just meeting the "Little Train (Engine) that Could." Upon walking into the train yard, I am enveloped with some kind of a transforming mist that goes down over the outside of me ever so gently touching my skin while at the same time, it seems to touch everything inside of me too as it travels internally with my breath. This is a wow experience in and of itself!

Here I am now standing (existing) in this newly experienced land. How and what am I **To Be** here? Am I alone here or are there others that I just don't readily see? While walking around some just to explore the surroundings, everything I look at seems a little blurry to my vision. The train track even seems **To Be** in sections all stacked in piles, not laid down ready for use. It appears there are multiple designs for the engines as well as a variety of passenger cars all just strewn around the expansive yard resembling no particular order. There seem **To Be** a few cabooses in the mix and even a few freight-type cars, flat cars, and perhaps some coal cars of some kind. Remember I said everything in here is kind of blurry to my vision.

I am standing inside these gates feeling a little confused as to why I am even in **Here**. It felt I was excited to come in **Here**, but this certainly doesn't seem like anything that sparked my heart interest earlier. It looks like **There** is some sort of a train station, depot, over **There**. I think I will go over **There** and sit for a moment. Maybe there will be someone in there who can help me grasp what this is all about. Upon arriving, I hear voices, but in looking around, I see no one. Even more perplexed by now, I do spot a row of chairs. I walk over to sit in one for a while to gather my thoughts. All of the chairs had two words painted on the back of them—**To Be**. Not understanding that or even giving it much attention, I sat down in one.

The first thing that I became aware of is that all of the chairs were full and everyone was talking but not necessarily to each other. This is where the voices I had heard upon entering had come from. Again, noticing that most of the chairs were full, I am certainly glad I chose an empty one to sit in and I hadn't plopped down on somebody's lap. After taking a few deep breaths and settling in a little more, I was amazed at how I immediately felt so comfortable, so peaceful, and so connected with this place and all these people who seemed to be talking even though it wasn't really apparent who they were talking to. I had a moment of gratitude that no one was rushing up to talk to me as I just wanted to sit quietly for a little while and take this all in somehow.

I don't know how long I had sat there before I heard a gentle, loving, excited voice ask, "Are you ready now?" Being a little startled by the intrusion, I was unclear about the meaning of the question.

"Ready." I ask, "Ready for what?"

"Ready to choose how and what you want **To Be** in this now of today," came the reply.

"Oh, I get it, kind of," I spurted as my somewhat seemingly stupid response. However, even so, I felt it being lovingly received by whoever I was talking to. It felt like I could even see a mischievous sparkle in their eyes. It was like I was connecting somehow with someone that I knew was really present but whom I could not readily see. This connection was all so real to me without any doubts. Glancing around then, I realized that every other person sitting in all those other occupied chairs was experiencing a virtually real connection with someone they were feeling connected to. Glancing around again, I became more aware of what I perceived I was actually seeing that I wasn't actually seeing. I knew many of the seats were occupied, but I didn't actually see physical bodies sitting there.

Now feeling really crazy, but enjoying every minute of it, I chose to keep playing whatever this was that I was playing and go be with my exciting fascinating connection. I sure hoped he or she was still **There (Here)**. I say he or she because since I hadn't actually seen the person. I didn't know which gender was appearing, but it felt as though it could be both or either. Oh, my, I really am flipping out, aren't I? Regardless, or oh well, whatever, I am going back down that rabbit hole, so to speak, to reconnect with my newly found playmate!

After getting comfortable in my chair once again, and after taking a few relaxing, clearing breaths, I immediately hear a jolly voice saying, "Hi, welcome, back. Are you ready now?"

"I sure am, lead the way," was my spontaneous response which came forth without any hesitation.

To this, I heard a hardy laugh and then a reply, "Okay, this could be a type of follow-the-leader game. That would work well if that is your choice of today, but why would you want **To Be** the follower and not the leader? I will not lead you or follow you. Rather, I will BE ONE with you as Creative Co-creators of Creation. I instantaneously got it! I turned within to my partner, my fellow conductor, as we gave a simultaneous wink of agreement verifying that we were in charge of the whole train. We had chosen shiny engines to pull fun passenger cars for all who wanted to share our journey—various kinds of freight and flat cars to house all of our appropriate doing projects—appropriate meaning those that flowed directives from our **To Be** chair sessions. No **To Do** car was ever disguised as an engine. We even had a caboose where we could recline, relax, and reflect on occasion as we were expressing 'job well done' or 'journey of all is going well.'

With this conductor insight, the entire train yard went into immediate transformation as the track for the journey went into place on the Earth and four bright shiny engines started the line. It was going to be a long train. Four more engines of a different color waited in line to come up at the rear. Passenger cars scattered throughout the configuration dispersed amongst the **To Do** cars. There were even several strange-looking smaller caboose-type cars intermingled throughout. They had some small windows that didn't afford much of a view. The value of these strange-looking cars didn't readily seem evident to many. However, as the conductor, as well as the designer of this train, my partner and I knew this was a whole and perfect creation. Here, the meaning of whole meant there had to be a room or a comfortable place for everyone who showed up to ride. Consequently, these unusual cars were for the worry-warts, the doom-and-gloomers, and those who otherwise regularly experienced life as a living hell.

It was interesting to see how these cars lined up amongst the other cars. They were next to some of the coal cars. There was even one old coal-stocked steam engine in that section where when these unusual car passengers needed **To Do** something to confirm their value, they could shovel coal as a perception that this kept their journey going. Another unusually designed car on the creatively all-encompassing train was the magic car. This was a car where one could quickly get what they thought they wanted. They then had to go to an experience chamber within the car where they explored a board of opportunities to pick some experience that would acquaint them with their magically filled new appearing life. Next, they had to evaluate each experience as to how it served their **To Be** life. Many adamantly wanted what they wanted and wanted it immediately which had them checking out this car for their journey through following their own perception of magic. If they did follow through and make it to the experience chamber, many recognized they had wanted what they wanted not because their heart of hearts had inspired them **To Do** so for them **To Be** more of what they had to offer themselves and life itself. This recognition offered them an understanding of what had motivated them internally to have the driving push to jump on the magic car. Initially, they weren't really being moved by what they really desired as their life; instead, they were motivated by what they didn't want as their life and just wanted to get away from it immediately or sooner! Another big factor pushing one to go to the magic car initially was (is) a foundation of fear. What was wanted for a change had to come immediately as there was a fear if it didn't show up fast, it would not happen at all! Therefore, magic was the potential answer for more than one scenario!

Oh well, and so it is; the train is ready to go. The journey agenda will be decided along the way as there will be many stops to let off and take on passengers of all kinds, and a changing out of the **To Do** cars. I am experiencing a sense that this entire whole and perfect adventure is my life as I'm meeting all of my life's needs and ways as I heard within the silence and saw in the invisible from my **To Be** chair.

Now, when will we be coming back? Well, that again is a wobbly one to answer. As we complete circles within the journey, it will appear as though we have returned to this station, but we really haven't. As the time passes with stops and starts, cars being switched out, passengers getting on and off, and the train whistle having a familiar tone, somewhere the circle completes. However, in completing our circle journey, it is never to go back to anything as the journey itself erased the agenda so thoroughly that it even pulled up the old train track. The part that seems familiar is so because what IS is! This train will always continue to circle within what IS, and the time frame of what IS is always Now. In any given moment, the 'just is' moment, we can be recognized, but our map's true purpose is to show us it can never take us back to the exact places we've been. Yes, we will be by this way again, but we won't be back. Clear? **To Do** cars when switched out and taken off the track metaphorically may have passengers in them who are going to sit off the track and play life over and over in that car that is sitting still in the belief that if they keep playing the same tapes over and over and making their own circle by looping around and around the same circle that they are still on the track going somewhere. There may be some on these cars that are sitting still and have been playing life on Earth for 90 years. Does that mean they have lived life for 90 years or they have lived one life 90 times? **To Be** circles in the invisible in order to establish the agenda of the **To Do** cars. The **To Do** are not aware of the **To Be.** Some are just hoping for or believing in magic or will be, or can be, as they seem very busy. However, they may be going nowhere other than circling inside a train car that isn't even on the track trying to create what IS from all that Was.

Wow, was I sitting in a **To Be** chair when I got all this information? If not, what car was I in, or which engine was I engineering to co-create the engine pull and keep the whole journey going? Perhaps, I am experiencing being in every car as well as the engine and the caboose!

Okay, now that you have heard the short tour guide synopsis, still want to use your ticket? Here I stop and chuckle within me because I know all must go on the trip. Whether ready or not, all will find themselves in some car singing or screaming their journey song. After experiencing all this phase of the journey has to offer, another train will just be created. Everyone will have found themselves at another train yard, depot, field with blurry cars, silent engines, stacks of tracks, and a depot full of **To Be** chairs. Each one will be there waiting for themselves to show up. I guess the familiar piece in the journey is the feel of the train yard scene and how it draws each in.

Could we create a train by just walking the train yards trying to pick out the cars we think we want? Not anymore because the older **To Do** mind which has so successfully designed the Human Doing has lost so much of its creative energy that it can no longer manifest its desires against all odds. Therefore, it looks like we have to get out of the big yard of 'Doing Vehicles' sitting beside their potential tracks and go inside to a **To Be** chair in order to manifest the creation. Maybe **To Be** stands for, or really means, Touching Only Being Essentials or Essence (your choice of words here).

Okay—All is RTG—Ready To Go—Now is the time. We don't know exactly where we are going, but we know we won't be back!

What is IS—INFINITE SOURCE
What was IS—INFINITE SOURCE
What will be IS—INFINITE SOURCE
Going Ready or Not
All Aboard the IS Train
INFINITE SOURCE IS LOVE!
EMBRACE YOUR JOURNEY!

LIVE AND LEARN
PART 8

Many aspects of life have been reviewed on these pages of Yes to Beyond. What, if anything, has come up for 'Your Individual Me to Me' journey as you review your existence as a Human Doing (Being) or a Human Being (doing)? What kind of a flow are we in right now as a collective co-creating a different order within the mass consciousness that has a power dynamic for all of us? Maybe the rivers of our Mother Earth home have a partnership clue reaching out to speak to us. Waters flow. Trickles flow. Streams flow. Rivers Flow. Ponds, lakes, and reservoirs are an accumulation of waters from various flows that are basically not consistent flows for multiple reasons serving multiple purposes. Flowing waters head toward the next bigger flow that is on the way to the ocean which is one of our biggest, if not the biggest, gifts of life in the accumulation and purpose of water. All water furnishes not only groundwater that is needed, but all water also puts moisture into the atmosphere to be used in many more necessary ways.

Having stated some of these concepts about water, I want to remind us that we too, as members of the tribe of Humanity, are also made up of a high percentage of water. Various sources share this saying the human body is 80% water, or at least needs to be in order to be of optimum health. We too are in a flow of some kind by just being alive on Earth and doing a journey of our choice and understanding. For me, as a complete nature lover and one who has water as my very best friend, I consider water as a Soul Mate of mine.

SOULS: THE RIVER'S AND MINE

Dear river, are you flowing away from something or toward
   something?
You go so fast, there is no way to stop, no way to grab a hold
   of anything.
You go over rocks, around rocks, have shallow pools and swift
   waterfalls.
You create beautiful music for all to hear.

I want to let go and be free to go with you, or perhaps as you,
With my flow being neither running away nor hurrying
   toward anything—just flowing.
Not stopping at any one place as a reality destination but
   moving to experience more.
Not missing what's ahead to explore because I stopped to
   experience no more.

There is no end to the road, no place to know when I have
   arrived.
There is no destination, just the journey presenting a way to
   thrive.
This trip is often a very big challenge for me
As I seem to need to stop for a definition of Who I Am to Be!

Oh River, I Love your music so very, very much!
As it feels every ear and every heart your song can touch
I have no riverbed to follow as in my journey I flow.
As I expand beyond what appears, may I too offer some song
   wherever I go?

Oh, River, the water comes to your flow from many places,
   even the skies above.
With your seemingly constant message being "stay in and as
   the flow to experience Love."
Oh, River, how do I do that when some of my sources of flow
   bring such sadness and pain,

As the whole Universe seems to turn upside down somehow
    seeking something to gain?

My flow seems pretty deep right now as all I have ever been,
    and all I want to seem to be standing side by side.
Oh, River, it even seems like there is so much, much more
    than all aspects of me along for the ride!
"So, what if there is?" I hear you say
The way to a New Creation is as everything arrives to play!

Unconditional means no judgment,
Now All that was, All that Is, All that is coming
Can All Unite to Play!
You may have no riverbed in which to flow, but as a Human
    in form, you have chosen to go!

So, how do I manage my journey?
"Stay conscious in Desire and Divine Guidance
As you persevere," was heard.
What else is there to do as all landscapes are changing and
    every mirror tilting?

LIVE AND LEARN
PART 9

I am coming to the ending of my sharing of words, thoughts, and experiences within my 18-year journey of reviewing my life as I had played it in this current reality. This journey was to explore what is true and what is not true; to take a look at Who I Am, and Who I Am not; to check into my inner self and see if it even makes any difference to me. Now that I have gone through many internal and external battles, and I have come to the connection and expression of uniting my Soul with that of the River's, how are my visible food for thought and invisible intuitive flow from the silence going to connect and facilitate me in regrouping myself as my journey continues to a New Reality Life, which for me is my LLC—Living Life Consciously? Perhaps I have at least one more puzzle piece to view and consider.

These words came to me fairly close to the 12/21/12 (December 21, 2012) ending marker of the first 18-year period of the 36 years of energetic change for Planet Earth. That time, and maybe these words, brought us to the crossroads where we were more ready to be prepared to participate with more clarity into co-creating the New Earth—The New Mass Consciousness.

ANGEL LIGHT IN THE
DUNGEON

Standing In-between the Worlds
Looking and Feeling For
A Direction to Take . . .

It's Dark. It's Cold. It's Silent, but it's Loud. How can there be a Loud Silence? What is it? Where is the sound coming from? I don't know—it's dark. I can't move around enough to see. I am cold. It is cold here—in this space. I say space—am I in just a space or is this an actual place? I don't know, I can't tell. All is dark inside and outside me it seems! Whether my eyes are open or shut, I see the same—Dark!

Maybe I am in a dungeon; maybe I am on top of a mountain; maybe I am nowhere to be seen—invisible. I have to be somewhere. There has to be something for seeing. Nothing—Something! No one—Someone! Invisible—Visible! Light—Dark! Hot—Cold! Where is this going? Where am I going? On a journey; there has to be an Angel light in this dungeon! All I can do is listen to the sound in the silence. Something is in here. I can hear it, not really hear with my ears, rather hear with my sense of it Being present. The Dark is still pitch black, but I am getting warmer! I feel like I turn my head to look around as there must be someone visible to me while I am still being invisible to others. Are there even any others? Yes, because I am never alone!

I ask out loud inside of me, "Are we having fun yet?" I feel applause. I look around and still see no one but feel many. I am comfortable. I am peaceful. I am safe. I am content. The sound in the silence has become a choir. I am singing in the choir as I hear my voice in harmony with All even though I don't know what part I am singing. In continuing expressing as tones and sound, I am All of the collective harmonized together even though I only share from, or as, one voice.

Stepping out of the choir, I sit in the audience to listen to All that I am hearing. The scene is beautiful, the sound is heavenly as the feeling experienced is Pure Love. I am the expression of the experience. I am the sound in the silence of the dark. I am a single voice in the choir with all others. I am singing my part in harmony as I am also All of the collective harmony. I am the singer. I am the audience. I am singing and listening. I am playing and observing. I am visible and invisible. I am beautiful. I am heavenly. Heavenly is Angelic. Heaven is an aspired ultimate. Angelic is of Angels.

I am totally without body now, therefore, I must be invisible. It is hard to determine this for sure as I am still so connected with my whole exploring experience of being in the dark, cold, silent, but not silent space or place. There is a piece of peace resonance in me even now that continues to vibrate, to dance, with All present. An awesome part I see from this Higher perspective of viewing is that I never quit singing in the choir when I stepped out to be a part of the audience to just listen. From this viewing sight (space), I also see me as a choir member looking and seeing me out in the audience even in real-time singing in the performance.

Now I see my Circle of Love Life unfold even more! Could it truly be that I was singing to me at the same time as I was listening to my own voice and experiencing beauty and heavenly sounds when I really didn't know which part I was singing and was just a part of the blend for the co-creation of the concert? I felt the meeting of our eyes. There was no clarity on the dynamics of me as a choir member or me as an audience attendee for the determination of who was looking at whom.

Simultaneously, now while singing within the harmonizing, my voice got clearer and purer. While listening to experience the beauty of the creation and feel the heavenly essence of it, all my heartfelt a deep soul felt warmth. My actual heartbeat rhythm began to change so it could take it all in for a higher expression. From my place of seeing, but not participating in the play, I saw the merging of it all. I was so flooded with Love that tears came!

Wait a minute, how can this be? Aren't I invisible? Here it was (is) appropriate to just allow the mystery of creation to do what's up for doing. Quantum is real and does work. Now going for yet another viewing from some other point of reference where there seems to still be some connection for expression as a further exploration of the experience. Follow along if you choose!

> I AM a Piece of PEACE
> I AM PEACE as the Piece
> I AM a Voice in the Choir. Is a voice our creation tone?
> I AM the Choir Song to All Voices. Is the choir All Tones as
>   the ONE?

I AM Visible and Invisible
I AM Here and There
I AM the Observer and the Player, Singer, and Audience
I AM Co-Creator and Creation

When is dark a dungeon housing fear?
When is dark a quantum void embodied with all the Creator's
creation tools?
Who decides? Each individual for themselves. That is why we
were given free choice.
Why is it Cold? Maybe the thermostat of the heart isn't turned
up high enough!

What is the sound in the silence? Each of us as a dot in life in the matrix of human design came in with a tone so in the ultimate silence, we (you) can sense/hear ourselves (yourself) as a creation tone. We can decide to play our life tone in any way we choose all the way from a place of seclusion to being in a choir of other voices. Even with the choice of choirs, we can choose what type of song our voice is going to sing out. In many ways, it can feel as if we are always auditioning and haven't quite reached our highest or higher potential yet, but we keep practicing or not.

What is Light? When there is some awareness that leads to being able to act outside of the dark—beyond the dark regardless of how one defines the dark.

What is an Angel? The perception of a Divine Entity that will Love us, take care of us, and help us get to heaven. Could it be even more? I say Yes! An Angel is an icon for self (SELF) Love. Looking more closely with **SELF** standing for **S**ource **E**mitting **L**ove **F**orever, you, me, they, them, us, all the way to I AM, are the uniquely designed pieces of SELF. A statement of truth for each and everyone of us is I AM SELF—**I AM S**ource **E**mitting **L**ove **F**orever!

Who is the Angel Light in the Dungeon?
Look in the mirror.
Who is the Angel Light in the void?

Look in the mirror to experience the merging of the image you see with the ultimate of creation as the Love that is All there is.

> I AM Visible—I AM Invisible
> I Am Here—I AM There
> I AM an Ultimate Creation
> I AM Love
> Love IS All There IS
> IS is INFINITE SOURCE!

Now to some quantum essence that has no definition, no structure, no place to play, and no need to play because all of creation IS automatically the play by design and in perfect order. I move on, in and from, this experience as it IS (infinite Source) now. Somehow, somewhere, for some purpose within the perfection of creator-creation, All that IS includes us. We as the tribe of humanity part of the Divine Human Being are the Finite of the Infinite!

The Creator—the always present Presence, never created Essence (essential), that never knew anything other than itself, and that was without any definition or conscious recognition. It was (is) pureness of neither, and/or both, light or dark that is truly beyond our comprehension. That is the ultimate mystery and will probably remain so for eternity. As a Being creation designed by and as a piece of the Essence Creator, what are we really Doing anyway?

THE END

I WISH YOU WELL!

Now that the Journey through these **Yes to Beyond** pages has come to an end, how are you going to map (script) out a New Road to Beyond where you are? Remember there is no right or wrong answer as each of our Book of Life is written and recorded individually, as no two are alike. Love is the Essence of our Life Domain regardless of our choices! That is our Truth for all of the time we are playing humans regardless of our chosen roles in our human scripted Earth-staged plays.

Revisiting All:
Super Market, Cabinet, Pantry, Refrigerator

What have you taken in for nourishment? Maybe some of the following either visible or invisible are on your list. Check it out and see if there is anything you could add to the list, or even mark off the list, as you do your reflection of the Yes To Beyond Journey through the nurturing of yourself from various places of nourishment.

SNACKS—**S**ource's **N**ew **A**nointing **C**onsciousness **K**nowledge **S**urfacing
SOUP—**S**ource **O**ffering **U**niversal **P**resence

Nourishment for Understanding

SELF—**S**ource **E**xpressing **L**ove **F**orever
DARK—**D**ivinity **A**ccessing **R**eality **K**nowledge
BLACK—**B**eing **L**ove **A**s **C**onscious **K**nowledge

STAR—What is the best way to be the main character of your own scripted shows within the tribe of humanity? **S**urrender **T**rust **A**llow **R**eceive.

Human Alterations (misconceptions) Regarding a Part of Existence

EVIL—reversed back to true reality is LIVE
DEVIL—reversed back to true reality is LIVED

When our choices are not appearing as LOVE but separated from LOVE, it is mankind that brought in the new words of description not Source (God).

Mankind does what it needs to do through free choice to create what LOVE isn't for us to see what it is. LOVE is ALL there is. As stated before, we are either LIVING within the reality of LOVE or we are searching for it according to our understanding of our own known core of wisdom. Live is **L**ove **I**nviting **V**ibrational **E**xploring, **E**xperiencing, **E**xpressing. Adding a Letter d to Live just means we do some of the three Es daily according to our choice!

Dynamics of Going to, and Standing at, the Edge!

RACES—**R**unning **A**round **C**lueless **E**scaping **S**igns
SHIT—**S**tuff **H**ot **I**n **T**ime! So much change inside and outside has (is) happening, that our container-structure of seemingly useless ways and stuff is actually heated up inside of us, with much metaphorically feeling heated up outside of us.

DOCK—**D**estination **of** **C**alibrated **K**nowledge! This journey is so devastating and exhausting, there just must be someplace to stop and regroup!

COMPOST—**C**ollection **of** **M**ultidimensional-**M**anifested **P**romises **O**ffering **S**ources **T**ruth! This shows up as a potential to recycle what no longer has any value through a system of regenerating it back to useable. This is a natural law system and does need a heat to use in the transfiguring, but it is different than the one in the garbage truck. Used up Love transfiguring back to (returning to) Useable Love requires the elemental fire of the Heart not the ashes of what was!

0 - (zero) —Appearing to have no set value in and of itself. Now at the very Edge feeling there is nothing there and no place to go, some new understanding has to appear or death is the only answer or direction. When all visible seems to be gone, and the surroundings have some familiarity of existence but nothing for playing out is visible, What Now?

See this as a birthing place, not a dying place! Zero is not the absence of everything. It is the pure quantum field of the essentials for everything that has been, is, will be, and even never will be! It is all the known and the unknown. Therefore, if you are finding yourself at the Edge, don't be afraid to jump. Right there beside you will be some Love to take your hand!

New Life Resume

Now on your (my) New Resume of Life, as One can now see, and maybe even know, ourselves as our own Observer, Leader, Various Playing Aspects, adult and childlike as we be our own cheerleader too on the journey of life that we have chosen in moving on to a New Road. In going even up more in the vibratory essentials of the Divine Human Being Matrix-template reality collective as a piece of the ONE, could each individual be a tone, a song, a choir-orchestra member, a conductor-director, and an audience participant enjoying, seeing themselves knowing the song and singing it?

How Big is ONE not only in size but in dynamics and realities as well? What does ONE really mean? It must have as part of its meaning that we are so much more than we have believed ourselves to be. We are not just one aspect of reality playing out a prerecorded, preprogrammed life in a vehicle costume known as our body, following a set of life rules according to the mass consciousness of the day! We must have a recognition of all our participating aspects in order for us to make up a recipe for our life that fully nourishes us! We can't fully utilize our cosmic and Earth kitchen without knowing all that we are and all that we need. We must go to the visible and invisible market and know what to buy or what to ask for. We must know that not everything will be in the refrigerator, or the cabinet, or the pantry. We certainly know that we need them all to take care of ourselves in the highest of ways. Perhaps our invisible kitchen is in the Best Informed (Higher Self) space of our intuitive giving and receiving Love Life reality! Wherever it is, we need it and have access to it!

Shift of the Ages

Our journey of the first 18 years of the 36 years of the Shift of the Ages has already happened for each one of us as an individual and a collective has already begun starting New. Consequently, we are where we are as a result of our choices and explorations, experiences, and expressions of the journey so far. As a reminder, the ending time of that first period was December 21, 2012. We have already stepped into the New! We still have a body and a knowingness that we are a physical, biological piece of existence. However, our past points of reference books have many, if not all, blank pages. Perhaps, one of the great gifts of these times for us is that even though many pages are blank, and even beyond cyberspace to the degree we understand it, we still have a code of some kind where and how we can be pulled or pushed out of the invisible into a visible reality and get going again!

Being HERE (**H**aving **E**verything **R**esetting **E**lectromagnetically) and in this NOW (**N**ew **O**rchestrating **W**hole), and feeling somewhat lost, are we in a womb or a tomb? Could it be both simultaneously? What is a birth process from conception to fetus, to embryo, to a beginning, and then through a period to completion of that life, to death? Perhaps, this is a life cycle that we can do over and over. In these two steps of our life cycle as our coming and going, one is a WOMB trip, **W**elcoming **O**f **M**y **B**ody, with the other being a TOMB trip, **T**ransitioning **O**f **M**y **B**ody. Both of these body trips are happening in present tense at the time of the happening, birth—beginning and death—ending.

This 18-year Yes to Beyond journey has been as though we stayed conscious in the tomb as our caterpillar reality was squeezed and most of our life as it had been known was crushed out and is being transfigured back to the immaculate love of our pure conception design from and as the Image of God. Within the tomb, we have taken all of our Stuff Hot in Time to the compost as it no longer serves us in any way. That Divine Process of Transfiguration is still alive in us even though we do not always recognize it.

We are standing naked outside the tomb unaware of what our butterfly life even is about. We don't even have a clear memory of what it felt like to have a metaphoric caterpillar existence. Something seems reversed here or something unusual! We came in through a tomb, (transitioning of my Body)! Or did we?

Regardless of what is seeming unusual, I am expressing a Welcoming of My Body! I must go now to get on the TO-BE TO-DO TRAIN. Maybe I will recognize some of me there!

A NEW ROAD
AN ALTERED VERSION

Are **You** off to see the Wizard, the wonderful Wizard of OZ?
If **You** are, how do **You** find Y**our** way, the yellow brick road
    may be a way
Unsure if I am going that way **You** say—I may be going a
    different way **You** say

Are **You** taking the road where every brick is a different color,
Some reflecting faces, some place, and some mirrored spaces?
Do **you** know this path does not lead to "over the rainbow;' it
    is the rainbow!

You ask is there a Wizard at the end of this road too?
Is it the same Wizard or one New?
Oh yes, there is most definitely a Wizard and I know that to
    be true!
Know that there is no end to this different way!

Skip and dance on **Your** journey and **You** will feel who **You**
    are.
As the mirrored spaces reflect the Wizard all along the
    way—**YOU!**

Again Remember
Your Life is Your Choice
and Your Choice is Your Life!

SOMEWHERE OVER THE RAINBOW

Somewhere over the rainbow
Way up high
There's a land that I heard of
Once in a lullaby
Somewhere over the rainbow
Skies are blue
And the dreams that you (I) dare to dream
really do (can) come true
Someday, I'll wish upon a star
And wake up where the clouds are far behind me
Where troubles melt like lemon drops
Away above the chimney tops
That's where you'll find me
Somewhere over the rainbow
Bluebirds fly
Birds fly over the rainbow
Why then, or why can't I?
If happy little bluebirds fly
Beyond the rainbow
Why, or why can't I?

YES TO BEYOND
Is Possible
Let's Join Hearts
and GO!

Thank you for turning some of the pages in this book **Yes to Beyond**. It is my desire that there was something that spoke to you in some ways as you checked into your own Book of Life in this changing time. We all are a valuable player in this change as we script our own Earth stage plays and play our individualized parts.

I LOVE YOU!

What am I really expressing when I say I Love you?
I am telling you that I feel and know you as a beautiful
piece of the Source of Creation Itself which is God!
You are made from the Creator's Image!
I am made from the Creator's Image!
That is the truth and not just theory!
When I connect with you in any way, be it side by side
or in my thoughts, my heart experiences a deep
tingling sensation whether we are rejoicing together,
crying together, or just chatting. This same Love goes to
any of you who found a potential cookie to enjoy or a morsel
of some kind that brought an in-sight or resonance to you
in your own life within these pages. Even though we may
never meet in person, we have met in the invisible realms
of reality as we are on our personal individual life journey
with the purpose being to make a difference as a New Potential
is emerging for all the Tribe of Humanity and Mother Earth!

I like it when my heart is open to giving and receiving what
our connection is representing. To me, that is Love Expressing,
and I can share it more somehow by telling you yet again
and again.

I LOVE YOU!

AS WE DEPART

I am sharing an experience that was my motivation for these As We Depart words being added to this book when the book seemed to already be completed. I shared it as I recognized it as a huge piece for me in my Yes to Beyond journey in that very current moment.

The actual experience as I find more of myself in the Yes to Beyond...

Right here and right now (May 2019) as we have come to some kind of departure from these pages, I want to introduce you to a very valuable and precious part of me- My Child Self. Please meet 4-year-old Norma Jean Sellard.

I am crying as I present her, a part of me, to you. My tears are drops of divine water that are flowing all the facets and dynamics of the essence of my Divine Human Being Life. They are representing love, reflections, beliefs, memories, thoughts, feelings, words, actions, reactions, and even more in the unknown to me. I can't attach a definition to why I am crying or even really feeling in this very moment. I just know to keep my kleenex box close by, and to let the tear river flow until it doesn't. These tears are a momentary expression (representation) in some way of every invisible and visible particle, wave, and cell known and unknown to me that I have explored, experienced, expressed, claimed, and resisted as a Divine Human Being. This form as me has been playing on planet earth this time for almost 75 years! I am truly experiencing a flood of tears!

In this here and now, I am feeling wrapped in the arms of love and looking into the innocent eyes of me as my inner child while my inner being is out of control. What is being revealed to me as I feel a magnified and expanded sense of my whole life this carnation on Mother Earth is that there is no place or structure to drop **ME** (**My E**verything) into!

Anyone who is here with me in any now, feeling the energy of this experience, we are not just sharing words or comparing words for similarities or not. Each eye viewing this and every heart feeling this in any way, is an invisible-visible light of form and energy participating as an intentional piece of ONE Whole!

I am sitting face to face, heart to heart, and as One with my child self, my inner child's presence. She appeared as a pure presence for me at the time of completing, I thought, the Yes to Beyond pages of the book to be published. She has been standing behind a short wall in front of me waiting to be not only seen, but really known, for decades of time now. Within these Yes to Beyond pages, I have revealed more than once my journey of frustration as I knew a book was inside of me. Time after time, I would engage in the process of bringing it forth, and all energy for doing that would just go away. I was left empty of feeling and void of any words coming forth. It was literally as if I would not only hit a wall in some way, but there was also a deep feeling that there just was no way around, through, or past this invisible but solid appearing wall.

That was my deeply experienced, invisible reality multiple times over the many years this book was in me to come out. From time to time, I had a subtle knowing that it just wasn't right timing yet. Even in feeling that as a piece of my (the) truth, I still also subtly knew there was more than that going on inside of me that I couldn't get past. That invisible wall really did seem to be very solid and real even in its invisibility.

As my life journey's dynamics continued to unfold throughout years of living, I eventually did come to the 'right timing' (starting Jan. 2019) for actually formulating a book that had (has) the opportunity to present some of Me to Me as well as relaying that some of those personal energy-nuggets could also be nutritional energetic breadcrumbs for others. I felt really uplifted and somewhat relieved! It felt as if this accomplishment had in some way taken a forever task off my shoulders! It even amazed me more than once, that in reality, the book was through guidance, to be focused on purging so much of what was termed as old energy as we have, are merging into the New within the Shift of the Ages. I knew I had consciously lived those 18 years of clearing. My purging hadn't all been through intellectual book learning or as the results of all my human doing 3D reality formulated happenings.

Feeling very gratified, I got the book manuscript submitted to the publisher. Finally, I had done it! As I soon realized, there was another unknown step to me that I still had to do before any book could be real in my hands signifying task complete. It was Author Profile, Cover information, Book Review, and several other similar tasks. Even though these were important but smaller projects, I absolutely could not get them done. Over time, as I sat down to accomplish getting them done, I would hit that well-known wall, lose all energy for the whole book project and go completely blank inside. After endeavoring many times to regroup somehow and get going again, I was unsuccessful repeatedly. I became very distraught but knew I couldn't give up this time! The reason known to me as to why I couldn't give up is that I had already paid for a publishing package. This had been my saving grace energetic not allowing me to quit in the middle of my very familiar shutdown voids.

The publisher was waiting for these submission papers with all of this information, and I couldn't get them completed!

In hours of the dark in the night as well as the depth of the darkest hole inside of me, I called out, cried out, asking what was happening in all of this. I was feeling a deep heartbreaking frustration. What I heard at some point was very clear. "The book can't be published!'"

In shock, I replied, "What does this mean? Why can't it be published, and where is this coming from?"

The immediate response was, "It is not safe for you to have it published! Don't do it!"

Whatever realm I was in, this shot through me like a bolt of lightning! After some non-determined lapse of time, clarity came to me in memory pictures and reality heart messages with some being from the past and some in the present. The responder was my inner child or child self of between 3 and 4 years old. In the Yes to Beyond pages, I shared with you a time when her (my) life was actually threatened in a very real way. In that moment, through the still present Universal instincts alive within the child, she did what she had to do to protect herself. Seventy years later, I experienced the replay of the exact moment of the threat with all of the details as well as the full feeling of the replay of her (my) immediate action or reaction. She had no idea what she had done wrong, but she had inner recognition or guidance telling her life for her was not safe. Somehow at 3-4 years old, she instinctively knew what that meant. Within that deep instinctive recognition, some dynamic took place, and many doors or paths into and out from her (my) heart were locked!

Over the years, as this child became me as an adult, all of those blocks invisibly thrown on possibly every path of giving and receiving that I have endeavored to participate on or with, the protected part of me was not freed up to play. How many blocks were furnished that constructed this wall, or these walls, have held me prisoner in my self-made prison that I wasn't even aware that I had truly started the process as a small child?

I now know the truth behind the directive that the book couldn't be published. I fully understood it as I had relived every piece of the awareness of how and why a piece of me had made that life directive 70+ years ago. It still held as truth inside of me even though I had forgiven all players, held no resentment, and moved on truly just seeing it as a memory that had happened. To me, it was healed and had been for years. Obviously, I had healed in my mental field and even my emotional element. However, my heart was still locked to allowing all the giving and receiving of love that my innocent creative child soul came to play in, with, and as. I can identify that I have been searching for those locked up energetics all of my adult life in every relationship I have been in and every scenario I have created or co-created!

The next morning, I clearly received the silent but heard message that my book could be (would be) published now, but it wasn't finished. It was to have another chapter. I contacted the publisher to see if I could add another chapter or change the original ending. I was told I could just do what I felt to do and resubmit the manuscript.

The Universe has been right beside me as I am consciously experiencing unlocking my heart. I am learning more and more that once we say Yes with intention to anything on our life journey path, there is some Universal Source right there beside us to move us along as long as we are setting intention for something that will not be harmful to ourselves, to anyone else, any animal, or mother nature. In unlocking my heart, I am experiencing the resolving and transfiguring of the walls that blocked the flow of love.

In moving forward, where am I now? I understand the situation as to how it happened. I understand that this is the time for an unlocking of doors within me that have kept me from giving the Love that I am and must give. There is also the unlocking of doors that have kept others from coming into my life because I couldn't receive them or what they had to give. I have played 70+ years without all of myself—without the benefit of the innocent beginning that was closed off early on in human life. What do I feel when I see that slight smile and those eyes that seem to be looking off somewhere—maybe just at the camera and maybe not?

While still in the depth of this situation, I felt to forgive myself and then to forgive my childhood self. However, I recognized that me as the adult had done nothing wrong, and that my childhood self just reacted or acted instinctively. She hadn't been old enough to have had any intellectual understanding of her immediate internal response. In this now, as the adult version of that small child, I look into her (my) eyes and have a very deep sense of compassion for her (me) then and me now which is her many years later. Compassion is defined as a sympathetic consciousness of others' distress together with a desire to alleviate it.

Now that my childhood, inner child, has gone through a reopening to an existence of being safe, and me as her adult self has grasped an understanding of much more of the human reality aspects of that human stage play, where is all the energetics of this whole scenario, happening, percolating now? The answer is, inside of me, the adult version of my childhood is beginning. I can't turn the clock or the calendar back over 70 years and replay as that 3- or 4-year-old, but I can have an invisible divine guidance furnishing support, understanding, and compassion, all of which is Love. As that adult now experiencing all of this, following are some of the things churning inside of me as the energetic keeper of the dynamic components of the revealed happening:

1. I have such a deep, deep feeling inside of me that even though I now have permission to do so, I cannot come out and be fully me. I have a strong contact with myself within myself but can't seem to be able to bring it out to connect with others in the way my heart desires.
2. There is the sense of a huge ball of various expressions of energy that are all woven together deep inside of me that is ready to explode.
3. I don't want to feel this big ball of fast-moving, interwoven energies inside of me anymore. This energy ball, or knot, continually requires me to search for something to do to get it to calm down as it feels it is impossible for it to go away.

What is really spinning and building momentum? Is it the old energy dissolving, resolving, and evolving? All of that movement is good! Or is it a new energy in the beyond as I consciously said, "Yes to Beyond" and moved on? Is the new very powerful mass of energy appearing as a powerful pressure rotation inside of me until it is integrated and balanced within me? Which perception is correct? How am I to know and what am I to do to make myself comfortable again? Could my answer be again, one more time, turn off my preprogrammed thinking mechanisms, surrender to the I don't know what I don't know, allow the answer to Be the answer, and then receive the truth of the outcome!

What is your inner child encouraging you to do from their innocence, purity, and imagination? Have you (are you) been disconnected from resonating with him or her as your beginning self on Earth? Did our preprogramming subconsciously take over and just direct our life voluntarily to ignore our new innocent one? At 3 or 4 years old, was my child self still an angel just observing life through her imagination as she watched all in her environment while endeavoring how to figure out what being a human in form really meant? At that point in her life, she would have had no intellectually learned tools, and very little if any, points of reference to replay for advice.

THE POINT OF THE WHOLE SCENARIO IS FOR US TO RECOGNIZE, WITHOUT ANY FEARS, WORRIES, OR DOUBTS THAT NOW IS THE TIME TO LIVE AS NEW EARTHLINGS ON A NEW EARTH!

I am inspired to write my next book. We are still participating in a part of the Shift of the Ages. We have done the first 18 years of the 36-year hub so-to-speak and are now well on our way into the second 18 years. Much is present for us to take in as new as we become New Earthlings in a New Earth!

www.ingramcontent.com/pod-product-compliance
Lightning Source LLC
Chambersburg PA
CBHW021617120626
46545CB00001B/269